D1235863

The Chess Terrorist's Handbook

by

International Grandmaster
Leonid Shamkovich

edited by
Paul Hodges

ISBN 0-939298-57-0

Published by:

American Chess Promotions

3055 General Lee Road

Macon Georgia 31204

USA

Cover design: Jim York

Typography and printing: JM Productions

PRINTED IN THE UNITED STATES OF AMERICA

Dedicated to the memory of
World Champion
MIKHAIL TAL (1936-1992)
The Greatest Chess Terrorist!

Contents

Foreword

by Don Maddox

As I reflect back over this project, Leonid Shamkovich and I had remarkably few differences of opinion during our collaboration. There was one, however. The title.

I thought a long time, looking for a title that would accurately reflect the spirit of what we were doing in this book. Finally, watching Leonid analyze one day in my study, I found myself drawn irresistably by the image of a quiet little man working anonymously in his home building bombs for other people to plant in public places.

It came to me that this is precisely what we were doing - building chess bombs for players to use against one another - and that "A Chess Terrorist's Handbook" was the title I had been looking for. Leonid, the quiet little man at the center of my vision, was not so sure.

"I don't know, Don," he said hesitantly. "I don't feel like a terrorist. Maybe we need a more dignified title."

But terrorists seldom think of themselves as terrorists. More often than not, they consider themselves artists or patriots, people with fanatical devotion to their craft and their cause, people to whom the "truth" is more important than their victims.

I am here to affirm that I have never met a gentler, more dignified man than Leonid Shamkovich, a man who loves chess with a passion that borders on the fanatic, and a man incapable of harming a hair on a human head .... away from the chessboard.

But I'm sorry, Leonid. I have watched you build the bombs, I have seen what they do to unsuspecting victims, and I have watched your remorseless pursuit of "truth" at the expense of the human ego across the board. You are, in spite of yourself, a chess terrorist, and this is "A Chess Terrorist's Handbook."

In the final analysis, I submit to the judgment of the reader. No matter how we label the tools of Leonid's craft, the goal is the same - to teach you to win chess games. You may choose, as Leonid does, to think of yourself as an artist; or you may lean back, close your eyes, and imagine a quiet little man, in the privacy of his study, building bombs.... Either way, the explosions are deadly.

Don Maddox
Manasquan, NJ, 1990.

Editor's Preface

or "How I Became a Chess Terrorist's Apprentice"
by Paul Hodges

I first met Don Maddox in July 1991 at the World Open where he was demonstrating the innovative products marketed by his fledgling company, ChessBase USA. In the coming months, Don and I became friends and collaborators on a number of chess projects in the local community in NJ (we live about four miles apart). As ChessBase USA grew at an explosive rate towards the end of 1991, it was clear that some of the many chess-related projects Don had taken on were going to overwhelm him. Among these ventures was his collaboration with Leonid Shamkovich on *The Chess Terrorist's Handbook* - ostensibly an annotated collection of some of Shamkovich's finest attacking games, but also intended as a guide to the regular club and tournament player as to the conduct of attack in the chess opening and middlegame. Don had just begun editing this work for Leonid but could no longer devote the time necessary to fulfill the important "behind the scenes" tasks of text preparation, proof-reading, editing, manuscript preparation and sundry other niggling little tasks that can distract the principal author from his main objective, and so in January 1992, I took over these duties - a month before I had even met Leonid. As I worked on the section involving the Sicilian Defence, I began to gain an inkling into Leonid's thought processes from his writings and crystal clear analyses - here was a chessplayer who seemed to revel in violence and "terrorism" on the chessboard. I would later meet Leonid for the first time in February 1992 at the classic US Amateur Team East tournament. As I talked with Leonid, and reviewed the work and revisions ahead, I could not help but contrast this gentle, charming, elder statesman of chess with the exuberant tactician I had come to know in his writings. Leonid Shamkovich may have been destined to become a Grandmaster but he was born a chess terrorist. For me, this collaboration has been a unique and enjoyable learning experience. Read on, and learn the ways of the chess terrorist ....

Dr. Paul J. Hodges
Brick, NJ, April 1992.

Leonid Shamkovich
International Grandmaster
Biographical Data

Leonid Shamkovich was born on June 1, 1923, in Rostov-on-Don, USSR, and began playing chess at the age of nine. In 1941, at the beginning of World War II, his family was evacuated to Tbilisi in Soviet Georgia, where young Leonid became a Candidate Master.

After the war, Shamkovich moved to Leningrad, where he graduated from the university with a degree in physics and earned his Master's title in three years. Soon he abandoned all pursuit of a "mainstream" career to become a chess professional, combining tremendous activity as a player with internationally recognized work as a theoretician.

Between 1954 and 1974, Shamkovich was extremely active in the USSR. He was twice Russian Republic (RSFSR) Champion (1954 and 1957) and Moscow Co-Champion with David Bronstein in 1963, narrowly losing a playoff 2.5 - 1.5. He participated in the famous Kiev USSR Championship with a stellar field of Soviet grandmasters, including Viktor Korchnoi, Leonid Stein, David Bronstein, Mikhail Tal, Efim Geller, Ratmir Kholmov, Alexey Suetin, and Evgeny Vasyukov. He went on to compete a total of six times in the USSR Championship, sharing 5th place in 1964.

In 1962, Shamkovich competed in his first international tournament, The Moscow International, finishing equal third behind Averbakh and Vasyukov and earning an International Master norm. In Marianske Lazne (1965), he finished third behind Vlastimil Hort and Paul Keres, achieving his first Grandmaster norm. At Sochi (1967), he tied for first with Krogius, Simagin, Spassky, and Zaitsev. During this same period, Shamkovich was also second and trainer to Tal (1965) and Stein (1972), publishing a prodigious number of theoretical works, including the book, *Sacrifice In Chess*. During 1969-1972, he won three international tournaments in Romania and Hungary.

In 1975, he emigrated to Israel, winning their Open Championship. The following year, he came to the United States via Canada and established permanent residence. He has been a U.S. citizen since 1983. Since arriving in the USA, he has won the U.S. Open twice (1976 and equal first with Anatoly Lein in 1977), qualified for the 1979 Interzonal in Rio de Janeiro, and competed in the 1980 Malta Olympiad. Shamkovich is still playing strong chess, writing internationally recognized books and articles, and serving as one of America's most qualified and experienced chess coaches.

Shamkovich is a popular author. His book, *Sacrifice In Chess*, was translated for publication in the USA. He has authored or co-authored works such as *The Tactical World of Chess*, *Fischer-Spassky, 1992*, and *The Schliemann Defense*, among others.

Leonid Shamkovich, Chess Artist

by Boris Gulko, IGM

Some people consider chess to be an art and others as a sport. I highly recommend this book of selected games by Leonis Shamkovich to both.

First of all, "The Prince," as Russian chessplayers used to call Leonid because of the aristocratic nature of his chess play, is a true chess artist. Thirty years ago, I saw the game Shamkovich-Sakharov and I still admire its beauty - Black attacked the White Knight on d4 with c7-c5 and Leonid answered with the cool e2-e3!! [This game can be found in Part VII - ed.] One of the most fantastic sacrifices I ever saw! A magnificent combination by Leonid in the game Fedorowicz-Shamkovich is one of the brightest in chess history. Have you seen the game A.Zaitsev-Shamkovich? [These games can also be found in Part VII - ed.] White was attacking the Black King with all of his pieces but Leonid produced the unbelievable defense g7-g5!! and defying all the odds, Black won! This game demonstrates to us the creative methods of Shamkovich. Leonid tries to find a paradox - an exception to the rules. He is the enemy of the commonplace.

This quality of Shamkovich's explains his tremendous achievements in opening theory. Shamkovichs games are interesting to players who want to improve their understanding of certain openings. Several years ago, Grandmaster Genna Sosonko found one of Leonid's ideas from an obscure game against Ravinsky in an old book. This discovery brought Sosonko several important points in tournament play.

Shamkovich has been considered one of the leading theoreticians during his career, and he employed an extensive opening repertoire. He used his knowledge to create many new ideas. Alekhine once wrote that White had to avoid the pin - Bg4 against Nf3 - in the central system of the Grunfeld Defense and had to develop his pieces with 7.Bc4 and 8.Nge2. Chessplayers strictly followed this advice for decades until Shamkovich first played 7.Nf3 and 8.Rb1. Now it is a very popular system and such grandmasters as Garry Kasparov, Boris Gelfand and Alexander Khalifman use it. For many years the system with 6.f3 in the Nimzo-Indian was considered to be harmless for Black until the game Shamkovich-Korchnoi, played in the early seventies. Leonid introduced the stunning pawn sacrifice - 9.e4! and once again gave food for thought to chessplayers for many years.

Although Leonid was Champion of Moscow and Russia, won many other international tournaments and obtained the grandmaster title, he manifested himself more as an artist, explorer and creator than simply as a sportsman.

So - enjoy beautiful attacks, paradoxical defenses, unexpected combinations, deep opening conceptions and the refined analyses of the unique Leonid Shamkovich!

Introduction to
"The Chess Terrorist's Handbook"

At the top level the game of chess is still a combination of error and opportunity, not the exercise in cold calculation many, even experienced, amateurs imagine. The career of the strongest player is, in some sense, a long education by trial and error.

I have been considering for some time writing a new kind of chess manual based on my forty years of experience against the strongest players in the world. The idea is to produce a practical manual based on personal experience, distilling lessons learned in combat against such players as David Bronstein, Mikhail Tal, and Boris Spassky during one of the greatest periods in chess history. But the purpose of this book is not to provide a 'Who's Who' of international chess over the past forty years. You will look in vain for the names of some of my most illustrious opponents in the index. I've chosen only the most logical, most instructive, and most contemporary examples from hundreds of games in my files. The result is, I hope, a manual that can be used by masters and amateurs alike to whet their appetite for struggle, to sharpen their opening play, to deepen their tactical sense, and to broaden their psychological repertoires.

The opening is, despite reams of theoretical analysis - and maybe because of it - still the most difficult and the most miraculous phase of chess. The maze of opening theory and its over-the- board challenges are very difficult for the practical player. The opening is replete, even in familiar seas, with so many threats and surprises that even the most experienced player finds himself marooned and helpless from time to time.

I have tried to illustrate in my examples the skills required to navigate the troubled waters of opening theory, choosing only the most contemporary and controversial examples from hundreds of Ruy Lopezes, Sicilians, and wide-open gambits. The first chapter charts some of the hazards lurking in the opening for unsuspecting victims - a selection of miniatures, quick kills that prove even strong players can find themselves wrecked barely out of the harbor.

In subsequent chapters, the reader will find instructive examples of attack and counterattack, of mistakes and combinations in the middlegame, and of typical middlegame motifs (chapters, for example, on kingside attack and the use of the long diagonal in the middlegame).

Getting ready to publish a book like this, you spend a lot of time packaging your successes as credentials for the task at hand. I find myself smiling inwardly. The truth is that the ups and downs in the dramatic structure of my chess career, both good results and bad, are part of my real credentials.

What I have to teach is learned from both winning and losing. I've spent a lifetime pursuing "truth" in opening and middlegame analysis, and I've learned essentially that the truth in chess is bigger than all of us, that sometimes the very security we take in our "knowledge" is the source of our undoing, making us careless and oblivious to danger.

If the reader emerges from this book with what Bobby Fischer calls a greater "sense of danger" and a more alert approach to the opportunities hiding in a chess position, I will have accomplished what few chess writers ever accomplish - I will have made you a better chessplayer.

This work is the most important of my chess career. My hope is that every game in the selection will offer some concrete, practical lesson to every reader, something you will carry away with you and apply to your own play the very next time you sit down at a chessboard.

Leonid Shamkovich
International Grandmaster
Brooklyn, NY, 1989.

Part I
Straight for the Jugular:
Chess Miniatures

The opening is strewn with land mines, some of them crude booby traps, others sophisticated snares for the unwary. "Miniatures" are short games with elegant finishes, generally less than twenty-five moves long, but sometimes extending further, especially as today's opening study pushes further and further into what used to be the sole province of the "middlegame".

Collections of miniatures are fairly common, but these selections often include the crudest of blunders in the opening, spectacular, but far from instructive. At best these games are opening curiosities, to be handled and wondered at, but hardly useful to the practical player.

The selection of miniatures you will find here have been hand-picked for their instructive value, each exhibiting a kind of clean, internal fighting logic and extraordinary decisions made in the heat of battle.

This is what separates the magic of the player from the wizardry of the problemist - the former's critical decisions must be made under threat of annihilation by a live enemy.

Many amateurs play the opening wearing "blinders", relying on rote memory and general principles to guide them through the first ten or fifteen moves. This chapter is testimony to untold volumes of missed opportunity. While many of us are skating blithely across the bookish surface of chess theory, the strongest players are constantly on the alert, ready to seize the advantage as early and as violently as possible.

I have purposely chosen examples from as many opening systems as possible to demonstrate that fortune favors the hungry hunter in all landscapes, from the quiet classicism of the Ruy Lopez to the hypermodern frenzy of the King's Indian, from the placid plains of the Caro-Kann to the frenetic fields of the Modern Benoni.

Before we get down to our real business, one quick miniature in a "lighter" vein built around the theme of Legale's Mate is my game against Ivashin.

RUY LOPEZ [C71]
Shamkovich-Ivashin
USSR Ch., Gorky, 1946

**1.e4 e5 2.♘f3 ♘c6 3.♗b5 a6
4.♗a4 d6 5.c4**

The Duras System of the Ruy Lopez.

5...♗g4 6.♘c3 ♘ge7?

Better is 6...♘f6, then ...♘d7.

7.d4! exd4 8.♘d5 ♖b8

8...♘g6! is better.

**9.♗g5 b5 10.cxb5 axb5
11.♗b3 ♘e5?? 12.♘xe5! f6**

If 12...♗xd1 13.♘f6+ gxf6
14.♗xf7+ mate - The very old
combination known as Legal's Mate.

13.♕xg4 ♘xd5 14.♗xf6!

1-0

RUY LOPEZ [C67]
Shamkovich-Blohm
American Open 1976

**1.e4 e5 2.♘f3 ♘c6 3.♗b5 ♘f6
4.0-0 ♘xe4 5.♖e1**

Modern practice more frequently
features the following positional plan:
5.d4 ♘d6 6.♗xc6 dxc6 7.dxe5 ♘f5
8.♕xd8+, with a slight advantage to
white. The text leads to dynamic play,
the theoretical foundation of which was
established in the last century by such
giants as Steinitz, Zukertort, Lasker,
Schlechter, Pillsbury and others, and
numerous contemporary Grandmasters.
Modern theory has decided black comes
close to equalizing in these lines, but I
intended to offer something unusual.

5...♘d6 6.♘xe5 ♗e7 7.♕h5!?

Ljubojevic's experimental move,
originated against Calvo in Lanzarote
1973 - that game continued 7...♘xe5
8.♕xe5 ♘xb5? 9.♕xg7! ♖f8 10.a4
♘d6 11.♘c3 with the dangerous threat
of ♘d5. More solid is the time-tested
7.♗d3, where 7...♘xe5 8.♖xe5 0-0
9.♘c3 ♗f6 is equalizing according to
ECO C67, but contains some hidden
reefs, e.g., 10.♖e3 ♘e8?? 11.♗xh7+!
crushing. I will return to another point

of this move in a later section on the Ruy
Lopez.

7...0-0 8.♗d3 g6?!

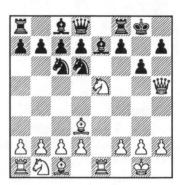

Theory suggests 8...f5 with an
unclear position.

**9.♘xg6 fxg6 10.♗xg6 hxg6
11.♕xg6+ ♔h8**

Although white has committed
himself to a series of sacrifices to
expose the black king, neither side
seems to be out of the opening, with
both queensides undeveloped. White
could settle for perpetual check, but if
he can deploy his pieces fast enough,
more is in the offing.

12.b3!

Black answers 12. ♖e3 with
12...♘f5! 13.♖h3+ ♗h4 with a clear
advantage.

12...♗f6?

This obvious reply is weak. Better is
12...♘f5! 13.♗b2+ ♗f6, when white
has to settle for a perpetual check: 14.
♖e3! ♘xe3 15. ♕h6+, etc. But not
14...♗xb2? 15.♖h3+ ♘h4 16.♕h6+

♔g8 17.♖g3+ ♔f7 18.♕h5+ with a stong attack for white.

13.♖e3 ♗g7

The only defense against 14. ♖h3+.

14.♗b2?

Attack requires absolute precision. Here white returns the favor he received at move 12. After 14.♖h3+! ♔g8 15.♕h7+ ♔f7 16.♗b2!, black is finished, e.g., 16...♕g5 17.♗xg7 ♕xg7 18.♖f3+; or 16...♘e8 17.♖f3+ ♔e6 18.♕e4+; or 16...♕e7 17.♕xg7+ ♔e8 18.♖e3, all winning for white. The activity of white's rook is deadly - as it plies from h3 to g3, f3 and e3 with devastating effect.

14...♖f6!

Black returns material to ransom his king.

15.♖h3+ ♔g8 16.♕h7+ ♔f8 17.♗xf6 ♗xf6?

This gives white a devastating attack. Instead, he should muddy the waters by sacrificing his queen with 17...♕f6! 18.♖f3 ♕xf3 19.gxf3 ♗xa1 20.c3, with a completely unclear position.

18.♖g3 ♘e7 19.♘c3!

Threatening ♘d5.

19...♕e8 20.♕h6+ ♔f7 21.♖e1

Miraculously, all of white's pieces are now in play against black's king. Black remains cramped and uncoordinated.

21...♕h8 22.♖xe7+!!

The key shot.

22...♔xe7 23.♘d5+ ♔e6

After 23...♔d8, white has 24. ♖h8+!!; and he follows 23...♔f7 with 24.♕g6+ ♔e6 25.♘xf6.

24.♘xc7+ ♔e7 25.♘d5+ ♔c6 26.♘f4+ ♔f5

The alternative 26...♔f7 fails to 27.♕g6+ ♔f8 28.♕d3! threatening 29.♘g6+ and 29.♕xd6+.

27.♕g6+ ♔xf4 28.d4!!

Flushing a covey of mating threats.

28...♗xd4 29.♕g5+ 1-0

CARO-KANN [B17]
Shamkovich-Kholmov
19th USSR Ch., Baku 1962

1.e4 c6 2.d4 d5 3.♘c3 dxe4 4.♘xe4 ♘d7

When this game was played, the theory of this system was not as well-defined as it is today. Black plans to play 5... ♘gf6 (not, however, after 5.♕e2 ♘gf6?? 6.♘d6 mate, as in a famous Keres game).

5.♗c4

The natural response, but today the eccentric thrust 5. ♘g5!? is also fashionable. A brilliant miniature played by Mikhail Tal in the 1986 USSR Championship highlights its potential: 5...♘gf6 6.♗d3 h6? 7.♘e6! ♕a5+ 8.♗d2 ♕b6 9.♘f3! fxe6 10.♗g6+ ♔d8 11.0-0 c5 12.c4 cxd4 13.♘xd4 e5 14.c5! ♘xc5 15.♗a5!, and black resigned (Tal-Oll). Another excellent example reached by a different move order (5.♗d3 ♘gf6 6.♘g5), is Geller-Meduna (Sochi 1986): 6...e5 7.♘1f3 h6 8.♘xe6! (anyway!)...♕e7 9.0-0 fxe6 10.♗g6+ ♔d8 11.♗f4 ♕b4 12.a3 ♕xb2 13.♕e2 ♘d5 14.♗d2 ♗d6?! 15.♕xe6 ♔c7 16.♖fb1 ♕xa1 17.♖xa1 ♘e5 18.♕xd6+ ♔xd6 19.♘e5, with a tremendous advantage for white. So the "amateurish" 5.♘g5!? (or 5.♗d3 ♘gf6 6.♘g5) can, in fact, become a very dangerous weapon in experienced white hands. The list of its victims is already long, including ex-World Champions Mikhail Tal and Anatoly Karpov. Karpov has, it seems, come close to finding an antidote by playing 5.♘g5 ♘b6, or 5.♗d3 ♘df6 6.♘g5 ♗g4. In 1962, however, we never seriously considered the early lunge with ♘g5, preferring 5.♗c4 or 5.♘f3.

5...♘gf6 6.♘g5 e6 7.♕e2

With the obvious threat 8.♘xf7.

7...♘b6 8.♗b3

Perhaps better is 8.♗d3, making

8...♕xd4?! 9.♘1f3 ♕d5 10.0-0 h6 12.♘xf7! ♔xf7 13.♘e5+ ♔g8 14.♗g6 with a strong attack, too risky.

8...h6 9.♘5f3 c5 10.♗e3 ♕c7 11.♘e5 ♗d6 12.♘gf3 0-0 13.g4!?

A lucky improvisation. The h6-pawn gives white some basis for a direct attack against black's kingside.

13...c4?

This is the fatal error, exchanging the c-pawn for white's g-pawn. Nine years later, Janos Flesch uncovered the correct move: 13...♘fd7!

14.♘xc4 ♘xc4 15.♗xc4 ♘xg4 16.♖g1! e5 17.0-0-0 ♘xe3 18.♕xe3!

This was an unpleasant surprise for Kholmov: 18... ♕xc4? 19.♕xh6 g6 20.♘g5 loses; and 18...e4 (black's best chance) is met by 19.♘e5 ♗xe5 20.dxe5 ♕xe5 21.♕xh6, with a strong white initiative.

18... ♔h8?

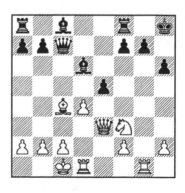

19.♖xg7!!

Severe punishment for black's flippancy. His king embarks on a final voyage.

19...♔xg7 20.♖g1+ ♔f6

The point of white's rook sacrifice is that black's king cannot return to its fortress: 20...♔h7 21.♘g5+ hxg5 22.♕xg5 mating; or 21...♔h8 22.♘xf7+, winning.

21.dxe5+!

After such a tremendous sacrifice of material, white must play extremely accurately. Weaker would be 21.♕xh6+ ♔e7 22.dxe5 ♕xc4 23.♕xd6+ ♔e8, and white's attack has evaporated.

21...♗xe5

White wins simply after 21...♔e7 22.exd6+ ♔xd6 23.♖d1+.

22.♕xh6+ ♔e7 23.♖e1! ♗e6

No better is 23...f6 24. ♕g7+! More resistance is offered by: 23...♕xc4 24.♘xe5 ♕e6 (a very elegant mate follows 24...♕xa2: 25.♘c6+ ♔d7 26.♖e7) 25.♘d3. But it's still just a matter of time until white wins.

24.♘xe5 ♖fe8

Black is hopeless in any case: e.g., 24...♖h8 25.♘g6+!; or 24...♖ad8 25.♕g5+.

25.♕g5+ ♔f8 26.♕f6!

The crucial "quiet move," threatening 27.♘g6 mate.

26...♖ec8 27.♘g6+ ♔e8 28.♗b5+ 1-0

We have already noted the long list of victims who have fallen under the banner of this system to white brilliancies in spite of its solid reputation. The most brilliant, perhaps, is Perenyi- Esperzhesy (Budapest 1974), continuing from move 7 above: 8.♗d3 h6 9.♘gf3 c5 10.dxc5 ♘bd7 11.b4 b6 12.♘d4 bxc5?? (12...♘d5!? is playable) 13.♘c6 ♕c7 14.♕xe6+!!, black resigns. The list of victims continues to grow after the modern 5.♘g5!? - for example, Tal lost to John Nunn in 20 moves (SWIFT 1988); and Karpov to Andrei Sokolov (Belfort 1988).

I added my own name to this illustrious list when, after defeating Tal on the black side of the system in the 39th USSR Championship, I ventured the same move again in the 40th USSR Championship (Baku 1972). In this game (included by Tal in his The Life and Games of Mikhail Tal), the Magician from Riga attacked as only he can. To this day, I cannot explain where I found the temerity to repeat this variation for a second time against the enraged Tal. But for the record, here is the game:

Caro-Kann [B17]
Tal-Shamkovich
40th USSR Ch., 1972

1.e4 c6 2.d4 d5 3.♘c3 dxe4 4.♘xe4 ♘d7 5.♘f3 ♘gf6 6.♘c3 e6 7.♗d3 c5 8.♕e2 cxd4 9.♘xd4 ♗c5 10.♘b3 ♗d6 11.♗g5 a6 12.0-0-0 ♕c7 13.♔b1 0-0 14.♘e4 ♗e5 15.f4! ♗xf4 16.♘xf6+ ♘xf6 17.♗xf6 gxf6 18.♕g4+ ♔h8 19.♖hf1 ♗e5 20.♗xh7! f5 21.♕h4 ♔g7 22.♖f3 ♖e8 23.g4 f4 24.g5 ♔f8

25.♖xf4! ♗xf4 26.♕h6+ ♔e7 27.♕f6+
♔f8 28.g6 ♗h6 29.♖f1! 1-0

The following game was remarkable
for the key role played by white's
bishops in spite of a relatively closed
position.

QUEEN'S GAMBIT [D46]
Shamkovich-Simagin
Moscow 1969

**1.d4 d5 2.c4 c6 3.♘f3 ♘f6
4.♘c3 e6 5.e3 ♘bd7 6.♗d3
♗b4!?**

Black avoids the Meran Variation
(6...dxc4 7.♗xc4 b5 8.♗d3 a6, etc.),
which is still current enough to be used
by Kasparov. But Simagin, my old
friend, always nursed a penchant for
opening variations off the beaten path.
With the text move, he inhibits the e3-e4
break and intends to withdraw the
bishop to d6 or c7 if necessary.

7.0-0 0-0 8.a3

Against Eric Marchand in the 1988
National Open, I played 8.♕c2,
managing to win after a false brilliancy
in the middlegame: 8...dxc4 9.♗xc4
♗d6 10.♘e4!? (TN?) ♘xe4 11.♕xe4
♕e7 12.♗d2 e5 (Black achieves his
thematic objective.) 13.dxe5?! (Better
is 13.♗c3.) ♘xe5 14.♗c3 ♘xf3+
15.gxf3 ♕g5+ 16.♔h1 (Black could
force a draw here with 16...♗xh2!
17.♔xh2 ♕h5+ 18.♔g1 ♕g5+, etc., but
he misses his chance.) 16...♗f5
17.♕d4 ♕h6 18.f4 c5 19.♕d5 ♕g6
20.f3 ♗e6 21.♕d2! (The spectacular
21.♕xd6 ♗xc4 22.♖g1! ♕xd6
23.♖xg7+ ♔h8 24.♖f7+ ♔g8 only
leads to a draw.) 21...♗xc4 22.♖g1

♔h8 23.♖xg6 hxg6 24.b3 ♗c7? 25.♕b2
and black resigned.

8...♗a5

More logical is 8...dxc4 9.♗xc4
♗d6, intending ...e6-e5.

9.♕c2 ♗c7?

Correct is 9...dxc4 10.♗xc4 ♗c7.

10.b3!

Black can no longer enforce the
freeing break in the center.

10...dxc4?

A more serious blunder. The position
demands a new strategic plan, such as
10...b6. Less convincing is 10...e5
11.cxd5 cxd5 12.♘b5! ♗b8 13.dxe5
♘xe5 14.♘xe5 ♗xe5 15.♗b2, when
white has a clear advantage because the
standard ...♗xh2+ combination fails in
this position.

**11.bxc4 e5 12.♗b2 ♖e8
13.♖ae1 exd4?**

Opening the game now favors white
because of his superior development,
but black has no adequate alternative
(e.g., 13...♕e7 14.♘e4; or 13...b6
14.♘e4).

14.exd4 ♖xe1

My usually aggressive opponent
hopes to simplify into a draw.

**15.♖xe1 ♘f8 16.♘e4 ♘xe4
17.♗xe4 ♗g4**

This pseudo-aggressive thrust only
fuels white's attack, but black has no

way to prevent the important d4-d5 advance.

18.d5! cxd5 19.♗xd5 ♗a5

Preventing ♕c3 and attacking the rook. After 19...♗xf3 20.♕c3! ♕g5 21.♕xf3, white is still winning.

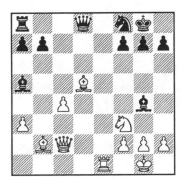

20.♕e4!

An unpleasant surprise for black, who cannot take the rook: 20...♗xe1? 21.♕xg4, winning.

20...♗xf3 21.♕xf3 ♕d7

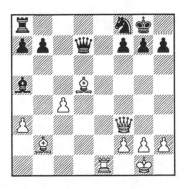

Considering this position over the board, I was tempted by this spectacular variation: 22.♕xf7+ ♔xf7 23.♖e7!!

♕xd5 24.♖xg7+ ♔h8 26.♖g3 mate. As I reached for my queen to execute this beautiful "windmill", I suddenly noticed the prosaic refutation 23...♘e6! 24.♗xe6 ♕xe6 25.♖xe6 ♔f7. What a pity!

22.♖e4!

Intending either 23.♕e2 or 23.♖f4. Black's position is desperate.

22...♖e8?

Hastening the end.

23.♕xf7+! 1-0

FRENCH DEFENSE [C08]
Shamkovich-McCarthy
New York 1976

1.e4 e6 2.d4 d5 3.♘d2 c5 4.♘gf3 a6 5.exd5 exd5 6.dxc5 ♗xc5 7.♘b3 ♗a7 8.♗d3 ♘f6 9.0-0 0-0 10.h3 ♘c6 11.♗g5 ♕d6 12.c4 d4?

Black understandably overlooks white's strong reply. White draws black's bishop to a vulnerable square and and uses a double attack to break open his opponent's kingside.

13.c5! ♗xc5

Forced: 13...♕d8 14.♖c1, and white wins the d-pawn; or 13...♕d5 14.♖c1 ♖d8 15.♖e1, with a good game for white.

14.♗xf6 gxf6 15.♕c1!

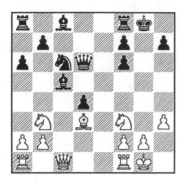

White threatens the bishop and
16.♕h6!

15...♘b4

Also losing are: 15...♗b4 16.a3 ♗a5
17.♕1h6; and 15...b6 16.♘xc5 ♕xc5
17.♕h6 f5 18.♖ac1.

16.♕xc5 1-0

MODERN BENONI [A66]
Shamkovich-Zheliandinov
RSFSR Ch., 1959

This popular defense leads to
double-edged play in which almost
anything is possible.

1.d4 ♘f6 2.c4 c5 3.d5 e6

It has long since become common
knowledge that advancing the e-pawn
before white plays ♘f3 is dangerous for
black because of the very central pawn
attack carried out in this game.

4.♘c3 exd5 5.cxd5 d6 6.e4 g6 7.f4 ♕e7?!

This is an unsuccessful attempt to
improve on such main lines as 7...a6
8.e5! and 7...♗g7 8.♗b5+ ♘fd7 9.a4.

With the text, black hopes to restrain the
e4-pawn and follow with ...♘bd7,
...♗g7 and ...0-0.

8.♘f3

The most logical move. Less
convincing is 8.♗b5+ ♗d7 9.♗d3?,
suggested by Kapengut in his Indian
Defences (Minsk, 1986) on the basis of
the game Reingard-Estrada (San Paulo,
1960): 9...b5? 10.♕e2 b4 11.e5! dxe5
12.d6, with a decisive attack for white.
Actually, the simple 9...♗g7 10.♘f3
♗g4 should solve black's problems.

8...♘bd7

Black still hopes to restrain the
central pawn advance.

9.e5!

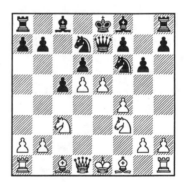

An even more brilliant alternative I
uncovered 31 years later (!) is 9.♗b5 a6
10.e5! with the idea 10...axb5
11.♘xb5, or even 11.0-0!? Ah, well,
"let's leave well enough alone" -
although this popular proverb is hardly
applicable to chess, where "second
best" is often a dead loss.

9...dxe5 10.fxe5 ♘xe5 11.♗b5+ ♘ed7+

Black can no longer escape: e.g., 11...♗d7 12.0-0 0-0-0 13.♘xe5 ♛xe5 14.♗f4 ♛d4+ 15.♛xd4+ cxd4 16.♖ac1!; or 11...♘fd7 12.0-0 Bg7 13.d6 ♛e6 14.♘d5! ♛xd6 15.♗g5!, threatening 16.♘f6+ or 16.♗e7.

12.♔f2 ♘g4+ 13.♔g3!

The king, feeling extremely fit, saunters forth to join the attack.

13...♘ge5 14.♘xe5 ♛xe5+ 15.♗f4 ♛f6 16.♛e2+

White also wins with 16.♖e1+ ♔d8 17.d6.

16...♗e7 17.d6 g5 18.♗e5 ♗xd6

Superfluous.

19.♗xd6+ ♔d8 20.♗c7+ 1-0

KING'S INDIAN [E80]
Platonov-Shamkovich
USSR Ch., 1971

1.d4 ♘f6 2.c4 g6 3.♘c3 ♗g7 4.e4 d6 5.f3 ♘c6

This well-known method of counterplay against the Saemisch variation prepares pawn breaks at either e5 or b5.

6.♗e3 a6 7.♘ge2 ♖b8

In preparing for this game, I was planning ...e5 prior to castling, although I had seen no previous examples of this approach and had not

worked out the details of the plan. As it turned out, this was a new theoretical idea.

8.♘c1

At the time, this maneuver was popular, freeing the bishop and transferring the knight to b3, increasing white's control over d4. Instead, contemporary players prefer the more active 8.♛d2 b5 9.0-0-0, without surrendering control of d4.

8...e5 9.d5 ♘d4!?

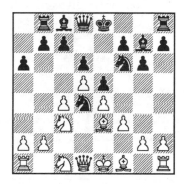

10.♘b3

Platonov declines the pawn sac without a moment's hesitation. The Ukrainian players were well-versed in the theory of the King's Indian and the importance of the bishop at g7. After 10.♗xd4 exd4 11.♛xd4, play might continue 11...0-0 12.♛d3 (otherwise, ...♘xe4) ...c5!, followed by ...b5 and active kingside play with ...♘h5 and ...f5. The black bishop at g7, unopposed by its white counterpart, is likely to dominate play effectively for a long time. Still, the question of this center sacrifice's soundness, especially with the high level of modern defensive technique, is still open. I remember Tigran Petrosian once voicing skepticism about black's chances, only to recommend the safer 9.♘b3 himself a few years later.

10...c5!

This is the point of black's opening plan. After 11.dxc6 bxc6, the rook on b8 is extremely active, and the possibility of a knight posted on d4 supported by two pawns is very unpleasant for white. Years later, in Velimirovic - Shamkovich (Rio de Janeiro Interzonal 1979), my opponent allowed a similar position: 1.e4 g6 2.d4 d6 3.h4!? h6 4.h5 g5 5.c4 ♗g7 6.♘c3 ♘c6 7.♗e3 ♘f6 8.f3 a6 9.♘ge2 ♖b8 10.♘c1 e5 11.d5 ♘d4 12.b4!? c5 13.♘b3 b6 with equality.

11.dxc6 bxc6 12.♘xd4 exd4 13.♗xd4 ♖xb2 14.♘b5?

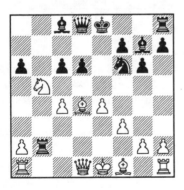

White was planning this resolute thrust when he played 11.dxc6. It looks very strong, since both 14...axb5 15.♗xb2 and 14...♕a5+ 15.♗c3 favor white. But the following makes it clear

that he should have tried 14.♕c1! ♖b7, with a double-edged game.

14...♘xe4!!

This paradoxical move was not easy to find over the board. I could not believe my eyes - can it really be possible to sac the knight before castling and in the face of white's active dark-squared bishop?

15.♗xb2

Other replies also favor white: e.g., 15.♘xd6+ ♕xd6 16.♗xb2 ♕b4+; 15.♗xg7 ♕a5+ 16.♗c3 ♘xc3 17.♘xd6+ ♔f8 18.♕d4 ♘b5+ (or 18.♕d3 ♘e4+) and 15.fxe4 ♕a5+.

15...♕a5+ 16.♘c3

And the roof caves in on white. Alternatives such as 16.♗c3 ♗xc3+ 17.♔e2 axb5 and 16.♔e2 ♗xb2 lead to the same result.

16...♗xc3+ 17.♗xc3 ♕xc3+ 18.♔e2 ♗e6! 0-1

The final stroke, threatening 19...♗xc4+. Leading to mate is 19.♕c1 ♗xc4+ 20.♔d1 ♘f2 mate.

"Congratulations!" exclaimed one of the other participants in the tournament. "You prepared an excellent opening variation."

"Thank you for the compliment," I replied ironically.

I couldn't help reflecting on a game I had lost many years ago to V. Ragozin after preparing a long variation in the Ruy Lopez. That is the last time I ever tried to catch an opponent with a long forcing variation prepared at home.

Frankly, I'm bowled over by contemporary professional players who manage this trick regularly against strong opposition. I am not at all sure such dogmatic preparation is good for chess progress, since it discourages opening improvisation and depends so heavily on existing theory as a launching pad for surprise continuations.

NIMZO-INDIAN [E20]
Formanek-Shamkovich
NY Chess Congress, 1978

1.d4 ♘f6 2.c4 e6 3.♘c3 ♗b4

There is little hope of crushing white in the opening phase of the game with this rock-solid defense, unlike the more dynamic King's Indian or Modern Benoni variations. Miniatures, of course, abound in every system. Three historical masterpieces with the Nimzo-Indian come to mind: Keres-Botvinnik (USSR Ch, Leningrad, 1941); Spassky-Fischer (W. Ch. Match, 1972); and Gheorghiu-L. Stein (Mar del Plata, 1965).

4.f3

This "old" move takes control of the key e4 square, but interferes with white's development unlike 4.e3, 4.♕c2 or 4.♘f3.

4...c5

Black blasts away at white's pawn center, but blockading the d4-pawn with 4...d5 is more popular. Which move is preferable? Since both involve maneuvering and tactical play, the choice is purely a matter of taste. A good

example of 4...d5 is the aforementioned Gheorghiu-Stein masterpiece: 5.a3 ♗d6!? 6.e4 c5!? 7.cxd5 exd5 8.e5? (8.dxc5!?) cxd4 9.♕xd4 ♕e7 10.♗f4 ♘c6 11.♗b5 0-0 12.♗xc6 ♗c5! 13.♘xd5 (13.♕d2 bxc6, with a plus for black) 13...♘xd5 14.♕xd5 ♖d8! (A new "in-between-move" - Stein never missed an opportunity to insert one of these moves.) 15.♕e4 bxc6 16.♘e2 (Black's attack is decisive after 16.♕xc6 ♗b7 17.♕a4 ♖d4) 16...♗a6! (A classic attacking formation - black's bishops X-ray the entire board, and white cannot castle.) 17.♗e3 ♖d5! 18.f4 ♖ad8 19.♗xc5 (White's position is hopeless in any case: e.g., 19.♔f2 ♖d2 20.♖ae1 ♖8d3 21.♗xc5 ♕xc5+ 22.♔f1 ♖xe2! 23.♕xe2 ♖d2! [GM Ray Keene]) 19...♕xc5+ 20.b4 ♕b6 21.♖c1 ♖d2, white resigned. My game took a more positional course.

5.d5 d6

Also very interesting is 5...♘h5!? 6.g3 (6.♘h3!?) ♗xc3+ 7.bxc3 f5 8.e4 f4!? 9.dxe6 ♕f6 (Moskalenko - Novikov, USSR, Lvov, 1988), although such an impudent counterattack seems premature to me.

6.e4 ♗xc3+ 7.bxc3 e5

This thematic push, in true Nimzovich spirit, attempts to close the center in the face of white's two bishops. Fischer chose the same plan in the cited game with Spassky after: 4.♘f3 c5 5.e3 ♘c6 6.♗d3 ♗xc3+ 7.bxc3 d6 8.e4 e5!. For some reason, contemporary masters usually avoid this solid move, preferring the sharper 8...♕a5 9.♗d2 (9.0-0) ♘bd7.

8.♗d3 0-0?

This is a serious inaccuracy. White should now have answered with 9.g4!, squelching black's kingside counterplay. Better for black is 8...♘h5!

9.♘e2? ♘h5! 10.0-0 ♛f6 11.g3

White blocks the positional threat 11...♘f4, but weakens his king's position. The "ugly" 11.♛d2!? is worth considering: e.g.,11...h6 12.g4 ♘f4 13.♘xf4 exf4 14.♛xf4 ♛xc3 15.♛d2 ♛xa1 16.♗b2 ♛xa2 17.♛c3! f6 18.♖a1 ♛xa1 19.♗xa1 ♘d7 20.f4 a6, with a double-edged and unclear position.

11...g5!?

The plot takes an unexpected turn. Black initiates an attack on the king's wing, where his own monarch resides. Such conceptions are more frequent in classical openings: e.g., 1.e4 e5 2.♘f3 ♘c6 3.♗c4 ♗c5 4.0-0 ♘f6 5.d3 d6 6.♗g5 h6 7.♗h4? g5 8.♗g3 h5! 9.♘xg5 h4! 10.♘xf7 hxg3!! 11.♘xd8 ♗g4 12.♛d2 ♘d4 13.♘c3 ♘f3+ 14.gxf3 ♗xf3, white resigned (Dubois- Steinitz, 1862). This brilliant miniature surfaces again and again as an opening trap, and we meet similar ideas in diverse opening settings, even more solid ones like the Nimzo-Indian. This game is a good example.

12.♗e3 ♚h8 13.♛d2 ♖g8

This is the point of black's plan, threatening 14...♘f4.

14.♚h1 ♘d7 15.♖f2 ♘b6

16.f4?

This attempt to dynamite black's (apparently) unstable kingside structure backfires. The correct move is 16.a4, but still promising for black is 16...♗d7 17.a5 ♘c8, followed by ...♘e7 and ...♘f4 after due preparation.

16...gxf4 17.gxf4 ♗g4!

This very unpleasant surprise creates several threats: e.g., 18.♖g1 ♗xe2 19.♗xe2 ♖xg1+ 20.♚xg1 ♖g8+ 21.♚f1 (or 21.♚h1 ♛g6 wins) 21...♛h4! 22.♗xh5 ♛h3+! crushing. Weaknesses of the pawns at e4 and c4 (typical for some Nimzo-Indian systems) counted in this variation.

18.f5 ♛h4 19.♖g1?

A blunder in a desperate position, if 19.♘g1 ♘g3+ 20.♚g2 ♘xe4! 21.♗xe4 ♗h3+ 22.♚h1 ♛xe4+, and black wins.

19...♛xf2! 0-1

White resigned in view of 20.♗xf2 ♗f3+ 21.♖g2 ♖xg2!

VERESOV SYSTEM [D01]
Shagalovich-Shamkovich
Grozniy Team Ch., 1969

1.d4 ♘f6 2.♘c3 d5 3.♗g5

Although this system has been well-known since the '60s, it has not been very popular. It does, however, appear occasionally in tournaments in the hands of even the strongest International Masters and Grandmasters. The obvious weakness of the system is the pawn at c2, and white cannot count on an advantage after such reasonable replies as 3...♗f5, 3...c5, or 3...♘bd7. This has been demonstrated over and over again in practice, but the eccentric nature of this system makes black's play far from easy if he is unprepared to meet it.

At this time, my opponent joined other strong Soviet masters from Minsk, including Veresov himself, as the world's leading authorities on the system. Oddly enough, Minsk's best player, GM Isaac Boleslavsky, never plays the Veresov, seldom adopting 1. d4, and has opposed it willingly and successfully many times.

3...♘bd7 4.♘f3 h6 5.♗h4 c6 6.e4!? g5 7.♗g3 ♘xe4 8.♘xe4 dxe4 9.♘e5

This gambit had been worked out in detail by Shagalovich and his friends. The alternative is 9.♘d2 f5 10.h4 f4 11.♕h5+ ♔e7 12.hxg5 fxg3 13.0-0-0 ♕e8 14.♕h4 ♔d8 15.♘xe4 ♗e7 16.♕xg3, with an unclear position (ECO DO1). White has two pawns and a strong initiative for the piece. Perhaps better than 9...f5 is 9...♗g7 10.♘xe4 f5. In any case, the text move seems

more logical and active. At the time, of course, I knew none of this.

9...♗g7 10.h4 ♘xe5 11.♗xe5 f6!?

I was surprised to learn after the game that this natural move was a new one in the position (12.♕h5+ ♔f8 is not dangerous for black). Theorists were recommending 11...♗xe5 12.dxe5 ♗d7 13.♕d2? gxh4 with equality. I am sure my opponent had something stronger in mind - such as 13.♕g4! ♗c6 14.♖d1! winning.

12.♗g3 0-0!

Black continues his development, counting on the bishop at g7 to protect his king.

13.hxg5 fxg5

Black opens lines for a counterattack since 13...hxg5 14.♕h5 is unpleasant for him. This move weakens black's center pawns at e4 and e6, but black expects dynamic counterplay.

14.c3 ♗d7 15.♗c4 ♕f6 16.♕e2 ♕f5

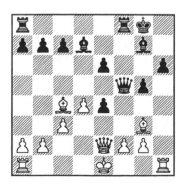

17.♗xc7?!

"Why not munch this key pawn before castling?" Shagalovich must have reasoned. Either 17.0-0 or 17.0-0-0 would have been better: 17.0-0 b5! 18.♗b3 b4 19.♗c2 ♗c6, with a double-edged position; or 17.0-0-0 b5 18.♗b3 b4 19.♗c2 bxc3! 20.♗xe4 ♕a5, and now if 21.♗xa8? ♕xa2 22.♗e4 ♕a1+ 23.♗b1 ♖b8 24.♕c2 ♖xb2! 25.♕h7+ ♔f8 26.♗e5 ♖c2+!! 27.♔xc2 ♕b2+ mating.

17...♖ac8 18.♗g3?

My opponent fails to sense danger. Correct was 18.♗d6 ♖fd8 19.0-0 (not 19.0-0-0? ♗a4!) ...♗c6 20.♗g3 ♗d5 21.♗xd5 (or 21.b3 b5!) exd5, and the queenside pressure gives black an advantage.

18...♖xc4!

This surprise shot obliterates white's most active piece and finally frees black's game.

19.♕xc4 e3!

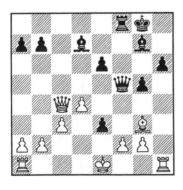

At move 17, white obviously

underestimated the potential power of this "weak pawn".

20.♕e2?

Oblivious, white continues to play for a win. This is a very common psychological mistake in the heat of battle - former World Champion Tigran Petrosian is the only player I've ever known who never fell into this trap. When his position became unexpectedly complicated, he used to systematically exchange pieces or offer a draw. The correct continuation here is 20.0-0 ♗b5 21.♕c5 ♗xf1 22.♖xf1: e.g., 22...exf2+ ♗xf2, with only a slight advantage for black.

20...exf2+ 21.♗xf2

Black meets the alternative 21.♕xf2 with 21...♕d5! 22.♕e2 ♗b5 or 22.♕e3 ♕xg2, with a strong attack in either case.

21...♗b5

A bishop laser!

22.♕d2

White offers a little more resistance with 22.♕e3, but also decisive is 23...e5!, opening new lines.

22...♕e4+ 23.♗e3

White overlooks the graceful finale, but also hopeless is 23.♕e3 ♕xg2.

23...♕h4+! 0-1

GRUENFELD DEFENSE [A16]
Nei-Shamkovich
Team Ch., 1955

The epic research of World Champion Garry Kasparov has made this a very popular opening today. In 1955, however, many aggressive players considered it their sworn duty to refute this brash system as quickly as possible. In this game, I took the opposite side of this debate.

1.c4 ♘f6 2.♘c3 d5 3.cxd5 ♘xd5 4.♘f3 g6 5.h4?

White is shooting blanks. An empty threat is h4-h5, and he weakens g4. Today, masters are choosing between 5.d4, transposing to the main-line Gruenfeld, 5.e4, and the aggressive 5.♕a4+!?

5...h6!

Not 5...♗g7 6.h5, with advantage to white. Sometimes, however, in similar positions this preventive move is unnecessary: e.g., 1.d4 ♘f6 2.c4 g6 3.♘c3 d5 4.cxd5 ♘xd5 5.e4 ♘xc3 6.bxc3 ♗g7 7.c4 0-0 8.♘e2 ♘c6 9.h4?! ♘a5 10.♗b3 c5!, seizing the initiative (Spassky-Stein, USSR Championship Playoff, 1964). The difference is that Nei was poised for sharp counterplay in the center. Here, discretion is still the better part of valor.

6.e3 ♗g7 7.♗c4 ♘b6 8.♗b3 c5 9.♘e4?

This is an invitation for black to sacrifice. White probably expected 9...♘bd7 10.d4, with good play. Unfortunately, the text involves a loss of time. Correct is 9.d4.

9...c4!

Black intends to take advantage of the weaknesses at d3 and g4, especially after the exchange of light-squared bishops. GM David Bronstein, in his latest Russian book, offers a similar idea in another position: 1.c4 ♘f6 2.♘f3 c5 3.♘c3 d5 4.cxd5 ♘xd5 5.g3 g6 6.♕b3!? ♘b4! 7.♘e4 ♗g7 8.♘xc5 ♕a5 9.a3 (Bronstein believes 9.♘d3 is relatively better, but black has more than enough compensation after 9...♘xd3+ 10.♕xd3 ♘c6, threatening ...♗f5.)...♘4c6 10.♕c4 b5 11.♕h4 b4 12.♘d3 ♘a6 13.♗g2 ♗d7 14.0-0 ♖c8 15.♘de1 ♘c5, with strong counterplay for the pawn. The book, "A Self-Help Manual of Chess", parodies philosophy in a children's book format, creating its own stylistic paradox.

The question of which came first, Bronstein's chicken or Shamkovich's egg, is less important than the fact that certain strategic ideas in the middlegame repeat themselves, but are almost never noted by commentators. Eventually, some enterprising theoretician will create a modern middlegame "album", classifying these ideas and positions. Up to now, no one has been willing to tackle this arduous task. Maybe today's computers will solve this problem.

10.♗xc4

Black has an excellent game after 10.♗c2 ♘c6.

10...♘xc4 11.♕a4+ ♘c6 12.♕xc4 ♗f5 13.♘c5 ♖c8!

White's queen invites one black piece after another to join the party with gain of tempo - a familiar opening motif.

14.g4

White still cannot escape the mounting pressure - the threat was 14...b6 15.♘b3 ♘d4.

14...b5! 15.♕xb5 ♗xg4 16.♘h2 ♗f5 17.e4

White's position is horribly compromised. A normal move such as 17.d4 fails to 17...0-0, threatening 18...e5 or 18...♗xd4. Nei hopes to solve his problems tactically. After 17...♗h3, white can force the exchange of queens with 18.♕d3, but black takes advantage of the weakened d4-square with a piece sacrifice.

17...0-0! 18.exf5 ♕d5 19.0-0 gxf5 20.d3 ♘d4 21.f3 ♘xb5 0-1

Thus far in this chapter, we have examined in detail ten different catastrophes in many different opening systems. The purpose of this thematic variety is to provide dynamic proof of the potential hidden in the full range of open, half-open, and closed openings.

Part II
Sicilian Ambushes: Studies in the Sicilian

The Sicilian Defense is currently the most frequently encountered system at all levels of chess. It offers a wide range of play, from lightning tactical strikes to cold calculated siege, from impetuous attacks by white to bold counter offensives by black. Both sides have an arsenal of deep strategic conceptions. In spite of the exploratory forays already completed by theorists into the Sicilian and dozens of books on Sicilian variations, chess players of all ranks are willing to trust their lives to its intricacies, occasionally still unearthing original ideas for both sides.

Part of the attraction of the contemporary Sicilian is that it can be adapted to various martial approaches. With white, you can opt for a military siege with the quiet Closed System (2. ♘c3) or the solid c3 lines, or you can storm the black defenses with the aggressive Open System (2. ♘f3 and 3. d4), preparing either a kingside or queenside offensive. With black, you have the same strategic choices - trench warfare with somewhat passive systems such as the Scheveningen, hoping to repulse white's initial charge before switching over to counterattack, or the combinative blitzkrieg of the Dragon Variation.

My young students sometimes ask me which variation in each case is best. I always answer, "Play what you know and understand best. One of the beauties of chess is that it always leaves us with choices, giving the widest possible rein to our individual personalities and imaginations."

I have always been a great admirer of this fighting system, and I used to try virtually every conceivable line, contriving to play more than a few instructive games and introduce more than one new idea to Sicilian theory. Today, however, I confess that I can no longer compete with contemporary Sicilian virtuosos, whose creative ideas abound in today's chess magazines and books. I have, therefore, chosen for this chapter only those of my games likely to add to my reader's arsenal of attacking ideas, making the Sicilian a more dangerous weapon in his hands.

THE SCHEVENINGEN VARIATION [B83]

Shamkovich-Panno
Natanya, 1975

1.e4 c5 2.♘f3 d6 3.d4 cxd4 4.♘xd4 ♘f6 5.♘c3 e6 6.♗e2 ♘c6 7.♗e3 ♗e7 8.0-0 ♗d7 9.♘b3 a6 10.a4 b6 11.f4 0-0

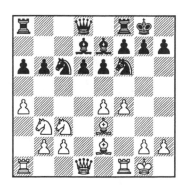

This is one of the most familiar and

popular Sicilian "tabiyas." For fifteen years, its interpretation remained fairly stable until Gary Kasparov took matters into his hands. He created a precise system of black counterplay that delivered repeated successes and furthered his drive toward the highest chess crown.

The main point of this plan is to thwart white's traditional attack with the g2-g4-g5 advance; transferring black's bishop from d7 to b7 after white has played ♘b3. Moves such as ...♖ab8 and ...♖fe8 forestall both white's kingside and queenside aggression.

Laying the groundwork with this plan, Kasparov plays the Sicilian middlegame with consummate confidence, as in the unforgettable 24th game in his 1985 World Championship match with Karpov.

Karpov-Kasparov [B85]
Moscow (m/24), 1985

1.e4 c5 2.♘f3 d6 3.d4 cxd4 4.♘xd4 ♘f6 5.♘c3 a6 6.♗e2 e6 7.0-0 ♗e7 8.f4 0-0 9.♔h1 ♕c7 10.a4 ♘c6 11.♗e3 ♖e8 12.♗f3 ♖b8 13.♕d2 ♗d7 14.♘b3 b6 15.g4 ♗c8 16.g5 ♘d7 17.♕f2 ♗f8 18.♗g2 ♗b7 19.♖ad1 g6 20.♗c1 ♖bc8 21.♖d3 ♘b4 22.♖h3 ♗g7 23.♗e3 ♖e7 24.♔g1 ♖ce8 25.♖d1 f5 26.gxf6 ♘xf6 27.♖g3 ♖f7 28.♗xb6 ♕b8 29.♗e3 ♘h5 30.♖g4 ♘f6 31.♖h4 g5 32.fxg5 ♘g4 33.♕d2 ♘xe3 34.♕xe3 ♘xc2 35.♕b6 ♗a8 36.♖xd6 ♖b7 37.♕xa6 ♖xb3 38.♖xe6 ♖xb2 39.♕c4 ♔h8 40.e5 ♕a7+ 41.♔h1 ♗xg2+ 42.♔xg2 ♘d4+ 0-1

This fantastic game provoked furious controversies, with Kasparov's direct and Karpov's indirect participation. The only comparable public debate I remember is the dramatic post mortem analyses following the 6th game of the Botvinnik-Tal match in 1960. In both cases, commentators world-wide wrestled furiously to prove that the winners played "incorrectly." Their arguments in both cases were far from convincing.

12.♖f2!?

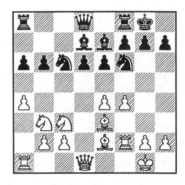

Usually you can expect to see the routine 12.♗f3 here. I intend to transfer the queen to a strong kingside attacking position with a gain of tempo.

12...♕c7 13.♖c1!

This is the point of white's plan. The pawn at c2 will soon require protection. Interestingly, Kasparov and Nikitin cite only 13.♕f1 ♘b4 14.♗f3 ♖ac8, leading to a double-edged game. This plan is weaker because the bishop at f3 hampers white's kingside attack.

13...♖fd8?

This validates white's attack. Correct is 13...♘b4 14.♗f3 (14.g4 d5! with counterplay) ♖ab8 15.g4 ♗c8 16.g5 ♘d7.

14.g4 ♗e8

Too passive. Deserving attention is 14...d5!?, though 15.exd5 ♘xd5 16.♘xd5 exd5 17.♗f3 clearly favors white.

15.g5 ♘d7 16.♕f1 ♘b4 17.♕h3

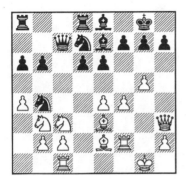

White has realized his idea and is preparing to storm black's kingside with f4-f5 (e.g., 17...♘c5 18.f5 cxf5 [18...e5 19.f6] 19.exf5 ♘xa4 20.g6!, with a crushing position). Advancing the f-pawn is also strong after 17...♘f8, but a good positional alternative is 18.♗f3 ♖ac8 19.♖cd1, leaving black without serious counterplay even though it is his best try.

17...g6?

Sometimes in sharp variations of the Sicilian, this risky move rescues black when the threat of ♘f5 looms. But here it cannot prevent the other threat of f4-f5, leading to a fatal weakening of black's kingside, especially on the a1-h8 diagonal.

18.f5 exf5 19.exf5 d5

This is a desperate attempt to free black's position.

20.fxg6 hxg6 21.♖f4!

The tactical point of white's attack; this move gains an important tempo for the transfer of the rook to a killing position at h4 by attacking the knight at b4. Less effective is the natural 21.♗d4 ♘e5.

21...♗c5

Black is hoping for 22.♘xc5 bxc5 23.♖h4 ♕e5, surviving.

22.♖xb4! ♗xb4 23.♘xd5

White's knight joins the attack with deadly effect.

23...♕e5

It is impossible to save the bishop - after 23...♕d6, either 24.♗d4 or 24.♖d1 is strong.

24.♘xb4

White has an extra piece. The rest is clear.

24...♘c5 25.♘xc5 bxc5 26.♘d3 ♕e7 27.♖e1 ♗xa4 28.♗f3 c4 29.♘f2 ♖ac8 30.♗d2 ♕c5 31.♗c3 1-0

While the original maneuver ♖f2 followed by ♕f1 cannot be unreservedly recommended to expert Sicilian attackers, it is well worth a try.

Seven years after my emigration from the Soviet Union, I resurrected the following system with white in my repertoire. Emerging well prepared from a memorable fight with Damjanovich, I won three games now cited in the opening books. In all three games, I played a2-a4, preventing ...b7-b5, while my opponents tried Korchnoi's ...g6, very popular at the time. I regarded this move critically, but was convinced of its vitality - with precise interpretation.

ATTACKING THE SCHEVENINGEN WITH ♕e1-g3

The maneuver ♕e1-g3 is an established attacking theme in the Sicilian Scheveningen. The queen simultaneously supports a possible e4-e5 and transfers to an active kingside role. In earlier games, white conducted the attack by pushing the f- and g-pawns instead of f- and e-pawns. Both plans are viable, depending on move orders and plans on both sides. If, for example, white has already played ♘b3 or black has avoided ...a6 and ...♕c7, the current approach is not very effective; g2-g4 would be more reasonable. I have played this system many times from the white side, creating several very nice instructive games. Against Jim Sherwin, I was determined to refute ...g6, apparently succeeding, but only after what has to have been the hardest work I've ever done over a chessboard.

Shamkovich-Sherwin [B85]
Lone Pine, 1976

1.e4 c5 2.♘f3 d6 3.d4 cxd4 4.♘xd4 ♘f6 5.♘c3 e6 6.♗e2 a6 7.f4 ♕c7 8.0-0 ♘c6 9.♗e3 ♗e7 10.♔h1 0-0 11.a4

Preventing ...b7-b5 which is possible after 11.♕e1 ♘xd4 12.♗xd4 b5.

11...♗d7 12.♕e1 ♘xd4 13.♗xd4 ♗c6 14.♕g3

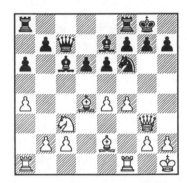

This is a key position. with several alternatives to Korchnoi's ...g6. In their book, for example, Gary Kasparov and Alexander Nikitin suggest 14...b6. White, however, gets a clear advantage after 15.e5! dxe5 (15...♘e8 16.f5!) 16.♗xe5 ♕b7 17.f5!, e.g., 17...exf5 18.♖xf5 ♘e8 19.♗c4, or 18...♔h8 19.♖af1 while 17...b5 loses a pawn after 18.axb5. A rare inaccuracy in an excellent book.

14...g6!? 15.f5!

Black has adequate counterplay after the quiet 15.♗f3 b5!, or 15.♗d3? ♘h5 16.♕f2 e5! The latter is no more effective if white has saved a tempo by omitting ♔h1. A good example is Evans - Shamkovich (USA Championship, 1980):

1.e4 c5 2.♘f3 d6 3.d4 cxd4 4.♘xd4 ♘f6 5.♘c3 e6 6.f4 ♘c6 7.♗e2 ♗e7 8.♗e3 0-0 9.0-0 ♗d7 10.♕e1 ♘xd4 11.♗xd4 ♗c6 12.♕g3 g6 13.♗d3? ♘h5 14.♕f2 ♘xf4! 15.♕xf4 e5 16.♕f2 exd4 17.♕xd4 ♕a5 (with excellent play) 18.♘d5? ♗xd5 19.♕xd5 ♕xd5 20.exd5 f5!, and black has a clear edge.

15...e5

Ineffectual is 15...♘xe4? 16.♘xe4 ♗xe4 17.f6 ♗d8 18.♕h4! e5 19.♗c3 ♕c6 20.♗f3 (better than 20.♕h6 ♗xg2+ 21.♔g1 ♗xf6) ...d5 (if 20...♗xf3 21.♖xf3 ♔h8 22.♕h6 ♖g8 23.♕xh7+!+-) 21.♗xe4 dxe4 22.♗xe5 ♔h8 23.♖a3! (threatening both 24.♖h3 and 24.♕h6) ...♕c4 24.♖g1 with a crushing advantage, e.g., 24...♕e6 25.♖h3 h5 26.Qg5 wins.

16.♗e3

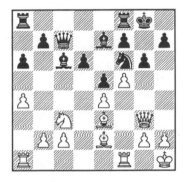

16...b5!?

Maybe black should finally grab the pawn at e4? No way! Two nice variations make it poisoned fruit: A) 16...♘xe4? 17.♘xe4 ♗xe4 18.f6 ♗d8 19.c4! d5 (or 19...♔h8 20.♗g5!) 20.♕h4 ♕d6 21.♗g5 ♗f5 22.♖f5 winning, or B) 16...♗xe4? 17.fxg6 ♗xg6 18.♖xf6! ♗xf6 19.♘d5 (a dream position for the knight in the Sicilian)...♕d8 20.♗b6 ♗h4 21.♗xd8 ♗xg3 22.♗f6! (with the winning threat of 23.♗e7 mate) ...♖fb8 23.hxg3 with a won game (two pieces vs. rook and a strong control over central squares).

A serious alternative is 16...d5!?

e.g., 17.fxg6 hxg6 18.exd5 ♘xd5 19.♗c4! ♗h4 (hoping for 20.♕xh4? ♘xe3) 20.♕g4 ♗d7!? (Black's final try, setting the trap 21.♘xd5? ♗xg4! 22.♘xc7 ♖ac8, regaining the piece with a good game. But not 21...♘xe3? 22.♕xg6+ ♔h8 23.♕h6+ ♔g8 24.♕xe3, when black's precarous king position leaves no serious chances of escape) 21.♕xh4! ♘xe3 22.♗xf7+! ♖xf7 23.♖xf7 ♔xf7 24.♕h7+ ♔f8 25.♕h6+ ♔f7 26.♕xe3 (with a decisive attack). Shamkovich-Grefe, Lone Pine, 1976 continued 26...♗c6 27.♕h6 ♖g8 28.♕h7+ ♖g7 29.♖f1+ ♔e6 30.♕h3+ ♔e7 31.♕h4+ ♔d7 32.♕f6 ♖e7 33.♕xg6 e4 34.♕g4+ ♔e8 35.♕g8+ 1-0.

Also doubtful is 16...♔h8 17.♕h4! ♕d8 18.♗g5 as seen in Shamkovich-Murray, Calgary 1975, when I should have answered 18...♖g8 with 19.♖ad1! with a clear advantage instead of 19.♖f3 as played. That game continued (after 18.♗g5) 18...♖g8 19.♖f3?! gxf5 20.♖xf5 ♖xg5! 21.♕xg5 ♗d7?! (21... ♘xe4!? 22.♕g4 ♘f6 with chances for both sides) 22.♖ff1 ♘xe4 23.♕h5 ♘f6 24.♖xf6?! (24.♕xf7!? is slightly better for white) ♗xf6 25.♖f1 ♗c6 26.♗d3 ♕g8 27.♘e4 ♗e7 28.♖xf7 ♗e8? (better is 28...♖f8!? with an equal game) 29.♘g5 ♗xf7 30.♘xf7+ ♔g7 31.♕h6+, 1-0.

The text move is apparently black's best chance.

17.♗h6 ♖fc8

Worth attention is the exchange sacrifice 17...b4!?, hoping for 18.♗xf8? ♖xf8 19.fxg6 hxg6 20.♗c4 ♔g7, with an edge for black. Very

strong, however, is 18.fxg6! hxg6
19.♗c4 ♔h7 20.♕h3 ♗d7 21.♕h4!

18.♗d3! ♔h8

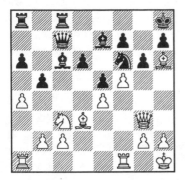

White answers 18...b4 with 19.♗c4!
bxc3 20.fxg6 ♔h8 21.♗xf7 hxg6
22.♗g7+! ♔xg7 23.♕xg6+ ♔f8
24.♗e6 ♗d8 (24...♗xe4 25.♕f7 mate,
Parma-Hamman, BDR 1978) 25.♕g8+
♔e7 26.♕f7 mate. No better is
19...♘h5 20.♕g4 ♘f6 21.fxg6!

19.♕h3?!

Even the smallest inaccuracy can
spoil an attack, poised on the razor's
edge between life and death for both
players. Only after the game did I realize
that 19.♕h4! was stronger, and two
years later I was able to use this
discovery against Vranesich in
Hamilton, Canada (1978): thus 19.♕h4!
♖g8 20.♗g5 ♕d8 21.axb5 axb5
22.♖xa8 ♗xa8.

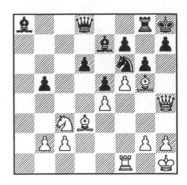

(analysis)

In this complex and critical position,
the game continued 23.♗xb5?! gxf5
24.♖xf5 ♖g6? 25.♗c4! d5 26.exd5
♖xg5 (Too late) 27.♕xg5 ♘xd5
28.♕d2 ♕c8 29.♖xf7 ♘f4 30.♖xf4
exf4 31.♕d4+ 1-0, but instead of
24...♖g6? (as played) my opponent had
the resource 24...♖xg5! e.g., 25.♕xg5
♘xe4 26.♕h5 f6 or 26...♘xc3 27.bxc3
f6 holding in both lines. Let us return to
our analysis diagram. Many years after
the game, I was able to solve this
analytical problem. Thus, 23.♘d5!! and
now A) 23...♗xd5 24.exd5 gxf5
25.♗xf5 ♖xg5 26.♕xg5 ♘xd5
27.♕h6! ♘f6 (or 27...♕g8 28.♗e4
♘f4 29.g3 ♘g6 30.♗d5 winning)
28.♗xh7! ♘xh7 29.♖xf7 and white
wins, or B) 23...♘xd5 24.fxg6! (if
24...fxg6 25.♖f7 ♖g7 26.♗xe7 ♘xe7
27.♕f6! wins) ...♖g7 25.gxf7! ♖xg5
(after 25...♕f8 26.♗xe7 ♘xe7
27.♕xe7 ♕xe7 28.f8♕+ ♕xf8
29.♖xf8+ ♖g8 30.♖xg8+ ♔xg8
31.♔g1 (White has a won endgame)
26.exd5 and white wins.

So how does white achieve an
advantage and which move is better?
Now it is clear - just 19.♕h4!

We will see soon why 19.♕h3?! is
weaker.

19...b4! 20.fxg6 fxg6?

Who can believe black had to take the knight? Better was 20...bxc3! ignoring, at first site, deadly threats against his king e.g., 21.♖xf6! ♗xf6 (21...cxb2?? leads to mate after 22.♗g7+!) 22.♗g5 fxg6 23.♗xf6+ ♔g8 24.♗c4+ d5 25.exd5 ♕f7 26.♗xe5 ♗xd5 27.♖f1? ♗xg2+!!, winning (but not 27...♕b7 28.♕e6!!, and white wins). Better is, of course, 27.♗xd5 ♕xd5 28.♗xc3.

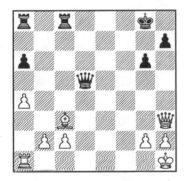

(analysis)

White has the strong bishop and two pawns vs. rook, but black is not worse anyway. For this reason 19.♕h3?! was not the best choice. My opponent missed this possibility, and the balance of the game now tilted decisively in my favor.

21.♕e6! ♖f8

White has a big edge after 21...bxc3 22.♖f6 cxb2 23.♖b1 ♕d7 24.♕xd7! ♗xd7 25.♖f7 ♖e8 26.♗c4!, planning ♗xg7.

22.♗xf8 ♖xf8 23.♘d5 ♗xd5 24.exd5 a5 25.♖f3 ♔g7 26.♖af1 ♗d8 27.♕h3

White's position is winning.

27...♕c5 28.b3 ♕xd5 29.♗c4 ♕e4 30.♕e6 d5? 31.♗xd5 ♕d4 32.♗c4 e4 33.♖f4 ♕c5 34.g3 e3 35.♖1f3 ♗b6 36.♖xf6 e2 37.♖f7+ ♖xf7 38.♕xf7+ ♔h6 39.♕f4+ ♔g7 40.♕f6+ ♔h6 41.♕h4+♕h5 42.♕xh5+ ♔xh5 43.♗xe2 ♔g5 44.♔g2 h5 45.♖f7 1-0

Shamkovich-Damjanovich,M [B85]
Sochi, 1967

1.e4 c5 2.♘f3 e6 3.♘c3 ♘c6 4.d4 cxd4 5.♘xd4 a6 6.♗e2 ♕c7 7.0-0 ♘f6 8.♔h1 ♗e7 9.f4 d6 10.♗e3 0-0 11.♕e1

Why not? Black seems to be begging white to light this fuse. Nevertheless, more accurate is 11.a4.

11...♗d7 12.♕g3

12...♔h8?!

I was very surprised to see this passive anti-positional move even though the idea behind it is clear - to prevent the potential threats ♗h6 and e5. More aggressive (and more risky) is

12...b5!? allowing the methodical break 13.e5! dxe5 14.fxe5 ♘xe5! (14...♛xe5?? 15.♘xc6 wins). This sharp line is analyzed in detail by Kasparov and Nikitin in their book, with such variations as 15.♗f4, 15.♗h6, 15.♘f3 and 15.♖xf6, but no one has demonstrated any clear advantage to white. For example, 15.♖xf6 ♗xf6 16.♗f4 b4 17.♘e4 ♔h8 18.♘f3 ♛xc2 and black maintains a balance. In this line, the attempt 18.♗d3 ♛a5 19.♘xf6 gxf6! (Not 19...♘xd3 because of 20.♛h4 with a crushing attack) 20.♛h4 ♘g6 21.♛xf6+ ♔g8 22.♗h6 ♛e5! parrying all threats. Of course, such analysis requires deep research and examination, however one cannot help admiring the resources in black's position after 13.e5. Black has, however, more adequate methods of defense at his disposal, e.g., 12...♘xd4 13. ♗xd4 b5, so I was surprised recently to find the text occurring several times in serious practice, notably in Larsen-Hort, Bugojno, 1978, which went 12...♔h8 13.♖ad1 b5 14.e5 dxe5 15.fxe5 ♛xe5? (Better is 15...♘e8) 16.♗f4, with advantage to white.

13.a3!?

White prepares to transfer his bishop from e2 to a strong position on d3, especially unpleasant for black's king in the corner. A good alternative is the "book" 13.♖ad1, as played by Larsen.

13...♖ac8

More accurate is 13...♖ab8.

14.♗d3 b5 15.♖ae1 ♛b8

Black plans to counterattack with ...b4.

16.e5! ♘g8?

This is a horrible move, depriving the king of g8. ♖elatively better is 16...dxe5 17.♘xc6 ♗xc6 18.fxe5 ♘h5 19.♛g4 g6 (if 19...♛xe5 20.♗d2 ♘f6 21.♛h3! wins) 20.♗h6 ♘g7 21.♗g5 ♛c7 when white maintains some edge after 22.♗e4.

17.♘xc6 ♗xc6 18.♗d4!

White has achieved a perfect attacking position.

18...b4 19.f5!!

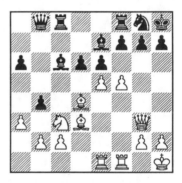

After the game, a spectator asked me, "Did you calculate the piece sacrifice when you played 16.e5 or earlier?" This is a typical question based on the assumption that Grandmasters always calculate ten moves or more in advance. Usually there is no necessity for extended calculation except in the most complicated or forcing positions. I was aware of the possibility for this advance earlier, but I considered it in detail only after my opponent played 18...b4. Human beings possess a very powerful instrument known as "intuition" which guides their calculations and makes them more trustworthy. This is the current difference between strong contemporary chess computers - whose intuition is zero, but whose ability to calculate is staggering - and human players. I have known only two players who calculate almost on the level of computers - even better if we exclude absurd half-moves - World Champions Mikhail Tal (in his prime) and Gary Kasparov. Both of these chess giants, of course, always maintain a practical balance between calculation, intuition, and preparation in their own games.

19...bxc3

Against 19...exf5, I had prepared the simple and elegant win 20.♖xf5 bxc3 21.exd6 ♗f6 22.♕h3! (threatening 23.♕xh7+!! ♔xh7 24.♖f5 mate) ...h6 23.♖xf6.

20.f6!

This is the point of the attack. White is clearing the way to black's king for his bishops, in particular for the bishop at d4, the key piece to his offensive.

20...♗xf6

The attempt 20...gxf6 fails to 21.exf6 ♘xf6 22.♖xf6 e5 23.♕h3!.

21.exf6 g6 22.♗xg6!!

Because white mates after 22...fxg6 23.f7+ e5 24.♖xe5 ♖xf7 25.♖e8+ ♖g7 26.♖f7+!.

22...e5 23.♖xe5!

This is the most logical finish, but the prosaic 23.♗xh7 ♘xf6 24.♖xf6 is equally decisive.

23...♗xg2+

Black despairs - also losing is 23...dxe5 24.♗xe5 ♕b7 25.♗e4!, or 24...♕b5 25.♗d3!.

24.♔xg2 dxe5 25.♗e4! ♘xf6 26.♗xe5 1-0

THE KERES ATTACK [B81]

Shamkovich-Benko
Pasadena 1978

1.e4 c5 2.♘f3 e6 3.d4 cxd4 4.♘xd4 ♘f6 5.♘c3 d6 6.g4!? a6

Theory has yet to decide which plan is better - 6...a6, followed by ...♘fd7 after white advances to g5, or the prophylactic 6...h6. Both plans have advantages and disadvantages. The latter in particular weakens the kingside with repercussions in the middlegame. The disadvantages of the text surface in the game.

7.g5 ♘fd7 8.♗e3 b5

This is black's most active continuation, preparing both 9...b4 and 9...♗b7.

9.a3 ♘b6 10.♖g1 ♘8d7 11.f4 ♗b7 12.f5 e5

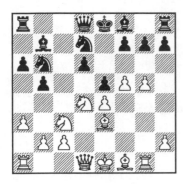

Black follows the book recommendation. Black gets reasonable counterplay from 13.♘b3 ♖c8 14.♗d3, theoretical orthodoxy at the time.

13.♘e6!!?

This crude invasion of black's camp by the knight was familiar to me from other Sicilian systems. After some thought, I decided to pull the trigger here. I wasn't sure it was an original idea, but the surprised look on Benko's face suggested that it might be.

In any case, white succeeds in disrupting the black king's position, disturbing for some time any hopes it might have held for peace. It is very strange that this logical move had not been tried before.

14...fxe6 14.♕h5+ g6?

Now black is in desperate trouble. Correct was 14...♔e7 (see the supplemental analysis below).

15.fxg6 ♔e7 16.gxh7 ♗g7 17.0-0-0 ♕e8 18.g6

A very unusual situation - white builds a stone wall in black's camp.

18...♘f6?

Black blunders, but it is already difficult to offer improvements: e.g., 18...♖c8 19.♗g5+ ♘f6 20.♗xf6+ ♗xf6 21.♕h6!, and black cannot stop the g6-pawn since the exchange-sac 21...♖xc3 22.bxc3 ♕c6 is insufficient.

19.♕xe5! ♕c6

On 19...dxe5, white has the surprising 20.♗c5 mate! Black creates more resistance with 19...♘c8, although both 20.♕g5 and 20.♗h3 dxe5 21.♗c5+ ♘d6 22.♖xd6 are very strong.

20.♖xd6!

The rest is clear.

20...♕xd6 21.♗c5 ♖ad8 22.♗h3 ♗c8 23.♗xd6+ ♖xd6 24.♕g5 e5 25.♕xe5+ ♗e6 26.♗xe6 ♖xe6 27.♕c5+ ♔e8 28.♕f5 ♖e7 29.♖d1 ♘fd7

White already has a large material advantage (queen plus 5 pawns vs. rook, bishop, and knight), and, more importantly, black's pieces are uncoordinated.

30.♘d5 ♘xd5 31.♕xd5 ♗e5 32.♕c6 ♔d8 33.♖d5! ♖f8 34.♕a8+ 1-0

Let us return to the critical position after 14.♕h5+:

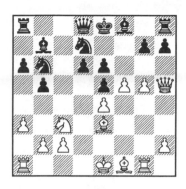

(analysis)

This anti-theoretical piece sacrifice provoked immediate criticism from my more classically oriented peers. Immediately after the game, Benko and GM Bill Lombardy grilled me - "Why did you sac the piece here?" With my limited English, the best I could reply was, "An attack against the black king."

Even as dynamic a player as Robert Byrne found fault with the idea. In his New York Times column, he noted: "The main question for the attack was what could be done if Benko had chosen the correct defense with 14...♔e7! One suggestion was 15.fxe6 ♔xe6 16.♗h3+ ♔e7 17.♖gf1 ♕e8 18.g6 ♔d8 19.♖f7 ♗e7, but Shamkovich failed to demonstrate white's compensation for the piece sacrificed."

A few months later in *Chess Life* (January 1979), I published detailed analysis demonstrating the power of the piece sacrifice. This analysis was cited by Kasparov and Nikitin in their valuable book *Sicilian: ...e6 and ...d6 Systems*, concluding: "This is beautiful and complicated, requiring practical tests."

The World Champion and his

co-author were absolutely right. The analysis required not only practical tests, but some important corrections (!).

Here is the main line of my analysis: 14...♔e7 15.fxe6 ♔xe6 16.0-0-0! ♔e7 17.g6 (A very attractive alternative is 17.♗h3 ♕e8 18.g6, hoping for 18...♘f6?? 19.♕xe5+!, but 18...♔d8 is much better.) ...♘f6 (if 17...♕e8 18.♕g5+) 18.♗g5

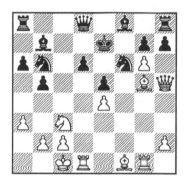

(analysis)

This critical position deserves special consideration. Black has two reasonable alternatives: 18...♕e8 and 18...♔d7. Which is better? In my original analysis, I gave preference to 18...♕e8, citing such complex and interesting variations as 19.♗h4 ♘d7 20.♗h3 ♔d8 21.♗xd7 ♔xd7 (21...♕xd7? 22.♕xh7!, winning) 22.♗xf6 gxf6 23.♕f5+ ♕e6 24.g7 ♕xf5 25.gxh8=♕! ♗h6+ 26.♔b1 ♗xe4 27.♖g7+ ♗xg7 28.♕xg7+ ♔e6 (28...♔c6 29.♘xe4 ♕xe4 30.♕e7) 29.♘xe4 ♕xe4 30.♕c7, and white wins. In spite of his two extra pawns in the major piece ending (an extraordinary metamorphosis from opening analysis), black cannot escape.

Now I believe only 18...♔d7! gives

black real chances to repulse the white attack: 19.♗h3+ ♔c7 20.♗xf6 ♕xf6 21.♖df1 ♕d8 22.♖f7+ ♔b8 23.♕xh7 ♖xh7 24.gxh7, and here 24...♕h4! 25.♖xf8+ ♔a7 26.h8=♕ ♕xh8 27.♖xh8 ♖xh8 with a balanced endgame is better than my original suggestion 24...♗e7? 25.♖gxg7, leaving white with the advantage.

So our analysis ends, after a rip-roaring roller-coaster of a ride fraught with danger and adventure on all sides, especially for black! It demonstrates the accuracy of the experimental sacrifice 13.♘e6!!? in spite of its apparent risk and illustrates once again the relative value of initiative over material.

THE NAJDORF VARIATION

The perennial popularity of this system, originated in the mid-fifties by a group of Argentine players led by the famous GM Miguel Najdorf, is unique in chess annals. It has become the most commonly played Sicilian system because of its chameleon-like flexibility - black can transpose on occasion to other variations, such as the Scheveningen and Boleslavsky systems; he can develop his knight on c1 to either c6 or d7; and he can even try the bold ...b7-b5 thrust before committing his knight on b8 (as in Polugaevsky's system). In turn, white has a free choice between such independent lines as 6.♗g5 (mainline), 6.♗c4 (similar to the Sozin), 6.♗e2, 6.♗e3, 6.f4 and 6.g3.

The mainline was subjected, from the beginning, to enormous practical experiment and analytical scrutiny.

Many articles and books were written just on 6.♗g5 and its different branches.

Over the years, I naturally came to use the Najdorf and took an active part in its theoretical development with my widely published analysis (see later in "How to Build an Opening Arsenal: Lessons in Opening Research").

For many years, the critical branches, both in theory and practice, have been the lines after 6.♗g5 e6 7.f4, leading either to the famous "Poisoned Pawn Variation" 7...♕b6 8.♕d2!? or to the "normal Najdorf" after 7...♗e7 or 7...♘bd7. I seldom met either variation in my practice. Here is one example cited in The Encyclopedia of Chess Openings:

Shamkovich-K. Grigorian [B99]
USSR Ch, Leningrad, 1971

1.e4 c5 2.♘f3 d6 3.d4 cxd4 4.♘xd4 ♘f6 5.♘c3 a6 6.♗g5 e6 7.f4 ♗e7 8.♕f3 ♕c7 9.0-0-0 ♘bd7 10.g4

Some theorists consider 10. ♗d3 a stronger reply.

10...b5 11.♗xf6 ♘xf6

Not 11...♗xf6? 12.♗xb5!, but a good alternative is 11...gxf6.

12.a3

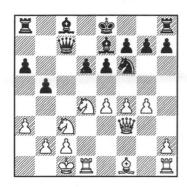

12...♖b8 13.f5

This was a relatively new try designed to prevent the maneuver ...♘fd7-e5 (or c5) because after the more usual (to this point) 13.g5 ♘d7 14.f5 ♘c5, the game is too complicated and murky (see ECO B99, note 24).

13...0-0 14.g5 ♘e8 15.♖g1 b4 16.axb4 ♖xb4 17.♖g3 ♕c5

ECO suggests 17...g6! as a good alternative. After 18.b3? as played in Perez-Quinteros, Torremolinos 1975, black should play 18...d5! with excellent counterplay.

18.♘b3 ♕e5 19.♗d3 a5 20.♘d2 a4

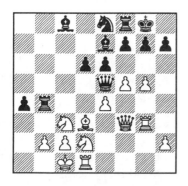

21.f6 ♗d8 22.♘c4 ♕c5

In Informant 12, Grigorian suggested the bold exchange sacrifice 22...♖xc4!? 23.♗xc4 a3 24.bxa3 gxf6.

23.e5! g6 24.♘e4 ♕a7 25.exd6 ♗b7 26.♕e3 ♗b6 27.♘xb6 a3!

An unexpected in-between move. This pawn becomes very dangerous.

28.♘d7

White accepts the challenge.

28...axb2+ 29.♔d2 ♖d4

With the threat of 30...♗xe4.

30.♘dc5?

More efficient was 30.♘ec5! followed by 30...e5 31.♕xe5 or 30...♕a5+ 31.c3 ♕a2 32.♔e1, winning.

30...e5 31.♘xb7 ♕xb7 32.♖gg1 ♘xd6 33.♘xd6 ♖xd6 34.♕xe5 ♖fd8

Black has some compensation for the sacrificed piece (a dangerous pawn at b2 and white's precarious king position), but not sufficient to justify the sac.

35.♕c5 ♕b8 36.♖ge1 ♖d5 37.♕e7 ♖xg5 38.c4! ♖g2+ 39.♔c3 h5

After the game, Grigorian suggested 39...♖xh2 40.♗xg6? ♖h3+!, when black holds. But he overlooked 40.♗f5! when white is still winning (40...♕g3+

41.♖e3; 40...b1♘+ 41.♖xb1; 40...♖f8
41.♗b1 ♖c8 42.♖d7, etc.).

40.♗xg6! ♖f8 41.♗xf7+ ♔h7 42.♕xf8 1-0

In spite of this successful opening
experiment, I cannot claim that 13.f5
guarantees white any permanent
advantage.

But my most interesting games in the
Najdorf have involved deviation from
standard lines, as in the following
crusher.

Shamkovich-Yudovich,Jr. [B95]
RSFSR Ch., 1959

1.e4 c5 2.♘f3 d6 3.d4 cxd4 4.♘xd4 ♘f6 5.♘c3 a6 6.♗g5 e6 7.♕d3!?

This rare move has both advantages
and disadvantages when compared to
more standard lines. It doesn't interfere
with the advance of white's f-pawn like
the currently unfashionable 7.♕f3!?,
and it prevents the strong maneuver
7...♕b6 permitted by the more modern
7.f4. But the vulnerability of white's
queen has prevented the text move from
ever becoming truly popular.

7...♗e7

ECO recommends 7...h6 8.♗h4
♗e7. Also interesting is 7...b5!?
possibly followed by 8.a3 ♗b7 9.♕h3!
♗e7 10.♗d3 with good chances for an
attack. This line clearly demonstrates
the potential of 7.♕d3 - unfortunately,
ECO fails to mention 7...b5.

8.0-0-0 ♕c7 9.♗e2

This is the point of my plan - white is

poised to play ♕g3 without fear of
...♘h5.

9...h6?

Black parries one threat, but he
weakens the g6-square at the same time.
Safer was 9...♘bd7 or 9...♘c6.

10.♗h4 ♘bd7 11.f4 b5

This thematic Sicilian thrust was
necessary if black were to retain any
hope for counterplay.

12.a3!

The theoretical recommendation
(ECO B95) is 12.♗f3 with the insidious
trap 12...♗b7? 13.♘xe6! fxe6 14.e5!
dxe5 15.♕g6+ (see the comments to
9...h6) ♔f8 16.♗xf6 ♗xf6 17.♗h5!
with a very strong attack
(Mukhin-Platanov, USSR 1969). In
case of 12...♘c5 13.♕e2 ♗b7, the
advance 14.e5 would be very strong
indeed, because 14...dxe5 15.fxe5 ♘h7
(Kortchnoi) loses by force; 16.♘cxb5!
axb5 17.♕xb5+ ♔f8 18.♗xb7 ♕xb7 (if
18...♘xb7 19.♘xe6+! fxe6 20.♖d7
wins) 19.♗xe7+ ♕xe7 20.♘c6! ♕g5+
21.♔b1 ♘a4 22.h4 etc. So, 12.♗f3 is
apparently the best move, but the text is
a good alternative. Such "double
solutions" are not too surprising, as
black has already commited two
inaccuracies. What is more important is
that white must manage his attack very
precisely in both cases.

12...♗b7

This move prevents the combination
13.♘xe6? fxe6 14.e5 dxe5 15.♕g6+ as
white's bishop is still at e2, in contrast
to the Mukhin-Platonov game. Yet

12...♘c5 13.♕e3 ♗b7 should be more accurate.

13.♗f3

Black's position seems, on the face of it, quite solid - he has completed his development and seems ready to castle into a comfortable Sicilian middlegame. But let's look closely at this critical position. Black is in fact in a classical state of Zugzwang - any black move adds fuel to white's attack, making it more dangerous or even decisive. To make matters worse, black has difficulty preventing the thematic sacrifices at b5, d5 or e6, and white has the powerful central break e4-e5 held in reserve.

13...♖c8

If black plays 13...0-0, white has 14.g4! (another typical attacking pattern) ...♕b6 15.♗f2 ♘c5 16.♕e2 b4 17.axb4 ♕xb4 18.h4 ♖ab8 19.g5 with a strong attack that forestalls black's counter-threats. The more aggressive 13...g5!? is met with 14.e5! dxe5 15.♘xe6!, similar to the earlier mentioned Mukhin-Platonov game.

14.♗xf6!

The reason for this unexpected exchange is clear in the following lines:

A) 14...♗xf6 15.♘dxb5! axb5 16.♘xb5 ♕b6 17.♘xd6+ ♔e7 18.e5, and black is caught in a stranglehold. The counter-sacrifice 18...♘xe5 19.fxe5 ♗xe5 20.c3 is insufficient.

B) 14...♘xf6 15.e5 ♘d7 16.♘xe6 fxe6 17.♕g6+ (a variation on a familiar theme) ...♔d8 18.♕xg7 ♖e8 19.exd6 ♗xd6 20.♗xb7 ♗xf4+ 21.♔b1 ♕xb7 22.♕f6+, winning. Note that here 17...♔f8 fails to 18.♖hf1+.

C) 14...gxf6, when black's position deteriorates after 15.♗h5! (another thematic manouever) ...♘c5 16.♕h3, attacking the e6-pawn.

14...♘c5!

This in-between move is black's best chance.

15.♕e2 gxf6 16.♔b1

This useful prophylactic move, prevents both eventual threats of ...d5 (and if exd5), ...♕xf4+ and ...♘b3+ after b2-b4. E.g., if 16.♗h5 ♖g8 17.b4 ♘b3+! (but not 17...♘d7? 18.♗xf7+! ♔xf7 19.♕h5+ winning).

16...♕b6

Here occurs a critical position of the game. Both camps have manned battle stations. Black intends 17...b4 and white can try 17.b4. After 17.b4 black has 17...♘d7 18.♗h5 ♘f8 holding. More interesting is 18.♘d5!? exd5 19.exd5 with a strong iniative for the sacrificed piece. I rejected the thrust 17.♗h5(!) as after 17...b4 18.axb4 ♕xb4 black's counterattack seemed more than sufficient; e.g., 19.♖he1 ♖b8! Unfortunately, I overlooked the fantastic combination 18.♗xf7+!! ♔xf7 19.♕h5+ ♔g8 (or 19...♔f8 or 19...♔g7) 20.♘a4!! and white wins as 20...♘xa4 leads to mate after 21.♘xe6+ (or first 21.♕xg6+). It is very simple, isn't it? However it is well known that any concrete maneuver or combination looks more or less simple with the benefit of hindsight - I discovered this continuation many years later. Alas, I chose a third way.

17.♖he1?! 0-0?

A returned kindness. Black should have played 17...b4! 18.axb4 ♕xb4 not fearing 19.♘d5 (it was my idea) since 19...exd5 20.exd5 ♖c7 21.♘f5 ♘a4! wins for black. If 21.c3 ♕b6 22.♘f5 ♔d8! 23.♘xe7 ♖e8 with the same result. The attempt 19.♗h5 is too late due to 19...♖b8! (with the threat of 20...♗xe4. White could only maintain a balance with 19.♘a2 ♕b6 20.♘c1. Now white finds a crucial attacking plan.

18.♘d5!

A final thrust.

**18...exd5   19.♘f5   ♖fe8
20.♗h5! 1-0**

Black surrendered because he could not avoid catastrophe: e.g., 20...♘xe4 21.♕g4+ ♘g5 22.fxg5 hxg5 23.♗xf7+!, etc. This game illustrated almost all of the typical Najdorf attacking patterns, sacrifices and intangible errors, making it a perfect introduction to and instruction in Najdorf themes.

Let me offer another game, but in a lighter vein, from the same variation.

Shamkovich-Kremenetsky [B95]
Moscow, 1962

**1.e4 c5 2.♘f3 d6 3.d4 cxd4
4.♘xd4 ♘f6 5.♘c3 a6 6.♗g5
e6 7.♕f3**

This move was very popular at the time the game was played. Keres's super sharp 7.f4, originated in 1956, still had not achieved common acceptance.

7...♗e7

According to theory, the main line is 7...h6 8.♗h4 ♘bd7 with adequate counterplay in view of the threat 9...g5 10. ♗g3 ♘e5.

**8.0-0-0 ♘bd7 9.♗e2 ♕c7
10.♕g3 0-0?**

Black castles prematurely, but sometimes (especially often in the Sicilian) it's not easy to pick the right moment to castle. ECO recommends 10...♘c5 11.f3 ♗d7 12.♗e3 0-0! (Barle-Sax, Vrbas 1977). But I think 11.♗f3 is stronger, maintaining the tempting attacking possibility of h2-h4-h5.

11.f4 b5

As in the previous game, black is virtually forced to push this pawn if he wants counterplay. Weaker is 11...♘c5 12.♗f3.

12.e5!

The immediate break is required. After the timid 12.a3 ♗b7, then the break with 13.e5 is less intimidating.

12...dxe5 13.fxe5 ♘d5?

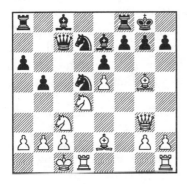

Black blunders. He must capture the pawn at e5 anyway but how to do it? The queen capture 13...♕xe5 fails after 14.♘c6 ♕c5 15.♗f3!, but the alternative 13...♘xe5 is not so clear: e.g., 14.♗f4 (the most natural reply) ...♗d6 (with the idea 15...♘d3+) followed by 15.♔b1 b4. If 15.♘f5!? exf5 (15...♘d3+? 16.♔b1 wins) 16.♖xd6 ♕xd6 17.♗xe5 ♕e6 18.♗f3 ♖a7!, and white's attack runs out of steam. After 14.♘f3 ♘h5! 15.♕h4 ♘f6, the game is equal (not 15...♗xg5? 16.♕xg5 winning) and 14.♗h6 can be met well with 14...♘e8 but white has 14.♗f3! (the unprotected black rook is an important recourse for white) ...♖a7 15.♗f4 ♗d6 16.♘de2!, threatening 17.♖xd6 and guarding against

16...♘d3+. 16...♘fd7 cannot help black because of 17.♘e4 ♗e7 18.♖xd7!

14.♗h6! ♕xe5

The exchange sacrifice after 14...g6 gives black no respite.

15.♘xd5 exd5

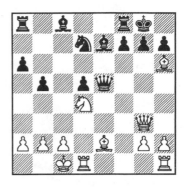

16.♘c6! ♕xg3 17.♘xe7+ ♔h8 18.hxg3 ♖e8

White wins after 18...gxh6 19.♖xh6 and 20.♖dh1.

19.♗g5 ♘f8

White mates after 19...f6 20.♖xh7+!

20.♗f3 f6 21.♗xd5 ♖a7 22.♖xh7+!! 1-0

Sometimes, a thematic threat (usually against the pawn at e6) will rear its head at an earlier stage in the Sicilian. A classic example follows:

Keres-Schajtar [B94]
Amsterdam, 1954

1.e4 c5 2.♘f3 d6 3.d4 cxd4 4.♘xd4 ♘f6 5.♘c3 a6 6.♗g5 ♘bd7?! 7.♗c4!

This very move has eliminated 6...♘bd7 from contemporary practice.

7...e6 8.0-0 ♕c7?

This leads to immediate disaster. Not much better is 8...b5 9.♗xe6! fxe6 10.♘xe6 ♕b6 11.♘d5! ♘xd5 12.♕xd5 ♗b7 13.♘c7+!, leading to mate-in-two. ♖elatively better is 8...♘b6 (D.♘.L. Levy), protecting the e6-pawn. But after 9.♗b3, white's prospects are clearly better.

9.♗xe6! fxe6 10.♘xe6 ♕c4 11.♘d5! ♔f7 12.♗xf6! ♔xe6

After 12...♘xf6 13.b3, black's queen is trapped.

13.♗c3 ♘f6 14.♗xf6 gxf6 15.♘b6 ♕c6 16.♘xa8

White already has both a positional and a material advantage.

16...♗e7 17.a4 b6 18.♕d5+ ♔d7 19.♖a3 ♗d8 20.♘xb6+! 1-0

The move 20...♕xb6 fails to 21.♕f5+ ♔c7 22.♖c3+, and 20...♗xb6 to 21.♕f7+ ♔d8 22.♕xf6+.

In the following game, black chose a more active defense, creating yet another weakness in his camp.

Shamkovich-Lebedev [B94]
USSR, Moscow Ch. 1955

1.e4 c5 2.♘f3 d6 3.d4 cxd4 4.♘xd4 ♘f6 5.♘c3 a6 6.♗g5 ♘bd7 7.♗c4 e6 8.0-0 h6 9.♗h4

A good alternative is 9.♗xf6 ♘xf6

10.♗b3 followed by a thrust with the f-pawn.

9...♘e5 10.♗b3

10.♗e2!? is in an interesting alternative.

10...♕c7 11.♕e2

This is acceptable play, but even better is 11.♗xf6 gxf6 12.♕h5! followed by 12...♘c4 13.♘cb5! axb5 14.♕xb5+ ♗d7 15.♕xc4, winning. Black should have tried 10...g5 11.♗g3 ♕c7 earlier - another example of how careful black has to be with the timing of even the most "natural" move in the Najdorf Sicilian.

11...♗e7 12.♖ad1 g5 13.♗g3 ♗d7 14.f4!

A critical break, getting ready to pressure the f-file.

14...gxf4 15.♖xf4 ♘h7

Black wisely tries to regroup. He cannot save the e-pawn after 15...0-0-0 16.♖df1 ♘e8 17.♖xf7!

16.♔h1 ♘f8?

Correct is 16...0-0-0 17.♖df1 ♖df8, with a passive, but defensible position.

17.♘f5!

Again, a thematic sacrifice. If white pussyfoots and allows ...♘fg6, black will be safe and very active. Now his position will go to ruin in a very few moves.

17...exf5

Inadequate is 17...♘fg6 18.♖ff1 0-0-0 because of the simple 19.♘xe7+ ♘xe7 20.♗xe5 dxe5 21.♖xf7.

18.♘d5!

Black cannot withstand the critical posting of this terrible knight.

18...♛b8

White wins after 18...♛a5 19.exf5 ♖c8 20.♗e1! ♛b5 21.c4 ♛c6 22.♘xe7 ♔xe7 23.♗b4!

19.exf5 ♗c6 20.♘xe7 ♔xe7 21.f6+ ♔e8 22.♖fd4 ♘fg6

The key pawn at d6 falls.

23.♖xd6 ♔f8 24.♗xe5 1-0

Shamkovich-Filtser [B94]
Moscow, 1968

1.e4 c5 2.♘f3 d6 3.d4 cxd4 4.♘xd4 ♘f6 5.♘c3 a6 6.♗g5 ♘bd7 7.♗c4 ♛a5

The theory of the time recognized this aggressive defense as best.

8.♛d2 e6 9.0-0

White creates active possibilities in the center and on the queenside with this move. A good alternative, however, is 9.0-0-0 (see the next game). This is an extremely rare case where castling on either side can be recommended.

9...h6 10.♗h4 g5?! 11.♗g3 ♘e5

This is more accurate than 11...♘h5?!, played by Petrosian against Tal (Bled 1959). The game

continued 12.♗xe6! fxe6 13.♘xe6 ♘xg3 14.fxg3 ♘e5 15.♖xf8+! ♖xf8 16.♛xd6 ♖f6, when according to John Nunn white should win with the prosaic 17.♛c7! ♛xc7 18.♘xc7+ ♔d8 19.♘xa8.

12.♗e2!

Taking control of the important h5-square.

12...b5 13.b4!?

This is the most energetic way to keep the initiative. Also playable is 13.a3 ♗b7 14.f4 gxf4 15.♖xf4, although black holds after 15...♗e7. With the text, white sacrifices a pawn, and the game becomes very complicated.

13...♛xb4 14.a4 ♘c4 15.♗xc4 bxc4 16.♖fd1 ♗d7 17.♖ab1

The tempting 17.e5 is weak because of 17...♘h5 18.♖ab1 ♛a5 19.exd6 ♘xg3 20.hxg3 ♗g7! 21.♖b7 ♖d8.

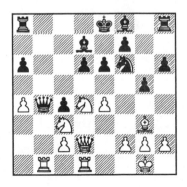

17...♛c5?

Black's position is already desperate

because of both bad development and weaknesses in his kingside. Nevertheless 17...♕a5! could offer more resistance, e.g., 18.e5 ♘h5!; 18.♘f5!? exf5 19.♗xd6 fxe4 20.♕d4 ♕f5 or 20.♘d5 ♕xd2 21.♘xf6+ ♔d8 22.♖xd2 ♗xd6 23.♖xd6 ♔e7 equal. The correct continuation of the attack would be 18.♖b7! intensifying all threats. The main lines run here 18...♗c8? 19.♘d5! winning; or 18...♘h5 19.♘f5! (this lunge a la Tal is very powerful on this occasion) ...♘xg3 20.♘xd6+ or 19...exf5 20.♗xd6 ♗c6 21.♖c7 with an unavoidable attack in both lines; or 18...♗e7 19.♘c6! ♗xc6 20.♖xe7+ ♔xe7 21.♕xd6+ (but not 21.♘d5+? since 21...♕xd5!) ...♔e8 22.♗e5! crushing. Considering these and similar variations, we can see again and again how difficult it is at times in dealing the final blow in the winning position when the weaker side has practical resources. This skill is a most certain quality required of a high class player.

18.e5!

Now 18...♘h5 is met with 19.♘e4!

18...dxe5 19.♘f3

Creating several threats: e.g., 20.♘e4, 20.♗xe5, and 20.♘xe5. Black's position is critical.

19...♗c6 20.♗xe5 ♗e7

Losing is 20...♗xf3 21.♗xf6 ♗xd1 22.♖xd1.

21.♗d4 ♕d6

The retreat 21...♕f5 22.♘e5 ♗d5 offers more resistance, but still good for

white is 23.♘xd5 ♘xd5 (23...exd5 24.♘c6) 24.♘g6! ♕xg6 25.♗xh8 f6 26.♕e2 ♔f7 27.♖b7 ♘f4 28.♕xc4 ♖xh8 29.♖xe7+!, winning.

22.♕e2 ♕c7 23.♘e5 0-0

Finally, black castles - but too late.

24.h4!

Completely destroying the black king's fortress.

24...gxh4 25.♖b6

Calling the last reserve into the attack.

25...♗d5 26.♘g4 1-0

After 26...♕d8, white has 27.♗xf6 ♗xf6 28.♖xd5!

Two years later, I chose the more straightforward 9.0-0-0, creating immediate threats on the d-file.

Shamkovich-Titenko [B94]
Moscow, 1963

1.e4 c5 2.♘f3 d6 3.d4 cxd4 4.♘xd4 ♘f6 5.♘c3 a6 6.♗g5 ♘bd7 7.♗c4 ♕a5 8.♕d2 e6 9.0-0-0 b5

After 9...h6 10.♗xf6! ♘xf6 11.f4, white has the unpleasant threat of 12.f5.

10.♗b3 ♗b7 11.♖he1 ♖c8?!

Black is impatient for counterplay. Better was 11...0-0-0 (not 11...b4? 12.♘d5! exd5 13.exd5+ ♔d8 14.♘c6+, winning) 12.a3 ♗e7 13.f4, and here instead of 13...h6 (Fedorowicz - Westerinen, New York 1977), deserving attention is 13...♕c7: e.g., 14.♗xe6 fxe6 15.♘xe6 ♕c4; but 14.♔b1 ♘b6; or 14.f5!, still leaves white with the edge.

12.e5!! ♘xe5

White can meet 12...dxe5 with 13.♗xf6 gxf6 (13...♘xf6 14.♖xe5, with a plus for white) 14.♘xe6, with a strong attack.

13.♘xe6! fxe6 14.♖xe5 dxe5 15.♗xf6 ♕c7 16.♗xe5 ♕f7 17.f4! ♗c6 18.♕e2 ♗e7 19.g4 (and 1-0)

Black has no defense against 20.f5. He resigned a few moves later.

Nunn and Stean concluded in their book on the Sicilian: "The fact that both 9.0-0-0 and 9.0-0 seem to be good for white has dissuaded black players from adopting this line." The last two games support their diagnosis. Maybe black

should simply avoid the pseudo-active 7...♕a5.

But if e6 is such a convenient target for white after 6...♘bd7 7.♗c4, why not try to complete your development without this ill-starred move? I tried one time to navigate this tricky channel by employing a special move order.

Soloviev-Shamkovich [B90]
Moscow, 1956

1.e4 c5 2.♘f3 d6 3.d4 cxd4 4.♘xd4 ♘f6 5.♘c3 a6 6.♗c4 b5 7.♗b3 ♗b7?!

Safer is 7...e6, transposing to a sharp variation of the Najdorf/Sozin variation. But I had a special trick up my sleeve.

8.0-0! ♘bd7 9.♗g5

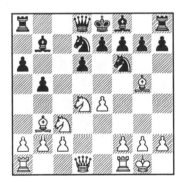

The most aggressive and logical move with the idea to destroy black's defense before he complets his development. Aronin in ECO (B90) suggested 9.Qe2 g6 10.f4, but after 10...e5, black holds.

9....g6!? 10.a4!

This is better than 10.♕e2 in the

original game, Levenfish-Aronin (USSR Ch. 1950), where 10...♗g7 11.♖ad1 0-0 12.a4 bxa4! gave black sufficient counterplay. In my game 10...bxa4 would be dubious since 11.Bxa4 ♗g7 12.♘c6! Qc7 13.♘d5 ♘xd5 14.exd5 gives white a clear plus.

10....b4 11.♘d5 ♗g7

But not 11....♘xe4? 12.♗xe7 ♗xe7 13.♖e1 with a winning attack.

12.♘xb4 ♗xe4?

More promising was 12...♕a5, but 13.♘d5! favors white anyway, e.g., 13...♘xd5 14.exd5 ♗xd5 15.♖e1 e6 16.♗xd5 ♕xd5 17.♘xe6! wins. If 15...♗xb3 16.♖xe7+ ♔f8 17.♘xb3 ♕xg5 18.♖xd7 and white has a clear plus.

13.♖e1 ♕b6

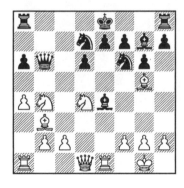

Now white unleashed a fantastic combination.

14.♗d5!! ♘xd5

After 14...♗xd5, white wins with 15.♖xe7+!! ♔f8 16.♘xd5 ♘xd5 17.♖xd7 ♕xd4 (17...♗xd4 18.♕f3

also wins) 18.♕f3! ♗f6 19.♖d1 ♕e5 20.♗xf6 ♕xf6 21.♕xd5 ♔g7 22.c3.

15.♘xd5 ♗xd5 16.♖xe7+ ♔f8 17.♖xd7 ♗xd4?

My only real chance for defense was 17...♕xd4, followed by 18.♕xd4 ♗xd4 19.♖xd6 ♗xb2 20.♖b1 ♗c3 21.♖xd5 ♔g7.

18.♗e3!!

The final point, based on double attacks. Black's risky opening plan has been refuted.

18...♗xe3 19.♕xd5 ♔g7 20.♕xf7+ ♔h6

Here white can win with 21.♕g7+ ♔h5 22.♖d1!, but my opponent, a strong master from Moscow, made several technical errors, allowing the well-deserved win to slip away.

Moral: Play carefully indeed if you want to omit ...e6.

Here is a game in which the pawn-thrust f4-f5 plays a key role in a "methodical" kingside attack.

Shamkovich-Grefe [B93]
New York, 1978

1.e4 c5 2.♘f3 d6 3.d4 cxd4 4.♘xd4 ♘f6 5.♘c3 a6 6.f4 ♕c7

More common is 6...e5. An interesting alternative is 6...♕b6!?

7.♗d3 g6 8.♘f3 ♘bd7 9.0-0 ♗g7 10.♔h1 0-0 11.♕e1

With the idea of e4-e5.

11...c5

11...e6!? is possible.

12.f5!?

A new move. Prior to my encounter with Grefe 12.♕h4 b5 13.fxe5 dxe5 14.♗h6 was known when after 14...♗b7? 15.♘g5 white had a clear advantage but the position is not so clear after 14...b4!? 15.♘e2 ♘h5! 16.♗xg7 ♔xg7 17.♘g5 ♘df6!

12...b5

12...gxf5 is met by 13.♘h4!

13.a3 ♗b7 14.♗g5 ♗c6

Black wants to regroup with ...♕b7, followed by advancing with ...a5 and ...b4. If 14...h6 then 15.♗d2 menacing ♕h4.

15.♘d2 ♕b7 16.♕h4

White has the initiative.

16...a5 17.♖ae1 b4 18.axb4 axb4 19.♘d1 ♖a1

Not 19...d5 20.♘e3!

20.♘e3 ♖xe1 21.♖xe1 d5 22.♖f1! dxe4

If 22...♘xe4 23.♗xe4! dxe4 24.f6 ♗h8 25.♘f5! gxf5 26.♕g3 winning.

23.♗c4 ♔h8

24.♗b3!

And not the impatient 24.♗xf7?! ♖xf7 25.fxg6 ♖f8 26.♘g4 e3! with unclear consequences.

24...♗b5 25.♖f2 ♕a7 26.♘dc4 ♕a6 27.g4!

White's attack has become very menacing. Black's kingside is near the breaking point.

27...♖e8

If 27...♖c8 28.♗xf6 ♗xf6 29.g5 continues the assault.

28.fxg6?

A time trouble error. Stronger is 28.♖d2! with a winning position.

28...fxg6 29.♖d2

Two threats. 30.♘d6 and 30.♖d6.

29...♗f8?

Also in time trouble, my opponent returns the favor. 29...♖e6! with complications was correct.

30.♔g2?

And now I should play 30.♖d6!

30...♗e7?

In the heat of the moment, with time trouble dictating events, black makes one last slip.

31.♖d6!

Now it is clear again.

31...♗xc4

If 31...♗xd6 32.♗xf6+ wins.

32.♖xa6 ♗xa6 33.♗a4 1-0

"With my knight on f5, I am sure of the power of my attack." - Garry Kasparov. Perhaps simplistic and meant as a joke, but occasionally true. In the following encounter, the knight on f5 lends great energy to the attack. After 18...♘c5, note that most of white's forces, led by the stallion on f5 are poised to storm black's kingside.

Shamkovich-Morales [B93]
Mexican Open, 1978

1.e4 c5 2.♘f3 d6 3.d4 cxd4 4.♘xd4 ♘f6 5.♘c3 a6 6.f4 e5 7.♘f3 ♕c7 8.♗d3 ♗e7 9.0-0 0-0 10.♔h1 b5

Another try is 10...♘bd7!? with the idea of ...♘c5.

11.fxe5! dxe5 12.♕e2 ♘bd7

12...b4? 13.♘d5 ♘xd5 14.exd5 ♗d6 15.♗xh7+! or 14...♘d7 15.d6! ♗xd6 16.♗xh7+! gives white a clear plus.

13.♘h4! ♖e8?

Better was 13...♘c5 14.♗g5 ♗e6 15.♘f5 with only a slight plus for white.

14.♘f5 ♗f8 15.♕f3!

White is clearly better.

15...♗b7

15...b4 is refuted by 16.♘d5 ♘xd5 17.exd5 with two threats: 18.d6 and 18.♘h6+.

16.♗g5

Threatening ♘h6+.

16...b4 17.♘d1 ♖e6 18.♘de3 ♘c5

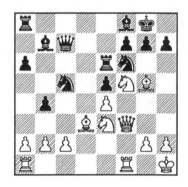

Now the attack surges into the black king's shelter.

19.♘h6+! ♔h8 20.♘d5! ♗xd5

20...♘xd5 21.♘xf7+ ♔g8 22.exd5 e4 23.♕h3 ♖g6 24.♗c4 is very good for white.

21.exd5 e4

If 21...♖d6 22.♘f5 or if 21...♖b6 22.d6 wins.

22.♕h3! ♖b6 23.♗c4!

At last this bishop finds an active role, threatening 24.d6.

23...♘cd7

Trying to hold on with 24...♘e5. If 23...♘a4 24.♗b3 ♘c5 25.d6 wins.

24.♘xf7+ ♔g8 25.♗b3 ♗d6 26.♘xd6 ♕xd6 27.♗f4

White's position is dominating. Two strong bishops and an extra pawn.

27...♘e5

If 27...♕f8 28.♗c7 ♖b7 29.d6+ wins.

28.♕e6+!

It is time to trade queens.

28...♕xe6 29.dxe6 ♘g6 30.♗g5 ♘g4 31.♗d8!

The final touch.

1-0

Shamkovich-Lebedev [B60]
USSR, 1962

1.e4 c5 2.♘f3 ♘c6 3.d4 cxd4 4.♘xd4 ♘f6 5.♘c3 d6 6.♗g5 ♕b6 7.♗xf6

Another attempt to refute the black queen's early sortie is 7.♘db5!? a6 8.♗xf6 gxf6 (8...axb5 is strongly met by 9.♘d5!) 9.♘d5 ♕a5+ 10.♘bc3 (weak is 10.b4? ♘xb4 11.♘bc7+ ♔d8 12.♕d2 ♘xc2+) ...f5 11.♕h5 ♗g7

with chances for both sides as in Tatai-Larsen, Siegen Ol. 1970.

7...gxf6 8.♗b5!

A more poular plan is 8.♘b3 e6. The bishop move aims at a favorable pawn sacrifice after 8...a6 9.♗a4 ♕xb2 10.♘ce2 or, as occurs in the game, at rapid and easy development. Interestingly, 8.♗b5! is not mentioned in ECO (B60).

8...♗d7 9.♘de2 h5?!

More logical is 9...e6 is to cover the d5 square.

10.0-0 0-0-0?

Again 10...e6 is preferable. Castling long puts even more pressure on the black queen, constraining her still more.

11.a4 ♕c5?

Even now 11...e6 was stronger, but black had to contend with threats of a4-a5 or ♖a1-a3-b3.

12.♘d5 a6

White was threatening 13.c3 followed by b4 capturing the queen. Now, however, Black's b6 square is fatally weak.

13.c3! ♖h6

13...axb5 would be followed by 14.b4 ♕a7 15.axb5 with a rout.

14.b4 ♕a7 15.♕d2 e6

Too late; this move can no longer save the day.

16.♗xc6 ♗xc6

16...bxc6 is met by 17.♘e7+! (a decoying idea: 17...♗xe7 18.♕xh6 wins) ♔c7 18.b5 with an attack.

17.b5 ♗e8?!

Not too good. Better was 17...exd5 18.bxc6 bxc6 19.exd5 c5.

18.b6 ♕b8 19.♘d4! exd5 20.exd5

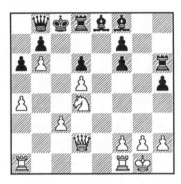

By sacrificing his knight, white has walled in the opponent's queen in her own camp. Attempts to spring her free with 20...♔d7 21.♕d3 ♕c8 22.♕f5+ or 20...♖d7 21.♖fe1 ♔d8 22.♘f5 are doomed to failure. Now white can easily create decisive threats in the center and on the kingside where he actually enjoys a tremendous material advantage.

20...♗d7 21.♖fe1 ♖e8 22.♘f5 ♖g6 23.♖xe8+ ♗xe8 24.♖e1 ♗d7

On 24...♔d8, white wins with 25.♕e2 ♗d7 26.♕xh5.

25.♕e2

Threatening 26.♕e8+!

25...♖g5 26.♘e7+

Black had been hoping for 26.♕e8+?! ♗xe8 27.♖xe8+ ♔d7 28.♖xb8 ♖xf5 29.♖xf8 ♖xd5 with a chance of saving himself in the rook endgame.

26...♔d8 27.f4 ♖g4 28.♕e4 f5

Black has no good moves at his disposal. If 28...♗g7 or 28...♗h6, white has the deadly 29.♕h7!

29.♕e3

Not the hasty 29.♘xf5? ♕c8! setting the black queen free. Precision and accuracy are paramount until the very end.

29...a5

A desperate attempt to activate the queen via a6. If 29...♗h6, the simplest win is 30.♘xf5 ♗c8 31.♕d4! threatening both 32.♕f6+ and 32.♕h8+. Black is in no position to parry both thrusts.

30.h3 ♖g7

If 30...♖xf4!? white emerges triumphant with the sophisticated maneuver 31.♕xf4 ♗xe7 32.♕e3! ♗f6 33.♕h6 ♗e7 (If instead, 33...♗e5 34.♖xe5! dxe5 35.♕f6+ wins) 34.♕xh5! ♕c8 (free at last, but to no avail) 35.♕xf7 ♕c5+ 36.♔h1 ♕xb6 37.♖xe7 winning.

31.♘xf5 ♖h7 32.♕d4 ♗e6

Despair.

33.♕f6+ ♔d7 34.dxe6+ fxe6 35.♕xe6+ ♔c6 36.♖b1 1-0

The break b7-b5 is very typical for the Sicilian as an attractive method of counterplay. Such action requires due preparation, in case white should play a2-a4, breaking up the black queenside pawns. White may also play e4-e5 to play on the weakened long diagonal (h1-a8). In the next game, white managed a more sophisticated method of realizing his advantage in development.

Shamkovich-Marchand [B28]
NY State Ch., 1977

1.e4 c5 2.♘f3 a6 3.♘c3 b5?

The text move, aiming for the rapid development of the queenside, is clearly premature. However, white must abstain from passive and stereotyped play or black will easily obtain a good position.

4.d4 cxd4 5.♘xd4 ♗b7 6.♗g5!

Pinning the e-pawn and inhibiting further development by the enemy pieces. Both 6...♘f6 7.♗xf6 gxf6 8.♕h5 and 6...♕c7 7.♘d5 ♗xd5 (7...♕e5 8.♗e3) 8.exd5 ♕e5+ 9.♗e3 ♕xd5 10.♗e2, threatening 11.♗f3 will be to white's advantage.

6...♕a5!? 7.♘b3 ♕b6 8.♗e2 e6 9.0-0 b4?!

This attempt to disorganize white's uncoordinated forces violates the principles of development in the opening. Black should instead be looking for ways to bring his own pieces into action effectively. Now white uses his minor pieces to harass the black queen, exchange off the active

light-squared bishop and to create threats against the king.

10.♘a4 ♕c6 11.♘a5 ♕xa4 12.♘xb7 ♕c6

Black's plan is clear now. On 13.♘a5 he intends 13...♕c5 with a double attack against white's knight and bishop, although white can defend both by 14.♗d8! ♘c6 15.♘xc6 dxc6 16.♗h4 ♘f6, when the position is roughly level. However, white's knight finds a more romantic and dangerous course.

13.♘d8!!

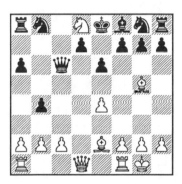

An unusual square for the knight at such an early stage of the game! A real "Trojan Horse" - only here does the knight find sanctuary, where it attacks the e- and f-pawns.

13...♕c7 14.♗h5!

This unexpected maneuver was inspired by the famous game, Keres-Kotov, Budapest, 1950.

14...g6 15.♕f3 d6

15...f6, placing three of white's pieces under attack, would offer a more stubborn resistance. However, after 16.e5! ♕xd8 (inferior are both 16...♔xd8 17.♗xf6+ ♘xf6 18.♕xf6+ ♔e8 19.♗f3! picking up one of the black rooks and 16...gxh5 17.exf6 ♔xd8 18.f7+ ♔c8 19.♕xa8 ♘e7 20.♗f6 winning) 17.exf6 ♔f7 18.♖ad1! ♘c6 (if 18...gxh5 19.♕xh5 is mate) 19.♖fe1 ♘xf6 20.♗g4 gives white a powerful attack for the piece.

16.♗g4

Forcing black to turn his attention to the e-pawn. White threatens 17.♗xe6 fxe6 18.♕xf8!+ winning two pawns.

16...h6 17.♗h4 ♗g7

After 17...g5 white continues with 18.♘xf7 ♕xf7 19.♗h5.

18.e5

Before sacrificing at e6, white forces the advance of the enemy d-pawn.

18...d5   19.♗xe6! fxe6 20.♘xe6 ♕b7 21.♘xg7+ ♕xg7 22.♕xd5

Black's position has collapsed.

22...♕a7 23.♖ad1 g5 24.e6

Threatening 25.♕d8 mate.

24...♔f8 25.♕f3+ 1-0

Black's position is hopeless. If now 25...♔g7 26.♖d7+! wins the queen while 25...♔e8 meets 26.♕h5+ ♔f8 27.♖d8+ ♔g7 28.♖d7+! with the same idea. Faced with imminent disaster, black resigned.

In the above game, white adopted a method of attack very common in this type of complex position. The technique involved called for concentration on both of black's weaknesses and creation of threats against them. Taking advantage of black's weakening of the long diagonal by the premature advance 3...b5, white, at an opportune moment, combined threats on the black e- and f-pawns. White's attack would certainly have lacked a sound foundation without this tactical motif.

MAROCZY BIND

In this section, we will examine three games which take place on the battlefield known as the Maroczy Bind, a system whereby white establishes pawns on c4 and e4 against black's "Dragon" formation. The flexibility of white's system is illustrated by the kingside attacks that we witness in Shamkovich-Waterman and Shamkovich-Kagan and the more positional approach that we see in Shamkovich-Pupols.

In the first game, white performs an unuusual tactical operation of "rescuing the rook."

Shamkovich-Waterman [B39]
Lone Pine, 1975

1.♘f3 c5 2.c4 ♘f6 3.♘c3 g6 4.d4 cxd4 5.♘xd4 ♘c6 6.e4 ♗g7 7.♗e3 ♘g4 8.♕xg4 ♘xd4 9.♕d1 ♘e6 10.♖c1 ♕a5 11.♗e2

White may also consider 11.♗d3!? ♘c5 12.♗b1 ♘a4 13.♗d2 with advantage.

11...d6 12.0-0 ♗d7 13.♘d5!

This was a new move in this position. White can count on no advantage after 13.♕d2 ♗c6 14.f3 0-0 15.♘d5 (15.♖fd1 may be slightly better for white) ...♕xd2 16.♘xe7+ ♔h8 17.♗xd2 ♗xb2 with equality.

13...♗xb2

White has dangerous compensation after 13...♕xa2 14.b4!

14.♖b1 ♗g7

A similar sacrifice of the b7-pawn was seen in the classic game Botvinnik-Portisch (Monte Carlo 1968 - Inf 5/44).In this game black did not succeed as well. In both games , we will see that the "trapped" rook fights actively for his life and causes black many problems.

15.♖xb7 ♗c6?

Black errs but even after 15...♘d8 16.♕b3 (but not 16.♗d2? ♕xa2 17.♖b3 [17.♖b1 ♖c8 intending ...♘c6 is good for black] ...♗a4! with advantage to black) ...♘xb7 17.♕xb7 ♖c8 (not 17...♖d8 18.c5! dxc5 19.♗b5 wins) 18.♗xa7 e6 19.♘b6 ♖d8 20.c5 dxc5 (20...♗b5 21.♘c8!) 21.♘xd7 ♖xd7 22.♗b5 ♕d8 23.♗xc5! white has a crushing position.

16.♖xe7+ ♔f8

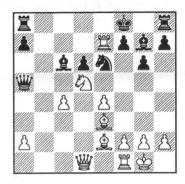

White's rook appears precariously placed, but ...

17.c5!!

"Rescuing the rook."

17...♘xc5

Others are no better, e.g., 17...♗xd5 18.♕xd5 ♔xe7? 19.cxd6+ winning. If 17...dxc5 18.♖xe6 fxe6 19.♘f4 ♔e7 20.♘xe6! (the most energetic attacking method) ...♔xe6 21.♗c4+ ♔e7 22.♗g5+ ♗f6 23.e5!! ♗xg5 24.♕d6+ ♔e8 25.♕xc6+ ♔e7 26.♕b7+ winning. This attack with mass sacrifices is very instructive.

18.♗c4 ♗xd5

No respite. 18...♕d8 is met by 19.♕f3 f6 20.♕xf6+!! ♗xf6 21.♗h6+ mating.

19.♕xd5 ♔xe7 20.♕xf7+ ♔d8 21.♕xg7

Black is busted.

21...♖e8 22.♗d5 ♖b8 23.♕xh7

A simpler task was afforded by

23.♗g5+ ♔c8 24.♕xh7 ♘xe4 25.♗c6
♕c7 26.♕h3+ winning.

23...♘xe4 24.♗c6! ♕c7

If 24...♖e7 25.♕xg6.

**25.♕xc7+ ♔xc7 26.♖c1! ♘c5
27.♗xe8 ♖xe8 28.♗xc5 dxc5
29.♖xc5+ ♔d6 30.♖c1**

White has a winning endgame. The
game concluded.....

**30...♖e2 31.♖a1 a5 32.a4 ♖e4
33.f3 ♖c4 34.♔f2 ♔c5 35.g4
♔b4 36.h4 ♔b3 37.♔g3 ♔b2
38.♖h1 ♖xa4 39.h5 gxh5
40.gxh5 ♖c4 41.h6 ♖c8 42.h7
♖h8 43.♔g4 a4 44.♔g5 a3
45.♔g6 a2 46.♔g7 a1♕
47.♖xa1 1-0**

Another sharp kingside attack.

Shamkovich-Kagan [B36]
Natanya, 1975

**1.e4 c5 2.♘f3 ♘c6 3.d4 cxd4
4.♘xd4 g6 5.c4 ♘f6 6.♘c3
♘xd4 7.♕xd4 d6 8.♗e3 ♗g7
9.♗e2 0-0 10.♕d2 ♗e6
11.♖c1 ♕a5 12.b3 ♖fc8 13.0-0
a6**

Black is aiming for the pawn break
...b5.

14.f4!

The best and most aggressive course
of action for white. Too slow is 14.f3 b5!
when black actually stands slightly
better.

14...b5 15.f5

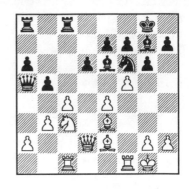

The more direct thrust with this pawn
is a prelude to a sharp attack.

15...b4?

A blunder as black's rook on f8 can
no longer defend his king's fortress.
Correct is 15...♗d7 16.fxg6 hxg6
17.c5!? ♗e6? (17...b4!? is probably
better) 18.♗f3 with advantage to white
as in Tal-Parma, Bled 1961 (see ECO
B36). Instead, I offer the following,
more forceful idea after 15...♗d7 i.e.,
16.fxg6 hxg6 17.♗h6!? b4 (not
17...♗xh6 18.♕xh6 b4 19.♖xf6! bxc3
20.♖xf7! (crushing) ...♔xf7 21.♖f1+
♗f5 22.♖xf5+ gxf5 23.♗h5+ ♔g8
24.♗g6! mating) 18.♗xg7 ♔xg7 (if
18...bxc3? 19.♕h6 is winning) 19.♘d5
with a small plus and enduring
initiative. Very interesting also (after
15...♗d7) is 16.b4!? preventing the
counterattack with b5-b4. The game
Ivanchuk-Anand, Moscow Intel PCA
1994 continued, 16....♕xb4 17.e5 dxe5
18.fxg6 ♗e6! 19.gxf7+ ♗xf7 20.♗h6
♗xh6 21.♕xh6 ♗xc4 with an edge for
black. More accurate would have been
16.fxg6! hxg6 17.b4! ♕xb4 18.e5! and
now both 18....dxe5 19.♖xf6 ♗xf6
20.♕xd7 and 18....♘e8 19.♘d5 ♕xd2
20.♗xd2 (threatening 20.♘xe7+ and

20.♘b6) clearly favor white. The new idea of Ivanchuk in combination with the advance f4-f5 is extremely important to theory.

16.fxe6 bxc3 17.exf7+ ♔f8

17...♔xf7 18.♖xc3 is clearly good for white.

18.♕c2 ♕e5 19.♗f3 d5!?

Black is also craving the iniative.

20.♖cd1!

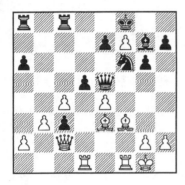

White is not distracted. A mistake would be 20.cxd5? ♘xd5 with black standing well.

20...dxc4

20...dxe4 21.♗d4 ♕e6 22.♖fe1 is good for white.

21.♗d4 ♕b5?

A mistake. A better chance was afforded by 21...cxb3!? but even after 22.♕xb3! (22.axb3 ♕a5 is unclear) ...♕a5 23.e5 ♖ab8 24.exf6! ♗xf6! (24...♖xb3 25.fxg7+ wins) 25.♕c2

♖b2 (or 25...♗xd4+ 26.♖xd4 ♕c5 27.♕f2 winning) 26.♕c1 wins.

22.b4! ♖d8 23.♕xc3 ♖ac8 24.a4! ♕b8

After 24...♕xa4 25.e5 ♘d5 26.♗xd5 ♖xd5 27.♕h3! wins. The game concluded ....

25.e5 ♘d5 26.♗xd5 ♖xd5 27.♕h3 h5 28.♕e6 ♖xd4 29.♖xd4 ♗xe5 30.♖d7 ♗xh2+ 31.♔h1 1-0

For our final inspection of the Maroczy Bind, we examine the quieter strategies available to white in the following interesting example.

Shamkovich-Pupols
US Open, 1987

1.e4 c5 2.♘f3 ♘c6 3.d4 cxd4 4.♘xd4 g6 5.c4 ♗g7 6.♗e3 ♘f6 7.♘c3 ♘g4 8.♕xg4 ♘xd4 9.♕d1 e5?

A questionable, but "theoretical" move. Better is 11....♘e6.

10.♗d3 0-0 11.0-0 f5

11....d6!? is worth considering.

12.exf5 ♘xf5?

Correct is 12...gxf5!? 13.♘d5 d6 14.♗xd4 exd4 15.♖e1 with a slight plus for white. The text weakens the light squares.

13.♕d2 ♘xe3 14.♕xe3 d6 15.♗e4 ♗e6 16.b3 ♕e7 17.♖ad1 ♖fd8 18.♗d5 ♖d7 19.♘e4!

White's minor pieces dominate the board.

19...♔h8 20.♗xe6 ♕xe6 21.♖d5!

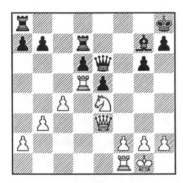

A complete blockade and domination a la Nimzovich.

21...b6 22.♖fd1 ♖ad8 23.h3 ♗f8 24.♕d3 ♕f5 25.b4 a5 26.bxa5 bxa5 27.c5!

Blockade and destroy! The game is over.

27...♖c7 28.cxd6 ♖b7 29.f3 ♖b4 30.♕c3 ♗g7 31.♕c7 ♖bb8 32.d7 ♕f4 33.♔h1 and black very soon resigned (1-0)

SICILIAN COUNTERATTACKS

Finally, we will close our survey of the Sicilian by examining four models of Sicilian counterattack drawn from my own praxis.

Hermlin-Shamkovich [B88]
Vilandy, Estonia, 1972

1.e4 c5 2.♘f3 ♘c6 3.d4 cxd4 4.♘xd4 ♘f6 5.♘c3 d6 6.♗c4 e6 7.♗b3 ♗e7 8.♗e3

8.f4 and 8.0-0 are common alternatives.

8...a6 9.f4

Against the Yugoslavian Grandmaster Velimirovic's patented attack 9.♕e2, black has two promising lines to generate counterplay, e.g., 9...♘a5!? 10.0-0-0 ♕c7 (intending 11...b5) and 9...0-0 10.0-0-0 ♕c7 11.g4 ♘d7! 12.g5 ♘c5, both leading to unclear situations.

9...♘xd4 10.♗xd4 0-0 11.♕f3

Theory also mentions 11.0-0 b5 12.e5 (the slower 12.a3 ♗b7 13.♕d3 a5! is promising for black) ...dxe5 13.fxe5 ♘d7 14.♘e4 ♗b7 15.♘d6 ♗xd6 16.exd6 ♕g5! with a complex and unclear game in the offing (see Short-Kasparov, 14th Match Game, 1993 and Klovsky-Shamkovich in the Supplementary games section).

11...b5!

After the game I was surprised to learn that this methodical move and successful improvisation was a theoretical novelty. Its purpose is clear: to develop comfortably the light-squared bishop.

12.e5

Another attractive try is 12.♗xf6 ♗xf6 13.e5 (it occurred in Short-Kasparov, 12th Match Game,

1993 - for details see the Supplementary games section), but 13...♗h4+! 14.g3 ♖b8 15.gxh4 ♗b7 16.♘e4 dxe5 leads to a complicated game with roughly even chances. I am very proud that World Champion Garry Kasparov adopted my old idea with success.

12...dxe5 13.fxe5

13.♕xa8 ♕xd4 is good for black, but white should take the opportunity to remove his king from the center while he can, i.e., 13.♗xe5! ♕b6 14.0-0-0 (14.♕xa8? ♗b7 15.♗d4 ♕c6 16.♕a7 ♘d7! 17.♗e3 ♘c5 [with the idea of 18...♖a8] is dangerous) ...♗b7 15.♕g3 ♖ad8, with mutual chances.

13...♕xd4 14.exf6

If 14.♕xa8 ♕xe5+ is very good for black.

14...♗c5!

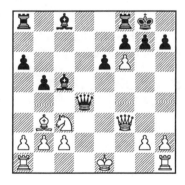

15.fxg7

The rook is still immune. 15.♕xa8? ♕f2+ 16.♔d1 ♗e3 17.♘e4 ♖d8+ wins quickly.

15...♖d8! 16.♖d1 ♕e5+

17.♘e4 ♖xd1+ 18.♔xd1 ♕xe4 19.♘xe4 ♗e7

Black has a strong bishop-pair and a clear advantage.

20.♘d2?

Better was 20.♖e1 ♗b7 21.♖e2, but black maintains his plus with 21...a5!

20...♗b7 21.♘f3 a5! 22.a4 ♖d8+ 23.♔c1 b4 24.♖d1 ♖xd1+ 25.♔xd1 ♗f6 26.♔c1 ♗c6!

Immobilizing white's bishop. The game is won.

27.♔d2

White hopes to win black's a-pawn with this king march, but black has prepared a nice tactical rejoinder.

27...♗xb2 28.♔d3 ♗xg7 29.♔c4 ♗c3 30.♔c5 ♗e4 31.♘d4

For if 31.♔b5 e5 32.♔xa5? ♗xc2! wins by forcing a winning pawn promotion. (33.♗xc2 or 33.♗a2 allows 33...b3+, etc.).

31...♗xg2 32.♘c6 ♗xc6 33.♔xc6

There will be no salvation in this reduction to opposite-colored bishops.

33...e5 34.♔b5 e4 35.♔xa5 e3 0-1

After 36.♗c4 b3+ is a familiar winning theme, so white resigned.

In the following game, black

counters white's initiation of a classical kingside attack with 17...f5!? The idea is two-fold: to stop the dangerous pawn break f4-f5 and secondly to activate black's counterattack. A few years later, Kasparov realized a similar idea even more convincingly in his famous game vs. Karpov (24th Match Game, Moscow, 1985).

Hebert-Shamkovich [B44]
Lone Pine 1981

1.e4 c5 2.♘f3 ♘c6 3.d4 cxd4 4.♘xd4 e6 5.♘b5 d6 6.c4 ♘f6 7.♘1c3 a6 8.♘a3 b6!?

I think this move, which is very popular at the present time (1992) is more accurate than 8...♗e7, as for example seen in Karpov - Kasparov (3rd Match Game, 1984). Black tries to mobilize his pieces as quickly as possible.

9.♗e2 ♗b7 10.0-0 ♗e7 11.f4 0-0 12.♗e3 ♘b8!

A subtle regrouping of the knight. From c5, the knight will augment pressure on white's e-pawn.

13.♗f3 ♘bd7

Black has equalized.

14.♕e2 ♖c8

Also playable is 14...♕c7. Black can also consider 14...♖e8!? (eyeing the queen on e2) so as to meet 15.g4 with the thematic break 15...d5!

15.g4 ♘c5 16.♕g2

16.♗f2 ♘e8 17.g5? is strongly countered with 17...e5! with advantage.

16...♘e8

Premature is 16...d5?! 17.cxd5 exd5 18.e5 ♘fe4 19.♘e2 and white stands well.

17.g5 f5!?

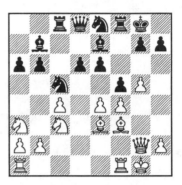

Black's critical idea, that we have already introduced.

18.exf5

Weak is 18.gxf6? ♗xf6 19.♖ac1 ♗xc3 20.♖xc3 ♘f6 with an edge for black. Possible is 18.♖ad1 g6 with a complex and unclear game.

18...♗xf3 19.♖xf3 ♖xf5 20.♕e2?

Better was 20.♘c2 ♖f7 21.♘d4 g6! 22.b4 ♘d3 with an unclear position.

20...♘c7!

Threatening to break with ...e6-e5.

21.h4 d5! 22.♖d1 ♕f8

Black enjoys a clear advantage.

23.♘c2

White hurries to return the "offside" knight to play. If instead, 23.cxd5 exd5 24.♘c2 ♘5e6, the weakness of f4 becomes apparent.

23...dxc4! 24.♕xc4

On 24.♘d4, I was contemplating the promising exchange sacrifice, 24...b5! 25.♘xf5 ♕xf5.

24...b5 25.♕e2 e5 26.♖df1 e4! 27.♖g3

27.♖3f2 ♘d3 28.♖g2 ♘xb2 29.♘xe4 ♘d5 gives black a strong attack.

27...♘7e6 28.♖g4 ♘d3 29.♕d2

No hope is offered by 29.♘xe4 ♘dxf4 30.♕h2 ♖xc2! 31.♕xc2 ♘h3+ 32.♔g2 ♖xf1 33.♔xh3 ♕f3+ with decisive penetration.

29...♘e5!

Winning. With black's next move, this knight completes an impressive tour de force (♘b8 - c6 - b8 - d7 - c5 - d3 - e5 - f3). The material gain is decisive. The game concluded ....

30.♖g3 ♘f3+ 31.♖gxf3 exf3 32.♖xf3 ♖d8 33.♕f2 ♗c5 34.♗xc5 ♕xc5 35.♘e3 ♘d4 36.♖g3 ♖f7 37.g6 hxg6 38.♖xg6 ♘f5 39.♘g4 ♕xf2+ 40.♔xf2 ♖d2+ 41.♔e1 ♖xb2 42.♘d5 ♖xa2 43.♘e5 ♖f8 44.♖g5 ♔h7 45.♖h5+ ♘h6 0-1

In conclusion, let me present the absolutely unusual game Ravinsky - Shamkovich, a "Sicilian Ambush"

played many, many years ago (semi-final of the USSR Ch. Vilnius, 1953). In this game, I improvised a new version of the Semi-Accelerated Dragon (SAD) and won. However, practically nobody (except Viktor Korchnoi) payed attention to this game at the time. It was published only in the 1953 Russian Yearbook and "filtered" into Western magazines much later. It is very interesting that the noted theorist GM Gena Sosonko did not have any idea about this original system and this game until I showed it to him in 1986. Soon after, he used the system against De Firmian (Wijk Aan Zee, 1986), repeating my game until the twentieth move and won convincingly - a rebirth of the modernized SAD. However, Sosonko lost with the system a few rounds later to GM Nigel Short and a few years later (1991) in New In Chess #22, he published a sharp criticism of the System and claimed it does not deserve any special place in opening theory at all ("forever"). I think my colleague may have been too subjective, as nevertheless this system has provoked new interest amongst Sicilian afficionados. I learned recently that Yugoslav GM Velimirovic had adopted the black side a few times with success. Let us return to the original game in question ...

Ravinsky-Shamkovich [B34]
Vilnius, USSR, 1953

1.e4 c5 2.♘f3 ♘c6 3.d4 cxd4 4.♘xd4 ♘f6 5.♘c3 g6!? 6.♘xc6 bxc6 7.e5 ♘g8

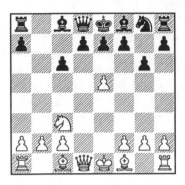

8.♗c4 ♗g7 9.♕f3 f5!?

The beginning of a new plan. Usual were 9...e6 and 9...f6 which are inferior.

10.♗f4 e6 11.0-0-0

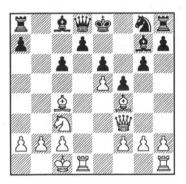

Probably the best move. In the above mentioned Short-Sosonko game, there followed 11.0-0 ♘h6 12.♖ad1 ♕c7 13.♖fe1 ♘f7 14.♕g3 (13.h4!?) ...0-0? 15.h4! ♔h8 16.♘a4! and white got a clear advantage. However by playing the thematic 14....g5! black might seize the initiative, although after 15.♗xg5 ♗xe5 (not 15...♘xe5? 16.♗d8! winning) the moves 16.♖xe5!? or 16.f4 require detailed analysis.

11....♕c7

Later on, plans involving ...♕a5 were developed.

12.h4! ♘h6!

The natural maneuver 12...♘e7 followed by ...♘d5 favors white, as shown in the game Suetin-Korchnoi, USSR 1954, while 12...♗xe5? fails to 13.♗xe5 ♕xe5 14.♗xe6!

13.♕g3

In case of 13.h5, the break 13....g5 (which I had planned over the board) seems risky to me now after 14.♗xg5 ♘f7 15.♗f4, e.g., 15....♗xe5 ♘xe5 (if 16....♕xe5 17.♗xe6!) 17.♕g3 d6 18.♗b3 as well as 15....♘xe5 16.♕g3 d6 (or 16....♗f6 17.♗xe6!) 17.♖xd6! Black should simply play 13....♘f7 14.hxg6 hxg6.

13...♘f7 14.♖he1

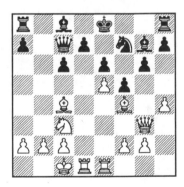

Black's knight has been successfully transferred to the optimal position at f7, where it takes firm control of the key squares at g5, e5 and d6. Meanwhile, White has firmly protected his central pawn which paralyzes black's position, but at the same time limits white's activity.

14...♖b8!

Finding a new target of counterattack - the white king's shelter.

15.♗b3?

Overlooking the major threat (33 years later, De Firmian would commit the same blunder against Sosonko........). Correct is 15.b3 (or 15.a3) ...0-0 with a double-edged game, when the mutual weaknesses of the d7- and e5-pawns counterbalance each other. Only practice will allow an adequate assessment of each side's chances in such a position.

15...♖b4! 16.♔b1

Preventing the threat 16...♖xf4 17.♕xf4 ♗h6. Anyway.........

16...0-0 17.a3 ♖xf4! 18.♕xf4 ♗xe5 19.♕d2 d5

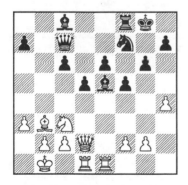

As a result of the exchange sacrifice for the central pawn black has obtained a powerful pawn center, freedom for his pieces and the prospect of a crushing attack on the b-file. The game is practically over. This position is remarkable in that it occurred in the aforementioned De Firmian-Sosonko game, a somewhat unique occurrence in the chess world for play to be repeated until the twentieth move in such a rare, unusual and "almost" unknown system.

20.♘e2 ♗d7 21.f4

If 21.h5 g5 would be strong.

21...♗f6 22.h5

A forlorn attempt to create counterthreats on the kingside.

22...♖b8 23.hxg6 hxg6 24.♘d4 ♕d6 25.♕e3 c5!

The entry into a final combination.

26.♘xc6 c4!

The point, for if 27.♗xc4 ♖xb2+ 28.♔c1 ♗xe6 29.♕xe6 ♕xa3 is crushing, e.g., 30.♖d3 ♖b1+ 31.♔d2 ♕b4+.

27.♘d4 cxb3 28.cxb3 ♕b6 29.♕d3

29.b4 would not help white, because of 29...a5 30.♘c2 d4!

29...a5 30.♖e3 ♘d6

The black knight transfers to a dominating position at e4.

31.g4 ♘e4

Threatening 32...♘f2.

32.♘c2 ♖d8!

Indirectly defending the d-pawn; because 33.♕xd5+? ♗e6 wins.

33.g5

33.♖g1 fails to the simple 33...♔f7.

33...♗b5

Snaring the queen.

0-1

Short-Kasparov [B88]
London (m/12), 1993

1.e4 c5 2.♘f3 d6 3.d4 cxd4 4.♘xd4 ♘f6 5.♘c3 a6 6.♗c4 e6 7.♗b3 ♘c6

Kasparov has chosen the more common and safe line, after miraculously escaping in Games 8 and 10.

8.f4 ♗e7 9.♗e3 0-0 10.♕f3 ♘xd4 11.♗xd4 b5

The original game was Hermlin-Shamkovich, which went 11...b5 12.e5 dxe5 13.fxe5 ♕xd4 14.exf6 ♗c5 15.fxg7 ♖d8! Also interesting is 13.♗xe5 ♕b6 14.♕xa8 ♗b7 15.♗d4 ♕c6 16.♕a7 ♘d7! 17.♗e3 ♘c5 with the idea 18...♖a8.

12.♗xf6! ♗xf6 13.e5 ♗h4+ 14.g3 ♖b8 15.gxh4 ♗b7 16.♘e4

The exchange sacrifice 16.♕g3!? is interesting, after 16...♗xh1 17.0-0-0 ♗a8 18.♖xd6 ♕e7 19.♖d1 g6, black is OK.

16...dxe5! 17.♖g1! g6 18.♖d1 ♗xe4

18...♕e7!? 19.h5 exf4 20.hxg6 hxg6 21.c3 is unclear.

19.♕xe4 ♕xh4+ 20.♔e2 ♕xh2+

20...exf4 gives black a small edge.

21.♖g2 ♕xf4

Kasparov suggests 21...♕h5+.

22.♕xf4 exf4 23.♔f3= ♖fd8 24.♖xd8+ ♖xd8 25.♔xf4 ♔f8 26.♔e3 ♔e7

Black's four connected passed pawns are very dangerous, so Short tries to create a passed pawn on the other side as quickly as possible.

27.c4! h5 28.a4 bxa4 29.♗xa4 h4 30.c5 ♖h8! 31.♖c2 h3 32.♗c6 e5 33.♔f2 h2 34.♖c1 a5!

Preventing b2-b4. Alternatives such as 34...♖b8 35.♗h1 ♖xb2+ 36.♔g3 or 34...f5 35.♗h1 e4 36.c6, hardly give black more chances for victory.

35.♗d5 ♖d8 36.♗g2 ♖d2+ 37.♔g3 ♔d7 38.♖a1 f5 39.♔xh2 ♖xb2 40.♖xa5 e4

Neither side can strengthen its position.

½-½

Short-Kasparov [B88]
London (m/14), 1993

1.e4 c5 2.♘f3 d6 3.d4 cxd4 4.♘xd4 ♘f6 5.♘c3 a6 6.♗c4 e6 7.♗b3 ♘c6 8.f4 ♗e7 9.♗e3 0-0 10.0-0-0

Short varies from 10.♕f3 as in game 12. His idea involves a breakthrough with e4-e5 or f4-f5.

10...♘xd4 11.♗xd4 b5 12.e5 dxe5 13.fxe5 ♘d7 14.♘e4 ♗b7

This position is well known to theory, e.g., 15.♕g4 ♗xe4! 16.♕xe4 ♘c5 Klovsky-Shamkovich, USSR 1971.

15.♘d6 ♗xd6 16.exd6 ♕g5 17.♕e2 e5 18.♗c3

The book line is 18.♗e3 ♕g6 19.♖ad1, but I am not sure that the new idea ♗c3-a5-c7 is stronger.

18...♕g6 19.♖ad1 ♔h8 20.♗d5 ♗xd5 21.♖xd5 ♕e6 22.♖fd1 ♖fc8

22...f5 23.a4 bxa4 24.♗xe5 ♖ae8 25.c4 ♘xe5 26.d7=, Christiansen - Spassov, Indonesia 1982. If 22...♖ac8 23.a4!

23.♗a5

Not 23.♗xe5? ♖e8-+

23...♖c6 24.b3 ♖ac8 25.♗c7 ♖e8 26.c4 bxc4 27.bxc4 f5

Threatening a pawn storm with e5-e4 and f5-f4 countering white's attack with ♕c2-a4 and c4-c5. It is not yet clear which attack is the most effective.

28.h3

28.♕c2!?

28...h6 29.♕c2 e4 30.♕a4

♖c5 31.♖xc5 ♘xc5 32.♕c6 ♘d7 33.♕d5 ♕g6!?

33...e3!?

34.♕d2?

34.c5! ♖e5 35.♕a8+ ♔h7 36.c6 f4 37.cxd7 ♖g5 38.♖d2 ♖c5! was not so clear and left black with real counterchances.

34...♖e5 35.♕e3 ♕e6 36.♖c1 ♖c5 37.♖c2 ♔g8 38.a4 ♔f7 39.♕f2 e3

A draw was agreed here, although black's position is already much better, maybe winning, e.g., 40.♕f3 ♖e5 41.♕e2 f4 42.a5 ♕g6 43.♔f1 f3! 44.gxf3 ♖g5.

½-½

Part III
Spanish Tortures: Explorations in the Ruy Lopez

1.e4 e5 2.♘f3 ♘c6 3.♗b5

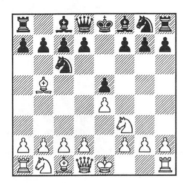

The Ruy Lopez (Spanish Game) is without question the most long-lived opening in chess history. It was discovered and analyzed in the 16th century by the Spanish priest Ruy Lopez, and has lived until the present time as one of the most popular openings for both white and black, dominating in popularity other lines in the Open Game such as the King's Gambit, Evans Gambit, Giuoco Piano, Two Knights Defence and the Scotch Game, etc. Very recently, one of the aforementioned older lines - the Scotch Game - has resurfaced and experienced a second youth thanks mainly due to revision and successful practice by Garry Kasparov and other GMs. But I do not believe that the success of this old system is stable enough to threaten the popularity of the Ruy Lopez.

The fantastic viability of the move 3.♗b5 and the numerous systems and variations associated with is best explained in that the Ruy Lopez is notable for an exceptional wealth of sophisticated, strategical and tactical ideas for both sides and at the same time offers solidity and soundness in the main systems. It is therefore not surprising that most of the greatest chessplayers in the world, e.g., Lasker, Capablanca, Alekhine, Smyslov, Keres, Tal, Spassky, Fischer, Karpov and Kasparov have all included the Ruy Lopez in their opening arsenals, often from both sides of the board. The author has been a witness to the long-term development and formation of theory in the Ruy Lopez and it is not by chance that I (LS) was drawn to this popular and dynamic system. I have played many Ruy Lopezes (mostly with white) with great success and will share some of the material from my Ruy Lopez archives that I believe will be of some significant interest to the reader. Our Ruy Lopez survey will begin with king-attacking games in Classical Systems.

CLASSICAL SYSTEMS IN THE RUY LOPEZ

Shamkovich - Gerensky [C78]
RSFSR-Bulgaria, 1959

1.e4 e5 2.♘f3 ♘c6 3.♗b5 a6 4.♗a4 ♘f6 5.0-0 b5!? 6.♗b3 ♗e7?!

Best here is the more usual 6...♗b7. Also possible is 6...♘xe4!? 7.d4 d5 transposing to the Open Ruy Lopez or even 6...d6!?

7.c3

7.d4! as in Shamkovich-Ervin (see below) is more accurate.

7...♗b7

An interesting alternative is 7...♘xe4!? leading to the gambit line 8.d4 exd4 (8...d5 9.dxe5 is again the Open Lopez) 9.cxd4 d5 10.♗f4 0-0 11.♘bd2 which, it seems to me, has never been examined in serious practice.

8.d4 ♘xe4?!

However, here this move is too active, as black loses control over the important d5-square. Safer was 8...d6.

9.dxe5 0-0 10.♗d5! ♘c5 11.b4!?

Played to displace the active knight at c5, but more solid was 11.♗e3 with an edge.

11...♘e6

If 11...♘a4!? 12.♕d3 (12.♗e3 is also good) ...♘b6 13.♗e4 g6 14.♗f4 is good for white.

12.♘a3! ♖b8 13.♕d3 a5 14.♕e4!

Protecting the b-pawn as 14...axb4 15.cxb4 ♗xb4? 16.♗xc6 wins for white, and further centralizing all forces.

14...♕c8 15.♘c2 ♘cd8 16.♘e3! c6 17.♗b3 c5

More stubborn was 17...d5 18.exd6 ♗xd6 but white maintains a strong attack with 19.♘f5 ♕c7 20.♗c2 g6 21.♘xd6 ♕xd6 22.♗h6.

18.♕g4!

Black cannot counter this decisive transfer of white's forces to the kingside.

18...♖e8 19.♘f5!

White's attack rapidly builds momentum.

19...♗f8

If 19...a4 20.♗c2 cxb4 21.♘xe7+ ♖xe7 22.♕h4 with a winning advantage for white.

20.♘g5! a4 21.♘h6+!

Another way is 21.♗c2!

21...♚h8

If 21...gxh6 22.♘xh7+! is simplest.

22.♗c2! ♘xg5

If now 22...gxh6? 23.♕f5 wins.

23.♗xg5 ♗d5

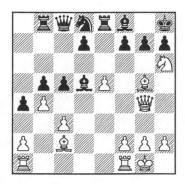

It is over. 23...♖e6 allows 24.♗f6! or if 23...♖xe5 24.♗xd8 and white is winning. After the text comes a final problem-like move and black is unable to prevent mate.

24.♗f6!! d6 25.♕h5! 1-0

There is no satisfactory answer to 26.♘xf7+ and 27.♕xh7 mate.

Shamkovich - Ervin [C84]
Lone Pine, 1975

1.e4 e5 2.♘f3 ♘c6 3.♗b5 a6 4.♗a4 ♘f6 5.0-0 b5!? 6.♗b3 ♗e7?!

The same inaccuracy as in Shamkovich-Gerensky. More promising is the Arkhangelsky variation e.g., 6...♗b7 7.♖e1 ♗c5 8.c3 d6 9.d4 ♗b6 10.♗g5 ♕e7 with counterplay.

7.d4!

More active than 7.c3 as played in the previous game. The point is that 7...exd4 8.e5 ♘g4 (or 8...♘e4 9.♗d5 ♘c5 10.♘xd4) 9.♖e1 are not good for black. Also good for white is 7...♘xd4 8.♘xd4 exd4 9.e5 and 7...♘xe4 8.dxe5 0-0 9.♖e1 ♘c5 10.♗d5. Hence black's more cautious reply.

7...d6 8.c3 ♗g4

White usually seeks to prevent this move by playing h3, but in this situation he can switch plans to a very promising pawn sacrifice.

9.h3! ♗xf3

What about 9...♗h5 (?) The continuation 10.g4!? ♗g6 11.♘h4 ♘a5! is not so clear (but not 11...♗xe4? 12.g5! with advantage). White should play 10.♖e1 0-0 11.d5 ♘a5 12.♗c2 or 10.d5 ♘a5 11.♗c2 0-0 12.♘bd2 with an edge in each case.

10.♕xf3 exd4 11.♕g3 0-0

On 11...g6, Tal-Temper, Vienna 1957 continued 12.♗d5 but stronger is 12.♗h6! as 12...♘xe4? is refuted by 13.♗d5! ♘xg3 14.♗xc6+.

12.♗h6!

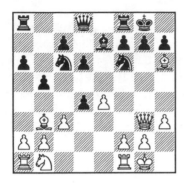

12...♘h5

It is ironic that one of the first victims of white's gambit plan was the author (LS). 12...♘e8 13.♗d5 ♕d7 14.♕g4! gave white a clear advantage in Nezhmetdinov-Shamkovich, RSFSR Ch. Kislovodsk 1956! Nearly twenty years later, I have the opportunity to "turn the table." The text is a slight improvement. A chess terrorist learns from his setbacks, and incorporates them into his own arsenal.

13.♕g4 dxc3 14.♘xc3 ♘d4

As compensation for his weak kingside, black has established an outpost for his knight at d4.

15.♕xh5 gxh6

15...♘xb3?? 16.♕g4 loses immediately.

16.f4!

Preparing a storm on the black king's position. Conversely, preserving the bishop with 16.♗d1 is a waste of time.

16...♘xb3 17.axb3 ♗f6 18.♕xh6?!

More accurate was 18.e5! dxe5 19.♖ad1 followed by ♘d5 with a strong initiative.

18...b4?

Simply forcing white to make a good move. Even so, the more natural 18...c6 is met by 19.♖f3! b4 20.e5! dxe5 21.♖d1! ♕b6+ 22.♔h1 with a crushing attack.

19.♘d5 ♗g7

Bad is 19...♗xb2? 20.e5!

20.♕h5 c6 21.♘e3 ♕b6 22.♖f3 ♔h8

The further concentration of white's forces is very instructive. Black cannot make use of a pin of the knight with 22...♗d4 because of the continuation 23.♖g3+ ♔h8 24.♔h1! ♗xe3 25.♕g5 ♗d4 26.e5! Black could try 22...f5!? but 23.♖g3 (not 23.exf5? ♖ae8 and black is doing fine) ...fxe4 24.♔h1 is strong.

23.♔h1 ♕d4 24.♖g3

Menacing 25.♘f5.

24...♖g8

More stubborn, but losing, is the brave 24...♕xe4 25.♖xg7! ♔xg7 26.♘f5+ ♔f6 (if 26...♔h8 27.♕g5 wins) 27.♘g3!! (27.♖d1 is not as strong and 27.♕g5+ ♔e6 is unclear) ♕g6 28.♕h4+ ♔g7 29.f5! ♕h6 (forced) 30.f6+! ♔g6 31.♕e4+ ♔xf6 32.♖f1+ winning.

25.♘c4

A little stronger was 25.♘f5 ♛xb2 26.♖d1.

25...♛f2?

The best chance was 25...♖ad8 but after 26.♛f3 white is in complete control.

26.♘xd6 ♖af8 27.♖g4 ♛xb2

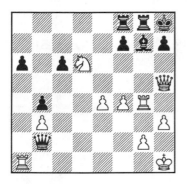

28.♖g1

A slight inaccuracy. 28.♖h4!! ♛xa1+ 29.♔h2 h6 30.♛xh6+! ♝xh6 31.♖xh6+ ♔g7 32.♘f5+ mate is forcing. After black's reply, white finds the path.....

28...♛xb3

Even if 28...♛f6 29.e5 ♛e6 30.♘e4! black's position would be desperate.

29.♖h4 h6

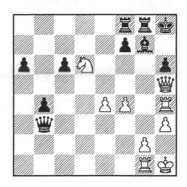

30.♛xh6+!! 1-0

As we have seen 30...♝xh6 31.♖xh6+ ♔g7 32.♘f5+ spells mate.

Shamkovich - Antoshin [C87]
Sochi, 1967

1.e4 e5 2.♘f3 ♘c6 3.♝b5 a6 4.♝a4 ♘f6 5.0-0 ♝e7 6.♖e1 d6 7.c3

The old plan 7.♝xc6+ bxc6 8.d4 also has a good reputation.

7...0-0 8.h3 ♘d7

A similar plan is popular at present, but with 6...b5 7.♝b3 d6 8.c3 0-0 9.h3 ♘d7 (e.g., Kasparov-Karpov, New York (m/8) 1990).

9.d4 ♝f6 10.♝e3 b5 11.♝c2! ♝b7 12.♘bd2 exd4?!

A questionable exchange as white has a permanent threat of e4-e5. Sometimes this exchange is strong as in the variation 6...b5 7.♝b3 d6 8.c3 0-0 9. h3 ♝b7 10.d4 ♖e8 11.♘bd2 ♝f8 12.a4 h6 13.♝c2 exd4! 14.cxd4 ♘b4 15.♝b1 c5 (e.g., Kasparov-Karpov, Lyons (m/20) 1990).

13.cxd4 ♘b4 14.♗b1 c5 15.a3 ♘c6

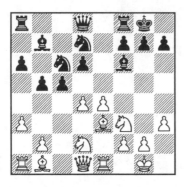

16.e5!

The basic objective of this thrust is to activate the "Spanish" bishop.

16...dxe5?

This reply leads to a terrible position for black. Correct was 16...cxd4 but 17.exf6 dxe3 18.fxg7 exf2+ 19.♔xf2 ♔xg7 20.♘e4 regaining the pawn is favorable to white.

17.dxc5!

After this strong move, white's pieces seize the key squares d5, d6 and e4.

17...♗e7 18.♘e4 f5?

This pseudo-active move weakens black's position beyond repair, but the more solid 18...♘f6 19.♘d6! did not promise black much.

19.♘d6 ♗xd6 20.♕xd6 f4 21.♗d2 ♖f6 22.♕d3 ♖h6

After 22...♘f8 the most logical

continuation would be 23.♗c3 ♕xd3 24.♗xd3 ♘g6 25.♗e4! with a dominating game.

23.b4 ♔h8 24.♗c3 ♕e7 25.♗c2 ♖d8 26.♕f5

The beginning of the final attack.

26...♖f8 27.♕g5 ♕f7

The queen trade with 27...♕xg5 28.♘xg5 leaves black without hope.

28.♖ad1 ♗c8 29.♗xe5! ♖h5

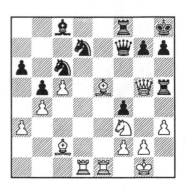

The last chance, as 29...♘dxe5 30.♘xe5 ♘xe5 31.♖xe5 is too bad for black.

30.♗xg7+! ♔g8 31.♗c3+ ♖xg5 32.♘xg5 ♕h5 33.♗b3+ 1-0

The triumph of white's bishop pair is very spectacular.

Shamkovich - Cobo [C67]
Salgotarian, 1966

1.e4 e5 2.♘f3 ♘c6 3.♗b5 ♘f6 4.0-0 ♘xe4 5.♖e1 ♘d6 6.♘xe5 ♗e7 7.♗d3 0-0 8.♘c3

This is of course more solid than the super-active 8.♕h5!? (see Shamkovich-Blohm in Part I).

8....♘xe5

Black is now at a crossroads - which is better: 8...♘xe5 or 8...♘e8 (?). Modern theory (ECO C67) reccomends 8...♘e8, referring to to Yanovsky-Lasker, Nurenberg 1896 which continued with 9.♘d5 ♗f6 10.♘g4 d6 (= ECO) and now Yanovsky gained the victory after the experimental exchange sacrifice 11.♖xe8!? ♖xe8 12.♘gxf6+ gxf6 13.b3 ♘e5 14.♗b2, but the new World Champion did not manage the game very well. Such an assessment (= ECO) does not seem to me to be a final one. What about 11.♗b5 (?). Both 11...♗xg4 12.♕xg4 and 11...♗e6 12.♘gxf6+ ♘xf6 13.♘f4! ♗g4 14.f3 ♗d7 15.b3 (with two strong bishops) are, in my opinion, favorable to white. In any case, contemporary players usually play the safer 8...♘xe5, as played by my opponent.

9.♖xe5 c6

Taking control over the key square at d5, but weakening the d6-square. However, black cannot practically avoid playing this move. Please consider the very interesting game, Nezhmetdinov- Kotkov, Krasnodar 1957, which continued 9...♗f6 10.♖e3 (threatening 11.♗xh7+ ♔xh7 12.♕h5+ ♔g8 13.♖h3 winning) 10...g6 11.♕f3! ♗g7 12.b3 ♘e8 13.♗a3 d6 14.♖ae1 and white had an edge (see Supplemental games). In his comments, Damsky suggested in his book of selected games of Nezhmetdinov that

11...♗d4 gave an equal game, but in fact 12.♖e2 ♘e8 13.b3 d6 14.♗a3 followed by ♖ae1 is good for white.

10.♕e2

White's concentration of pieces along the e-file is one of the major elements of his attacking plan.

10...♗f6 11.♖e3 g6 12.b3 ♘e8 13.♗a3 d6 14.♖ae1

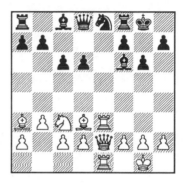

Both sides have developed their pieces, including such "enfants terribles" as the bishop once at c1 and the knight that was posted at d6. Nevertheless, white's position is very strong (space advantage, pressure along the e-file and against the weak pawn at d6), and the question is can black successfully consolidate his forces?

14...♗e6?!

More promising was 14...♘g7 as suggested by Maric in Informant 4, taking control over f5. If 15.♘e4 ♗e7 16.♘g3 ♗e6 17.♗c4 d5 equalizes but 15.♕f3! (with the threat of 16.♗xd6 ♕xd6 17.♘e4 winning) seems very strong as well, e.g., 15...♘f5 16.♗xf5 ♗xf5 17.g4 winning or 15...♗d4

16.♖3e2 f5? 17.♘d5! winning but 15...♗f5! 16.g4 ♗xd3 17.♖xd3 ♖e8! is possible.

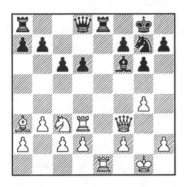

(analysis)

Black's position is still precarious, but maybe defensible. I recommend readers to consider and study such interesting lines as 18.♘e4 ♗e5 19.♘xd6 (If 19.♗xd6 ♗xd6 20.♘f6+ ♕xf6! is O.K for black) ...♗xd6 20.♖xe8+ ♘xe8 21.♗xd6 ♘xd6 22.♕f4 ♕a5 with equality. In any event, black suffers in this whole system because of his pinned d6-pawn. The text 14...♗e6 helps white to firmly seize the initiative.

15.♗c4!

Exchanging a clumsy bishop for an important defender of black's position.

15...♘g7 16.♘e4 ♗e7

Worse is 16...♗e5 17.♗xe6 ♘xe6 18.c3, with the powerful threat of 19.d4.

17.♗xe6 ♘xe6 18.h4!

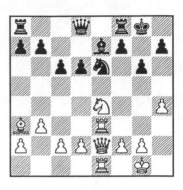

A very strong thrust designed to prevent 18...d5 since 19.♗xe7 ♕xe7 20.♘g5 wins for white.

18...♖e8

It is not easy to offer advice to black in this situation. For example., 18...♗xh4 19.♘xd6 ♕d7 (19...♕c7 20.♖xe6) 20.♕c4! ♗f6 21.♘xf7! winning. Black could have tried 18...♘d4 19.♕d3 ♘f5 20.♖3e2 but the pawn on h4 is still laced with poison, 20...♘xh4 21.♘g3! ♖e8 22.♗xd6 and 20...♗xh4 21.♘xd6 win for white, while 20...d5 21.♗xe7 ♕xe7 22.♘g3! is clearly better for white also. Nevertheless, the text is weaker.

19.g3 h6

Positional suicide. Maric offers 19...♘g7 but both 20.♗b2 and 20.h5 are strong continuations.

20.h5 g5 21.♕f3 ♖f8 22.♗b2!

At last the deadly threat of 23.♘f6+ becomes a reality. There is no defense.

22...d5 23.♘f6+ ♗xf6 24.♗xf6 ♕d7 25.♖e5 ♖ae8 26.♕g4

Threatening 27.♗xg5.

26...♕d6 27.f4! ♕b4 28.c3 ♕b6+ 29.d4 ♘xd4 30.♖xg5+ ♔h7 31.♖g7+ 1-0

The following game illustrates the risks for black if he plays too passively.

Shamkovich - Averbach [C67]
Moscow, 1974

1.e4 e5 2.♘f3 ♘c6 3.♗b5 ♘f6 4.0-0 ♘xe4 5.♖e1 ♘d6 6.♘xe5 ♗e7 7.♗d3 ♘xe5 8.♖xe5 0-0 9.♘c3

By a slightly different move order, we reach the position of Shamkovich-Cobo.

9...♖e8?!

9...c6 was Shamkovich-Cobo. If 9...♗f6, white has the possibility 10.♖e3 (threatening 11.♗xh7+) 10...g6 11.b3 intending 12.♗a3 with a good game.

10.♕e2

The best alternative is 10.b3! for example 10...♗f6 11.♖e1 ♖xe1+ 12.♕xe1 ♘e8 13.♗a3 d6 14.♕e4! with a crushing position, Geller-Panno, Varna Ol. 1962. A waste of time is 10.♘d5 ♗f8 followed by ...c6.

10...♗f8?

Worth consideration is 10...♗f6!? e.g., ECO gives 11.♖xe8+ ♕xe8 12.♘d5 ♗d8 with equality, although, in my opinion 13.b3 is good for an edge. Interesting is 11.♖e3!? ♖xe3 (11...♗d4? 12.♗xh7+ wins) 12.dxe3 with a small advantage for white.

11.b3 ♖xe5

If 11...g6 12.♗a3! ♖xe5 13.♕xe5 ♗g7 14.♕f4 with the advantage.

12.♕xe5 ♘e8?

A better try is 12...♕e8!? but 13.♕f4! ♕e1+ 14.♗f1 ♕e6 15.♕f3 maintains a plus for white.

13.♗b2 d6 14.♕e4 g6 15.♖e1 ♘f6 16.♕f3!

Stronger than 16.♕h4 ♗d7 17.♘e4 ♘xe4 18.♕xe4 when 18...♕e8! equalizes.

16...d5?

Black's last chance to fight was 16...c6! 17.♘e4 ♘e8 18.♘f6+ ♘xf6 19.♗xf6 ♕d7 with a positional inferiority.

17.♘b5 ♘h5

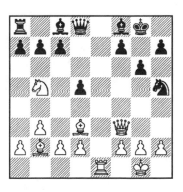

Instead 17...♘e8 18.♖xe8 ♕xe8 19.♕f6 loses instantly.

18.♖e5!

White's attack builds momentum.

Two threats viz., 19.♖xd5 and 19.♖xh5 gxh5 20.♗xh7+!

18...♘f6 19.♘xc7 ♗g4 20.♕f4 ♖c8 21.♘xd5 ♘xd5 22.♖xd5

After 22...♕xd5 23.♕f6 black is diagonalized!

1-0

Shamkovich - Martz [C67]
Lone Pine, 1975

1.e4 e5 2.♘f3 ♘c6 3.♗b5 ♘f6 4.0-0 ♘xe4 5.♖e1

5.d4 is examined in the next game.

5...♘d6 6.♘xe5 ♗e7 7.♗d3 0-0 8.♘c3 ♘xe5 9.♖xe5 ♗f6 10.♖e3 g6 11.b3

The most accurate is 11.♕f3! (see the game, Nezhmetdinov-Kotkov).

11...b6! 12.♗a3 c5!

Thoroughly shutting out white's dark-squared bishop.

13.♕g4 ♗d4 14.♖e2 ♗b7 15.♖ae1 f5! 16.♕f4 ♕f6

Threatening 17...g5.

17.h4 ♘e4!

A very strong invasion. The threat is 18...♗e5 and 19...♘xc3. White cannot take the knight because the f2-pawn falls under attack.

18.♗c4+ ♔h8 19.♘d5 ♕g7!

A new and unpleasant threat of 20...b5! appears. White's next is an attempt to complicate the position further.

20.d3!?

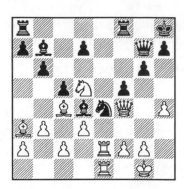

20...b5?!

The position is extremely complicated. Black should have played 20...♘xf2! 21.♖xf2 ♖ae8! e.g., 22.♖xe8 ♖xe8 and now 23.♔f1 ♖e5! wins (but not 23...b5? 24.♘c7!) or 23.♕d2 ♕e5! winning. Better is 22.♖ef1 b5 23.c3 ♗xf2+ 24.♔xf2 bxc4 25.♗xc5 ♗xd5 26.♗d4 ♖f6 27.bxc4 ♗c6 with an approximately even game. As we can see, black's success can be attributed to the terrible position of the offside bishop at a3. I have to note that my old recommendation of 21...b5 (Informant 19) is likely not so strong since 22.♖e7 ♖f7 23.♖xf7 ♕xf7 24.♘c7 bxc4 25.bxc4! ♖c8 26.♘b5 is unclear.

21.dxe4 bxc4 22.bxc4 fxe4 23.♕xe4 ♕f7 24.♔h2 ♗a6!

But not 24...♗xf2? 25.♗b2! winning.

25.f4 d6

If 25...♗xc4? 26.♗xc5! is better for white.

26.♖d2 ♖ae8?

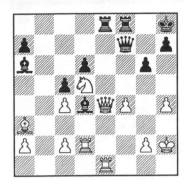

Better was 26...♗g7 27.♖de2 ♗d4 with equal chances.

27.♖xd4! ♖xe4 28.♖dxe4

Suddenly, the tables are turned. White is absolutely dominating.

28...♕g7 29.♖e7 ♕d4 30.♖b1 ♔g8 31.♗b2 ♖b8 32.♗xd4! ♖xb1 33.♗g7!

34.♘f6+ mate is coming.

1-0

Shamkovich - Lein [C67]
Tbilisi, 1970

1.e4 e5 2.♘f3 ♘c6 3.♗b5 ♘f6 4.0-0 ♘xe4 5.d4

This answer usually leads to a peculiar position after 5...♘d6 6.♗xc6 dxc6 7.dxe5 ♘f5 8.♕xd8+ ♔xd8, where black may hold with precise play, despite white's theoretical advantage. I remember only a few games of mine in this line, in particular a loss with black

to ex-World Champion Mikhail Tal who played a very strong endgame, and a win with white vs. GM Bisguier (New York 1977) which was a very sharp battle, that can be found in the Supplemental Game section. More interesting is the following game, where my opponent played the half-forgotten move 5...♗e7!?

5...♗e7!? 6.♕e2 ♘d6 7.♗xc6 bxc6 8.dxe5 ♘b7 9.♖e1

Making the advance ...d5 more difficult. A good alternative is 9.♘c3 0-0 10.♘d4 as in Keres-Unzicker, Hamburg, match 1956 (see Supplemental games).

9...0-0 10.♘c3 ♘c5 11.♗e3 ♘e6 12.♖ad1!

Better than 12.♘d4 when Keres gives 12...♘xd4 13.♗xd4 c5! 14.♗e3 d5 15.exd6 ♗xd6 with an unclear game.

12...d5

12...f6 13.♘d4! maintains an edge for white.

13.exd6 cxd6 14.♘d4 ♗d7

A later game went 14...♘xd4 15.♗xd4 ♗e6 16.♕f3 ♕d7 17.♕g3 and white is clearly better, because his bishop is too strong, Torre-Knezevic, Vrsac 1977.

15.♘f5 d5 16.♘xe7+ ♕xe7

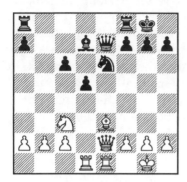

This theoretical position originated in our game. White is better, but how is he to blockade black's hanging pawns at c6 and d5?

17.♘a4

Seems sensible enough, threatening 18.♗c5.

17...♖fd8 18.♕f3?!

An inaccuracy. White should prefer 18.b3!? or stronger still 18.♗c5! ♕h4 19.b3 with an edge in each case, as black's "hanging pawns" are blockaded firmly.

18...♕b4?

An impulsive queen lunge and a prelude to a sequence of time-wasting maneuvers with the queen which only helps white to regroup his forces. Correct was 18...c5! 19.♘c3!? (not 19.♗xc5? ♕h4 winning) ...d4 20.♘d5 ♕d6 21.♗d2 with a murky position.

19.b3 ♕a3 20.♗c1 ♕e7

And definitely not 20...♕xa2?? 21.♗b2 sealing in the wayward queen.

21.♗b2 ♕g5 22.♕g3 ♕g6 23.♖d3 ♘g5 24.f3 ♗f5 25.♖d2 h6 26.♘c5!

26...♗xc2??

My aggressive opponent still tries to seize the initiative, but is trapped. GM Suetin suggested 26...♘e6 (Informant 8) but 27.♕xg6 ♗xg6 28.♘xe6 fxe6 29.♖xe6 ♗e8 30.♗d4 wins for white.

27.f4!

Decisive. White wins a piece. Lein expected only 27.h4? ♘e6! and black wins! The rest is clear.

27...♗e4

27...♘e6 fails to 28.♘xe6 fxe6 29.♖xc2!

28.fxg5 hxg5 29.♘xe4 dxe4 30.♖xd8+ ♖xd8 31.♗c1 ♖d5 32.♕b8+ ♔h7 33.♕xa7 1-0

White's concept in this game, including 17.♘a4, was approved by theory (ECO C67, note 103) and commentators. It appeared clear that white is really better after this methodical maneuver. But eight years later, in the game Karpov-Kortchnoi, Merano (m/2) 1981, the rivals repeated the variation until the 16th move. It is very likely the Challenger was going to improve black's play after 17.♘a4, but we do not know how he was going to do it because Karpov played 17.♕d2! and won the game (see Supplemental games). Krogius' suggestion of 17...♕f6 after Karpov's 17.♕d2 shouldn't solve black's problems because of 18.♘a4! e.g., 18...♖fe8 (threatening 19...d4!) 19.h3 h6 20.b4! with a winning game for white. So the game Karpov-Kortchnoi provoked some analytical and psychological questions; what is black's possible counterplay which Kortchnoi intended after the expected 17.♘a4 (?).

Black has at least two ways, offering chances to equalize the game.

A) 17...♕h4 and now 18.b3 d4! 19.♗d2 (or 19.g3 ♕f6) ...c5 20.♘b2 ♗c6 or 18.♘c5 ♘xc5 19.♗xc5 ♖fe8 with an equal position in each case, or

B) 17...♖fe8 18.b3 (18.♗c5? is refuted by 18...♕h4! 19.♕a6 ♘f4! with a strong attack and threatening 20...♘xg2! and 18.c4 d4! 19.♗c1 (19.♗xd4 ♕b4!) ...c5 20.♕c2 ♗c6 is also in black's favor) ♕f6 19.♗c1 (not 19.♕d2 d4! 20.f3 c5! and black wins) ...c5 20.♘b2 ♗c6 with level chances. Very likely Kortchnoi had prepared in answer to 17.♘a4 one of two replies (17...♕h4 or 17...♖fe8), but 17.♕d2 proved to be an unpleasant surprise for him. Such is the unusual and dramatic relationship between two games separated by a decade of time.

Shamkovich - Lein [C93]
USSR Ch. Leningrad, 1971

1.e4 e5 2.♘f3 ♘c6 3.♗b5 a6 4.♗a4 ♘f6 5.0-0 ♗e7 6.♖e1 b5 7.♗b3 d6 8.c3 0-0 9.h3 h6

This prophylactic move was very popular at the time until Zaitsev introduced 9...♗b7, which became even more fashionable when Karpov incorporated it as a basis of his "black repertoire."

10.d4 ♖e8 11.♘bd2 ♗f8 12.d5!?

White usually plays 12.♘f1 here, but this "semi-closing" of the position is a playable alternative.

12...♘e7

12...♘a5 is not as good as 13.♗c2 followed by 14.b4 concedes white too much space.

13.a4 ♗b7?!

ECO C93 mentions 13...♗d7 and if 14.c4 ♘g6 with equal chances.

14.c4

This move gives white an edge as 14...bxc4 15.♘xc4 and 14...b4 15.c5! favor white, but black could now try 14...c6!?

14...♘d7?!

Black seeks counterplay based on ...♘c5 and ...f5 - a natural but incorrect decision.

15.axb5 axb5 16.♖xa8 ♕xa8 17.cxb5 f5

The point of black's counterplay is to destroy white's pawn center at the cost of weaknesses to his kingside - a risky concept.

18.exf5 ♗xd5 19.♘e4! ♗xb3

In case of 19...♔h8 20.♘fg5! white's attack is very dangerous, e.g., 20...♗xb3 21.♕xb3 hxg5 22.♕f7! ♘f6 23.♘xf6 gxf6 24.♕xf6+ ♗g7 25.♕xg5 etc.

20.♕xb3+ ♕d5 21.♕c2 ♖c8

After maneuvering play on the queenside in the opening the theatre of operations transfers suddenly to the kingside. The purpose of the following piece sacrifice is to exploit the weakness of black's king position and the the lack of coordination of his pieces.

22.♗xh6! ♘xf5

Accepting with 22...gxh6 23.f6 ♘g6 (23...♘f5 24.♘eg5! hxg5 25.♕xf5 ♕f7 26.♘xg5 does not help) 24.♘eg5! e4 25.♖xe4 hxg5 (25...♘xf6 26.♖d4!) and now either 26.♖g4 winning or 26.♖e8! ♖xe8 27.♕xg6+ ♔h8 28.f7!! which is crushing.

23.♗d2

The simplest and apparently the best decision. The tempting leap 23.♘eg5!? is unclear after 23...g6! but not 23...gxh6 24.♕xf5 hxg5 25.♘xg5 or 23...e4 24.♖d1 ♕b7 25.♕b3+ ♔h8 26.♕e6 with white winning in both lines.

23...♘d4 24.♘xd4 exd4 25.♘g5

The critical blow. Black's kingside weaknesses prove fatal.

25...d3

If 25...♘f6 26.♕g6 threatening 27.♖e6.

26.♕a4 ♘f6 27.♖c1

The weakness of the pawn at c7 is an important winning resource for white. The threat is 28.b6.

27...♖a8 28.♕f4 ♖e8 29.♖xc7 ♕xb5

Black appears to have repulsed the main threats, but .....

30.♗c3 ♕b6 31.♖f7! d5 32.♕f5! d2 33.♗xd2

Black was hoping for 33.♖xf6?? d1♕+ 34.♔h2 ♕c7+ 35.g3 ♕h5! and black wins.

33...♖a8

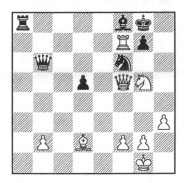

34.♖xf6!

The final breakthrough.

34...♖a1+ 35.♔h2 ♗d6+ 36.♖xd6 ♕xd6+ 37.♗f4 1-0

Shamkovich - O'Kelly [C94]
Palma de Mallorca, 1966

1.e4 e5 2.♘f3 ♘c6 3.♗b5 a6 4.♗a4 ♘f6 5.0-0 ♗e7 6.♖e1 b5 7.♗b3 d6 8.c3 0-0 9.h3 ♘b8

The very flexible Breyer system, which I believe will again become fashionable in the future.

10.d3

Avoiding the main lines resulting from 10.d4 ♘bd7 11.♘bd2 ♗b7 where, by the way, the theorists have yet to prove any serious advantage for white.

10...♘bd7 11.♘bd2 ♗b7 12.♘f1 ♘c5 13.♗c2 ♖e8 14.♘g3 ♗f8 15.♘h2

This methodical preparation for a kingside attack is very typical of this line, but more common here is 15.b4.

The next break is an adequate and natural reaction.

15...d5 16.♕f3

The position is dynamically balanced, but the struggle for the initiative has barely begun. Even so some years later, Kurajica-Unzicker, Hastings 1971/72 was agreed drawn (!) at this position.

16...♘e6 17.♘f5 ♔h8!

O'Kelly's original idea. Black is tenaciously preparing his king's defenses.

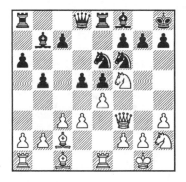

18.♘g4

Here 18.g4 and 18.h4 have been tried but without particular success, e.g., 18.g4 c5 19.g5 dxe4 20.dxe4 ♘d7 21.h4 ♕c7 with an unclear position, Ciocaltea-O'Kelly, Havana 1965 and 18.h4 c5 19.♗g5 ♘xg5 20.hxg5 ♘g8 21.♕g3 g6! and black is O.K, Browne-Portisch, Wijk Aan Zee 1972.

18...♘xg4 19.♕xg4 c5 20.h4 ♕c7 21.♖e3?!

Beginning the attack straight away,

but 21.exd5 ♗xd5 22.h5 (unclear) looks better.

21...g6 22.♖g3 ♘f4! 23.♔h2

Better was 23.h5 at once.

23...f6 24.h5!?

Playing va banque, otherwise after ...d4 or even ...h5 black will stand much better.

24...♘xh5 25.♖h3 gxf5?!

Risky. Black would do better to consolidate with 25...♕f7 with an advantage.

26.♕xh5 fxe4 27.dxe4 d4

27...dxe4 would be better.

28.♕h4

At last white has a real object of attack at f6. Now his problem is how to activate his bishop at c2.

28...♕e7?

Correct was 28...c4 29.♕xf6+ ♕g7 with a slight edge for black.

29.cxd4 cxd4

29...exd4 30.e5! is too dangerous.

30.♗b3!

Suddenly the tables are turned and black is in trouble. White's bishop pair is very active.

30...♗c8 31.♖f3 ♗g7 32.g4! ♖a7 33.g5 fxg5

33...♗e6 fails to 34.g6!

34.♗xg5 ♕d6 35.♖f6!

The crucial blow.

35...♕b4

If 35...♗e6 36.♖g1! would be very strong.

36.♖h1!

Preparing the final combination, which cannot be averted.

36...♖f8

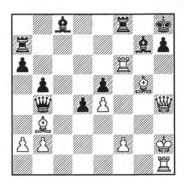

37.♕xh7+!! ♔xh7 38.♔g3+ ♗h6 39.♖hxh6+ 1-0

After 39...♔g7 40.♖fg6+ is mate.

Shamkovich - Ivkov [C92]
Rio de Janeiro IZT, 1979

1.e4 e5 2.♘f3 ♘c6 3.♗b5 a6 4.♗a4 ♘f6 5.0-0 ♗e7 6.♖e1 b5 7.♗b3 d6 8.c3 0-0 9.h3 ♘d7

This system is even more popular nowadays after Karpov adopted it in his 1990 challenge to Kasparov.

10.d4 ♗f6 11.d5!?

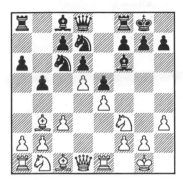

Again this "semi-closing" of the position leading to double-edged positions (instead of the more common 11.a4). The continuation leads to a build-up of forces on opposite sides of the board as white prepares an attack against the black king and black infiltrates with his rooks along the a-file.

11...♘a5 12.♗c2 c5 13.♘bd2 g6 14.b3 ♗g7 15.♘f1 ♘b6 16.♘g3 ♗d7 17.♗g5 ♕c7 18.♕d2 c4 19.b4 ♘b7 20.h4 a5 21.a3 ♖a6 22.♗e3 ♖fa8 23.♖ac1 axb4 24.axb4 ♖a2

In Informant 28 Ivkov assesses this position as favorable to black. I feel that white's play on the kingside culminating with 30.♘g5! is critical of this assessment.

25.h5 ♖8a3 26.♗h6 ♕d8 27.♗xg7 ♔xg7 28.♕e3 ♖b2 29.hxg6 hxg6 30.♘g5!

Ivkov was critical of this move in Informant 28 (30.♘g5?!).

30...♘c8

The critical moment. Here I played the fatal move...

31.f4??

...which was correctly criticized by Ivkov, as I had overlooked the deadly queen trade...

31...♕b6!

... after which my attack lost most of its momentum. I proceeded on with ...

32.♕xb6 ♘xb6 33.fxe5 ♖xc3 34.♖f1 ♗e8?

34...♘d8 is stronger according to Ivkov.

35.e6! f6 36.e5!

... but even so the rest of this game was a desperate struggle for me.

36...f5 37.♘3e4 fxe4 38.e7 ♘xd5 39.♖f8 ♘xe7 40.♖xe8 ♘f5 41.♖b8 ♖cxc2 42.♖xc2 ♖xc2 43.g4 ♘d8 44.♖xd8 dxe5 45.♖d7+ ♘e7 46.♘xe4 ♔f8 47.♖b7 c3 48.♔f1 ♖c1+ 49.♔e2 ♘c6 50.♘f6 ♖f1 51.♘d7+ ♔e8 52.♖c7 ♖f4

53.♖xc6 ♔xd7 54.♖xg6 ♖xb4
55.♔d3 ♖c4 0-1

But let us return to the critical position in the last diagram. Here white can practically win by force by bravely forging on with 31.♘f5+!!

The main variations run as follows:

31...♗xf5 32.exf5 ♖aa2 (32...♕f6 33.fxg6 fxg6 34.♘e6+ wins) 33.fxg6! ♖xc2 34.♖xc2 ♖xc2 35.gxf7 and now if 35...♕f6 36.f8♕+! and 35...♕e7 36.♕f3 ♘d8 37.♕f5! and 35...♕h8 36.f8♕+! ♔xf8 37.♕f3+ ♔g7 38.♘e6+ are all winning for white. Declining with 31...♔f8 32.♘h7+ ♔g8 33.♕h6! does not save the position for black, and 31...gxf5 32.♕g3 (threatening 33.♘e6+) ...♕f6 (if 32...♔f8 33.♘h7+ ♔e7 34.♕g5+ ♔e8 35.♕g7! ♔e7 36.exf5 is winning) 33.exf5 (threatening 34.♘e4) ...♗xf5 34.♘e6+ ♔h6 (or 34...♔h8 35.♗xf5 fxe6 36.♖e4! winning) 35.♖e4! fxe6 (35...♗xe4 36.♕h3+ wins) 36.♖h4+ ♕xh4 37.♕xh4+ ♔g6 38.♗xf5+ exf5 39.g4! opening lines for the final attack.

So by playing 31.♘f5!! white really would crush the insecure black fortress - almost a natural outcome of black's straightforward play on the queenside. Alas, it was not easy to find such a plan over the board. This encounter illustrates that it is never enough to simply achieve a winning position - you also have to be able to defeat your opponent!

Shamkovich - Benjamin [C96]
USA, 1976

1.e4 e5 2.♘f3 ♘c6 3.♗b5 a6 4.♗a4 ♘f6 5.0-0 ♗e7 6.♖e1 b5 7.♗b3 0-0 8.h3 d6 9.c3

♘a5 10.♗c2 c5 11.d4 ♘d7 12.♘bd2 cxd4 13.cxd4 ♘c6 14.♘b3 a5 15.♗d3 ♗a6

For 15...♖b8 see Shamkovich - Lower given below.

16.d5

16.♗e3 maintaining central tension is possible.

16...♘b4 17.♗f1 a4

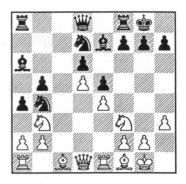

18.♘bd4!

Despite the apparent success of 18.♘bd4 connected to an original exchange sacrifice, this continuation does not seem to have been employed further in practice. Less incisive is 18.a3 ♘xd5 19.♕xd5 axb3 20.♗xb5 ♘f6 21.♕d3 ♗xb5 22.♕xb5 ♕b8 with equality.

18...exd4 19.a3 ♗f6?

Also poor is 19...♘xd5? 20.exd5. The critical line runs 19...♘c5!? 20.♘xd4 ♗f6 21.♗e3 ♗xd4 22.♗xd4 ♘b3 23.axb4 ♘xa1 24.♕g4! f6 25.♖xa1 with compensation for the sacrificed material.

20.axb4 ♕b6 21.b3! axb3

If 21...d3 simply 22.♖a2 is good.

22.♕xb3 ♘e5

If 22...♗b7 then 23.♗d2 intending ♖a5 is good.

23.♘xe5 dxe5

23...♗xe5 24.f4 ♗f6 25.e5 is good for white.

24.♖a5 ♕b7 25.♗d2 ♗d8 26.♖a3 ♗c7

If 26...♗b6 then 27.♖ea1 ♖a7 28.♕g3 f6 29.♕g4! is strong.

27.♖ea1 ♖a7 28.♕c2 ♗b6 29.♕c6!

Holding the endgame is a near impossible task for black.

29...♕xc6 30.dxc6 ♖fa8 31.♗e2!

Not the impulsive 31.c7? when 31...♗c8 holds. Now the threat of 32.c7 is very real and very final.

31...♔f8

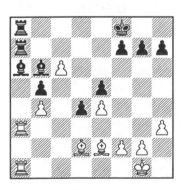

31...g6 fails to 32.♗g5 ♔g7 33.♗e7! followed by ♗c5.

32.c7! ♗xc7

There is no choice because 32...♗c8 fails to 33.♖xa7 ♖xa7 34.♖xa7 ♗xa7 35.♗g4! winning. The rest requires no comment.

33.♗xb5 ♗xb5 34.♖xa7 ♖xa7 35.♖xa7 ♗d8 36.f3 ♔e8 37.♖b7 ♗a6 38.♖b8 ♔d7 39.b5 ♗c7 40.♖f8 ♗xb5 41.♖xf7+ ♔c6 42.♖xg7 1-0

Shamkovich - Lower [C96]
US Open, 1977

1.e4 e5 2.♘f3 ♘c6 3.♗b5 a6 4.♗a4 ♘f6 5.0-0 ♗e7 6.♖e1 b5 7.♗b3 0-0 8.h3 d6 9.c3 ♘a5 10.♗c2 c5 11.d4 ♘d7 12.♘bd2 cxd4 13.cxd4 ♘c6 14.♘b3 a5 15.♗d3 ♖b8!?

Deviating from the 15...♗a6 of Shamkovich-Benjamin (see above).

16.♗d2!

A theoretical novelty. ECO C96 refers to the game Tal-Reshevsky, Amsterdam IZT 1964, where 16.♕e2 ♗a6? 17.♗d2! exd4 18.♘bxd4 ♘xd4 19.♘xd4 ♘e5 20.♖ad1 brought a clear edge to white, but better, to my way of thinking, is 16...♕b6 17.♗e3 ♕b7 keeping such threats as ...a4 and ...♘b4 in reserve.

16...a4 17.d5 axb3 18.dxc6 ♘c5 19.axb3!

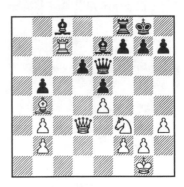

The point of white's opening idea - 19...♘xd3 is met by 20.♗a5! ♕e8 21.c7! winning.

19...♕c7 20.♕c2

Stronger than 20.♗f1 ♗e6!

20...♘xd3 21.♕xd3 ♕xc6 22.♖ec1 ♕d7 23.♗b4

Threatening 24.♘xe5.

23...♕e6

Better was 23...♖b7. The text allows an unpleasant incursion onto the seventh rank.

24.♖a7 ♖b7 25.♖c7 ♖xc7 26.♖xc7

The powerful posting of white's pieces, in particular the rook at c7, coupled with the weakness of the pawn at d6, gives white a clear edge.

26...f5?

Black looks for counterplay, but underestimates a fatal queen trade (as the reader already knows, I was to make a similar error against Ivkov a few years later). Even so, 26...♗d8 27.♖c3 is much to white's favor.

27.♕d5! ♕xd5 28.exd5 ♖e8 29.♘xe5 ♗f8

After 29...dxe5 30.d6 black cannot stop the pawn.

30.♘f7 ♖e7 31.♘h6+!

Forcing a simplification to a winning pawn ending under the most favorable circumstances.

31...gxh6 32.♖xc8 1-0

Black has no chance after 32...♔f7 33.♖xf8+! ♔xf8 34.♗xd6 ♔f7 35.♗xe7 ♔xe7 36.g4! creating a passed f-pawn.

The theoretical importance of the final game in this chapter is debatable, but it is representative of the double-edged middlegames that occur in the classical "Closed" lines of the Ruy Lopez. An exchange of tactical errors by the combatants leads to a dynamic and sharp middlegame with many pitfalls awaiting the unwary.

Shamkovich - Bisguier [C99]
US Open, 1978

1.e4 e5 2.♘f3 ♘c6 3.♗b5 a6 4.♗a4 ♘f6 5.0-0 ♗e7 6.♖e1 b5 7.♗b3 0-0 8.c3 d6 9.h3 ♘a5

An old system, named for Chigorin, which for many years has been a "tabiya" in the Ruy Lopez. To this day, no refutation has been demonstrated, but its popularity has been usurped by the Breyer variation (9...♘b8) and more recently by the sharp lines introduced with the Zaitsev system (9...♗b7).

10.♗c2 c5 11.d4 ♕c7 12.♘bd2 cxd4 13.cxd4 ♗d7 14.♘f1 ♖ac8

This is more flexible than 14...♖fc8 as it reserves the option of a later ...♖fe8. GM Bisguier's experience in this line is very deep as evidenced from the notes I have incorporated into this game. In fact, I am playing into the "teeth" of one his favorite defenses. An early example of 14...♖fc8 continued 15.♘e3 ♘c6 16.a3 a5 17.d5 ♘d8 18.♗d2 a4 19.♗b4 ♗f8 20.♗d3 ♘b7 21.♕e2 ♕b6 22.♘d2 with a small edge for white, Fischer-Bisguier, USA Ch. 1958-59.

15.♘e3 ♘c6

Previous tries include 15...♖fe8 16.b3 (after 16.♗d2 ♘c6 17.d5 ♘d4, black had a comfortable game in Darga-Bisguier, Bled 1961, or 16.d5 g6

17.b3 ♘b7 18.b4 ♘h5 19.♗d2 f6 20.♖c1 ♘d8 and black again held the balance, Robatsch-Bisguier, Hastings 1961-62) ...♗f8 17.♖e2 exd4 18.♘xd4 g6 19.♗b2 ♗g7 and now after 20.♕e1 ♘c6 21.♖d1, white had a small pull, Kavalek- Bisguier, Netanya 1971.

16.a3

The bishop on c2 is a target of black's counterattack in this variation. Removing the bishop from the line of fire with 16.♗b3 as in Parma-Prameshuber, La Havana 1966, is a possibility that can be seriously considered. Bisguier now takes action.......

16...♘xd4! 17.♘xd4 exd4 18.♕xd4 ♗e6 19.♗d2 ♘d7

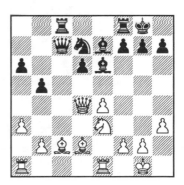

Black's threat is 20...♗f6.

20.♕d3

Of the alternatives 20.♗c3!? ♗f6 21.♕d3 ♗xc3 22.e5! g6 23.exd6 at first sight looks good for white, but in fact 23...♕a5 24.bxc3 ♕xc3, he can claim no advantage. Interesting is 20.♗b4 ♗f6! (weaker is 20...a5 21.♗c3 and the weakness of the pawns on a5 and b5 could become a decisive factor in the outcome of the game) 21.♕xd6 ♕xd6 22.♗xd6 ♖fd8 with a playable game for black. Note that the d6-pawn "weakness" is offset by the activity of black's pieces. My previous experience in this variation was 20.♖ac1 ♗f6 21.e5 dxe5 22.♗xh7+ ♔h8 23.♕b4 ♘c5, Shamkovich-Yudovich, Moscow 1962, and now 24.♗f5! would have given white the advantage, but black's play can be improved.

20...♘c5   21.♕e2   ♗f6 22.♖ab1 ♘b3?!

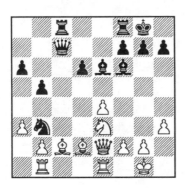

Exploiting the weakness of the b3-square, black threatens 23...♘d4. Here the reply 23.♗xb3 ♗xb3 24.♖bc1 would have given white a slight edge, because of the long-term static weaknesses of the d5-square and the d6-pawn. But I had taken a great interest in an attractive tactical idea...

23.e5?!

Giving full play to the "Spanish" bishop.

23...dxe5

Other answers favor white, e.g.,

23...♘d4 24.♗xh7+! ♔xh7 25.♕h5+ ♔g8 26.exf6 winning, or 23...♘xd2 24.exf6 ♘xb1 25.♗xh7+! crushing, and if 23...♗xe5 24.♕d3 wins.

24.♕d3

Here is the point of white's combination - the double threat of 25.♕h7+ mate and 25.♗xb3. Now if 24...g6 25.♗xb3 ♖fd8 26.♗d5 ♕d7 27.♗a5! winning.

24...e4! 25.♕xe4

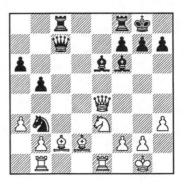

When I made this move, I suddenly realized that black can frustrate my attack with the queen sacrifice 25...♕xc2!! Indeed after 26.♘xc2 ♘xd2 27.♕e2 ♘xb1 the tables are turned in view of the tremendous activity of the black pieces e.g., 28.♖xb1 ♗f5 29.♖c1 ♗xb2 and black wins. The alternative 27.♕e3 (instead of 27.♕e2) would not help because of 27...♘xb1 28.♘d4 ♖fe8! 29.♘xe6 ♖xe6 30.♖c1 ♖d8! followed by 31...♘d2. Beware of falling into your own trap! However my opponent missed this brilliant shot and made a fatal error ...

25...g6? 26.♗xb3 ♗xb3
27.♘g4! ♗g7 28.♖bc1 ♕d8
29.♖xc8 ♕xc8 30.♗b4 ♖d8
31.♕f3!

White has built, step-by-step and by
force, a powerful attacking position. In
view of the threat of 32.♕xb3, black
cannot prevent the next important
invasion.

31...♗e6 32.♘f6+ ♔h8
33.♗c3!

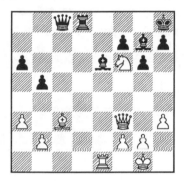

The "dark-squares" battery is ready.
In spite of the restricted material on the
board, black can hardly hope to save the
game, because of white's threats of
♖e4-h4 and ♕e4-h4. Some picant
variations: 33...♕c4 34.♖e4 ♕d3
35.♖h4 h6 36.♕f4 g5 37.♕xg5 ♕g6
38.♘d5! ♔h7 39.♗xg7 ♕xg7 (or
39...♔xg7 40.♕e5+ ♔h7 41.♘f6+
winning) 40.♘f6+ ♔h8 41.♘g4! with a
crushing attack.

33...h6 34.♕f4

An inaccuracy. Much better was
34.♕e3! ♕c4 35.♘d5! winning, while
34...♕b7 fails to 35.♘h5! ♗xc3
36.♕xc3+.

34...♖d3!?

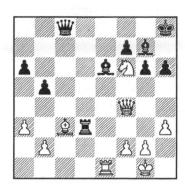

The best try. Meanwhile, 34...g5
loses after 35.♕e4 ♗f5 36.♕e3! e.g.,
36...♕e6 37.♘h5! winning or
36...♗e6 37.h4 gxh4 38.♘h5! or
36...♗g6 37.♕e7 ♖f8 38.♘e8!
crushing.

35.♘d5!

The alternative 35.♘h5? does not
work since 35...♗xc3 36.♕xh6+ ♔g8
37.bxc3 gxh5 is to black's advantage.

35...♔h7?

More resistance would have been
possible with the exchange sacrifice
35...♖xc3! (35...♗xc3? 36.♕xh6+
leads to mate) 36.♘xc3 ♔h7 when it is
not as easy for white to win because of
the strength of black's bishop-pair.
After this lapse, the end comes quickly.

**36.♗xg7 ♔xg7 37.♕e5+ ♔h7
38.♘f6+ ♔g7 39.♘h5+ ♔f8
40.♕h8+**

A dramatic and memorable game.

1-0

RARE AND UNUSUAL BLACK SYSTEMS IN THE RUY LOPEZ

An admirer and student of the Ruy Lopez should be prepared to meet a variety of unusual subsystems which do not conform to the classical formations illustrated in the previous examples. For instance, one such "opening surprise" appeared with success in the recent Candidates matches - the so called Arkhangelsk System 3...a6 4.♗a4 ♘f6 5.0-0 b5!? 6.♗b3 ♗b7 (Sax-Kortchnoi, games 2 and 4, where Kortchnoi used the eccentric 7...♗d6!? after 7.d3 and equalized comfortably. White avoids the theoretically disputed lines less often, but against great experts of the black side of this opening this approach is quite reasonable. An interesting example occurred in the recent Candidates semi-final matches when the British GM Short employed the half-forgotten line 3...a6 4.♗a4 ♘f6 5.0-0 ♗e7 6.♕e2, thus avoiding Karpov's favorite defenses to 6.♖e1. As a result, he crushed his mighty rival in games 6 and 8 - and this clever psychological ploy played a pivotal role in Short's historic victory in the match.

Let me present three games on this topic, where black deviates from the classical methods of defense in the Ruy Lopez.

Shamkovich - Stopa [C61]
USA, 1977

1.e4 e5 2.♘f3 ♘c6 3.♗b5 ♘d4!?

The very old Bird Defense, which appears from time to time in modern practice, but is viewed with skepticism by contemporary theorists.

4.♘xd4 exd4 5.0-0

Not 5.c3? since 5...♕g5! forcing the sad retreat 6.♗f1 (if 6.♗e2 d3! would be strong as well) ♗c5 with a good game for black. I'd like to remind you that a similar lunge of the queen may be met in other systems, such as the main line of the Schliemann Gambit 3...f5 4.♘c3 fxe4 5.♘xe4 d5 6.♘xe5 dxe4 7.♘xc6 ♕g5! and in the more obscure 3...♕f6?! 4.♘c3 ♘d4?! (more sensible is 4...♘ge7!? 5.d3 ♘d4 6.♘xd4 exd4 7.♘e2 with an edge for white, Bogoljubov-Ed. Lasker, New York 1924) 5.♘xd4 exd4 6.♘d5 ♕d8?!

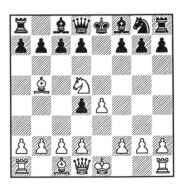

(analysis)

Also 6...♕g5 7.♘xc7+ ♔d8 8.♘xa8 ♕xb5 9.d3 b6 10.♗f4 d6 11.a4! is better for white according to Alekhine. It is a curiousity that Alekhine suggested (after 6...♕d8) in the tournament book the "howler" 7.♘f4?? overlooking the strong 7...♕g5! (Soltis) with the double attack against b5 and f4. Indeed after 8.♘d5 ♕xg2 9.♖f1 ♕xe4+ or 8.♗c4 ♕xf4 9.d3 ♕h4 black is winning. However, white should play instead 7.♕h5!! (threatening 8.♕e5+) with a strong attack e.g., 7...♗d6 8.e5! g6 (8...♗f8 9.e6! wins) 9.♕e2 ♗c5 10.b4! A natural and fitting conclusion to black's unique retrogade sense of development.

5...c6 6.♗a4 ♗c5 7.d3 ♘e7

A theoretical but questionable move - the best place for the knight is f6. The recent game Novik-Mejster, USSR Ch. 1991 is interesting as after 7...d6 8.f4 f5 9.♘d2 ♘f6! 10.♗b3 ♘g4 black achieved fine counterplay. (See Supplemental games).

8.♕h5

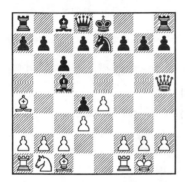

This bold lunge should now be a familiar motif. Black's development now becomes a complicated task as white prepares a dangerous concentration of forces on the kingside. Theory (ECO C61) approved of this plan but the recent game Kamsky-Ivanchuk, Tilburg 1990, varied with 8.f4 (! Kamsky) and achieved convincing success (see Supplemental games). But which move is better? Unfortunately, the young American GM did not expound further

on his comments (Informant 52) or as to why he rejected 8.♕h5.

He did not specify the variation 8.f4 ♘g6 9.♕h5. What about 9...♗e7, followed by 10.f5 ♘e5 11.♗f4 d6 12.♘d2 ♗f6 or 10.♘d2 d6 11.♘f3 0-0 12.♗b3 ♗f6 13.e5 (if 13.♗d2 ♗e6!?) ♗e7 (?). Let us leave the theoretical question opened - most probably both moves (8.♕h5 and 8.f4) are very strong.

8...d6 9.♘d2 ♗e6 10.♘f3 ♕a5

An attempt to complicate an inferior position. Keres and Geller have given in ECO 10...0-0 11.♘g5 h6 12.♘xe6 fxe6 13.♗d2 with a slight advantage, but more promising for white, it seems to me, is 13.♗b3 d5 14.♕h3 ♕d6 15.♗d2 followed by 16.♖ae1; as black's pawn on e6 is very weak.

11.♗b3 ♗xb3

The point of black's 10th move: white cannot recapture with the "normal" 12.axb3. On the other hand, black cannot castle at all, 11...0-0 fails to 12.♗xe6 fxe6 13.♘g5 (Not so clear is 13.♘xd4 g6). 11...0-0-0 12.♗xe6+ fxe6 13.♕h3 is not too pleasant for black either.

12.cxb3 ♕c7

The more active 12...♕b5 should be met by 13.♘g5 ♘g6 14.♕h3 ♘e5 15.♖d1 with the threat of 16.f4.

13.♘g5 ♘g6 14.f4 0-0-0 15.♗d2 ♕e7 16.b4 ♗b6 17.a4!

Black finds no peace - a strong attack is gathering on the queenside.

17...♕f6

Preventing 18.♖fc1.

18.♕h3+ ♔b8

19.e5!

The critical break, capitalizing on the weakness of the f7-pawn.

**19...♕e7 20.exd6 ♖xd6
21.♖ae1 ♕d7 22.f5! f6**

The only counterchance, hoping for 23.fxg6 fxg5 24.♕xd7 ♖xd7, minimizing the damage.

23.♘e4

Winning the exchange. The rest is clear.

**23...♘e5 24.♘xd6 ♕xd6
25.♗f4 ♗c7 26.♗xe5 fxe5
27.b5 cxb5 28.axb5 ♕b4
29.♕g4 ♕e7 30.♖f3 h5
31.♕g6 ♖h6**

32.f6! ♕b4 33.♕e8+ 1-0

Shamkovich - Fauber [C76]
US Open, 1987

1.e4 e5 2.♘f3 ♘c6 3.♗b5 g6!?

Another very old system, which was successfully employed by such great players as Steinitz, Pillsbury, Blackburne, Lasker and Alekhine. Nevertheless, it did not gain full approval of old theory. For instance, Alexander Alekhine pointed out in his comments to his famous game against Tarrasch (Karlsbad 1923 - see Supplemental games) - "The Pillsbury Defense, which he employed successfully in Hastings 1895. But the theory evaluates it - not without grounds - as an insufficient one.I managed it in this game especially to to check the innovation 4...♘d4." But the modern theory is not so severe because contemporary theorists and practical players have discovered new and attractive ways for black to generate counterplay. The greatest contribution in recent times was made by ex-World Champion Vassily Smyslov who played many nice games with it as black and made important refinements to the system. Nowadays the system bears his illustrious name.

4.c3

Now my opponent employed the modern move order.

4...a6! 5.♗a4 d6 6.d4 ♗d7 7.0-0 ♗g7

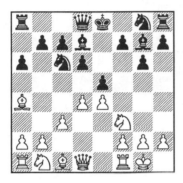

The game has transposed to the Alekhine System, where white has a rather wide choice: 8.d5, 8.♗b3, 8.♗g5, 8.♗e3 or 8.dxe5. Each line has its merits and defects, but theory had not yet determined the best plan for white. For an example of 8.♗e3, see the game Boleslavsky-Nezhmetdinov in the Supplemental games section. I chose the last line.

8.dxe5 ♘xe5

In contrast to other Ruy Lopez systems, this simplification does not promise black an easy route to equality. Even so, the sounder 8...dxe5 9.♗g5 also does not guarantee black a quiet life.

9.♘xe5 dxe5 10.f4!

At this moment, I recalled the splendid Fine-Alekhine encounter (AVRO tournament, Holland 1938) played some fifty years previously.

10...♘e7

Alekhine had chosen 10...♗xa4?! 11.♕xa4+ ♕d7 12.♕xd7+ ♔xd7 13.fxe5 ♔e6? 14.♗f4 and Fine won the ending. I once tried to rehabilitate this line with 13...♖f8 14.♗f4 ♘e7 15.♘d2 ♘c6 16.♘f3 h6, but 17.♖ad1+ ♔c8 18.b4! ♖e8 19.a4 ♖hf8 20.♖d5 g5 21.♗g3 g4 22.♘d4 still favors white.

11.f5!

This extremely strong move was originated by Keres against Goldenov (USSR 1952) which continued 11...f6 12.♗e3 ♗xa4 13.♕xa4+ ♕d7 14.♕xd7+ ♔xd7 15.c4! with a dominating position for white. Apparently, black is unable to improve his position any more after this move.

11...gxf5 12.exf5 ♘d5!?

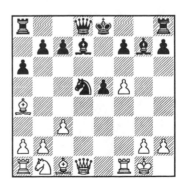

13.♗c2!

A strategical solution paralleling the technichal one of Geller (13.♕xd5) - see Supplementary Games. ECO C76 only mentioned 13.♗b3 ♘f6 14.♗g5 ♕e7 15.♘d2 0-0-0 16.♕e2 ♖hg8 with "an unclear position", Bronstein - Westerinen, Juurmala, Latvia 1978, although 17.♘e4 should yield white a clear advantage. Apparently 13...♗c6 is better. With the text white envisages taking control of the e4-square, in order to transfer a knight or bishop there and blockade black's center.

13...♗c6

13...♘f6 14.♗g5 ♗c6 15.♕e2 ♕e7 16.♘d2 with a clear advantage.

14.♗e4! ♕d6 15.♕f3 0-0-0 16.♘d2 ♗f6?

This bishop is a poor blockader. Instead 16...♗h6!? merits attention, e.g., 17.♘b3 ♗xc1 18.♖axc1 with a slight edge to white.

17.♘b3 ♘e7 18.♗e3 ♗xe4 19.♕xe4 ♕c6 20.♕xc6 ♘xc6

20...bxc6 21.c4! is unpleasant for black.

21.♘c5 ♗e7 22.♘e4!

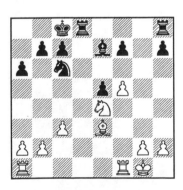

Completing the construction of the blockade. Despite material equality and the absence of concrete white threats, black's position is inferior, maybe losing.

22...♖d3 23.♔f2 ♖g8 24.h3 b6?

Better was 24...h5!?

25.♔e2 ♖d7 26.g4 ♗h4 27.g5!

This kingside pawn attack quickly decides the outcome of the game.

27...♖dd8 28.♖g1

Threatening 29.♖g4.

28...h6 29.gxh6 ♖h8 30.f6

Black's bishop is trapped again.

30...♔d7 31.♖g4 ♗xf6 32.♘xf6+ ♔e6 33.♖f1 ♘e7 34.♘h5 f5 35.♘g7+ ♔d7 36.♘xf5 1-0

In conclusion, I present the following curious miniature from my encounter with the famous American chess veteran who boldly employed his own lovely sharp system.

Shamkovich - Kewitz [C60]
New York, 1976

1.e4 e5 2.♘f3 ♘c6 3.♗b5 g6 4.c3 f5!?

This "confusion" of two independent systems - the Schliemann with 3...f5 and the Smyslov with 3...g6 looks a little unnatural and overly provocative - but is actually not too bad. As I said earlier, the Ruy Lopez allows for many black interpretations that require precise play by white in the struggle for the initiative.

5.exf5 e4 6.♘d4 ♘xd4 7.cxd4 ♕g5

The familiar motif of a double attack. The alternative 7...gxf5 is of interest but inferior: 8.♕h5+ ♔e7 9.d3! (Worse is 9.♕xf5 ♘f6 10.d3 d5 11.♕e5+ ♔f7 and black stands better) ...♘f6 10.♗g5 d5!? 11.♘c3 (not 11.♗xf6+ ♔xf6 12.♕h4+ ♔f7 13.♕xd8 ♗b4+! with a clear plus) ...♗g7 12.dxe4 dxe4 13.♗c4 with an overpowering initiative.

8.0-0 ♕xf5 9.♘c3 c6

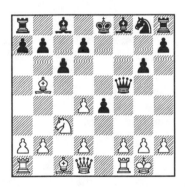

The critical position of this rare system has emerged.

10.♗a4?

A standard and stereotypical response that allows black to consolidate his position. The eccentricity of black's opening play demands a much more active and alert reaction by white. In keeping with the "romantic" spirit of the position would be the opening of lines even at the cost

of a piece, e.g., 10.f3 e3 11.dxe3 cxb5 12.e4 ♕h5 13.g4 ♕h4 14.♘xb5 ♕d8 15.♗f4 or 10.d3 cxb5 11.dxe4 ♕h5 12.g4 with a strong attack in both lines.

10...d5 11.d3 exd3 12.♖e1+ ♔d8?

A fatal error. Correct was 12...♔f7! 13.h3 (if 13.♖e5? ♕g4 black is better) ...♗d6 14.g4 ♕f6 15.♖e3 ♔g7 with an unclear position and good chances for black to solidify his game. Now the white forces bombard the hapless black king, which will find no shelter in the center.

13.♖e5 ♕f7 14.♕xd3 ♗d6 15.♗g5+!

A deadly blow as 15...♔c7 loses to 16.♖xd5! cxd5 17.♘b5+ ♔d7 18.♘xd6+ ♔xd6 19.♕g3+ mating, or 16...♗e6 17.♖xd6! ♔xd6 18.♕g3+ ♔d7 19.d5! and black collapses.

15...♘f6

The alternative 15...♗e7 cannot help black because of 16.♕g3! ♗xg5 17.♕xg5+ ♕f6 18.♕g3 ♘e7 19.♖ae1 ♘f5 20.♘xd5! ♕f7 (20...♘xg3 21.♘xf6 is desperate for black) 21.♕g5+ mating.

16.♕f3 ♖f8 17.♘xd5!

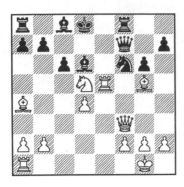

A final, not too complicated combination, winning material and exposing the black king to mortal threats.

17...cxd5

To no avail is 17...♗xe5 18.dxe5 cxd5 as white wins by force with 19.♗xf6+ ♔c7 20.♖c1+ ♔b8 21.♗d8!

18.♗xf6+ ♕xf6 19.♖e8+ ♖xe8 20.♕xf6+ ♗e7 21.♕f7

If, for example 21...♗d7 22.♕xd5 ♔c7 23.♕xd7+ ♔b6 24.♕b5+ ♔c7 25.♖c1+ ♗c5 26.♖xc5+ ♔d6 27.♕d7+ spells mate.

1-0

SUPPLEMENTAL GAMES

Shamkovich-Bisguier [C67]
New York 1977

1.e4 e5 2.♘f3 ♘c6 3.♗b5 ♘f6 4.0-0 ♘xe4 5.d4 ♘d6 6.♗xc6 dxc6 7.dxe5 ♘f5 8.♕xd8+ ♔xd8 9.♘c3 h6 10.h3 ♗b4?! 11.♘e2 g5 12.b3 c5 13.♗b2 ♗e6 14.c4 ♔d7 15.♖fd1+ ♔c6 16.a3 ♗a5 17.g4 ♘e7 18.b4!

cxb4 19.♘ed4+ ♔b6 20.♘b3 ♘c6 21.♖dc1 ♖hd8 22.♘fd4 ♘xd4 23.♗xd4+ ♖xd4 24.c5+ ♔c6 25.♘xd4+ ♔d5 26.♘xe6 fxe6 27.♖ab1 bxa3 28.♖xb7 ♔xe5 29.♖b3 ♔d4 30.c6 ♗b6 31.♖xa3 ♔d5 32.♔f1 ♖f8 33.f3 e5 34.♔e2 e4 35.fxe4+ ♔xe4 36.♖f1 ♖b8 37.♖f6 ♗d4 38.♖e6+ ♔d5 39.♖xh6 ♖b2+ 40.♔d3 ♖xg2 41.♖a5+ ♗c5 42.♖g6 ♖g3+ 43.♔e2 ♖g2+ 44.♔f3 ♖f2+ 45.♔g3 ♖c2 46.♖g5+ ♔c6 47.♖gxc5+! ♖xc5 48.♖xa7! ♖c3+ 49.♔h4 (+-) ♔d5 50.g5 ♔e6 51.♔g4 ♔f7 52.h4 ♔g7 53.♔h5 ♖c4 54.♖a5 ♖d4 55.♖c5 ♖d7 56.♖e5 c6 57.♖c5 ♖d6 58.♖c4 ♖e6 59.♔g4 ♖d6 60.h5 ♖d1 61.♖xc6 ♖g1+ 62.♔f5 ♖f1+ 63.♔e6 ♖e1+ 64.♔d6 ♖d1+ 65.♔e7 ♖d5 66.h6+ ♔h7 67.♔f6 ♖d7 68.♖e6 ♖d1 69.♖e7+ 1-0

Karpov - Kortchnoi [C67]
Merano (m/2), 1981

1.e4 e5 2.♘f3 ♘c6 3.♗b5 ♘f6 4.0-0 ♘xe4 5.d4 ♗e7 6.♕e2 ♘d6 7.♗xc6 bxc6 8.dxe5 ♘b7 9.♘c3 0-0 10.♖e1 ♘c5 11.♗e3 ♘e6 12.♖ad1 d5 13.exd6 cxd6 14.♘d4 ♗d7 15.♘f5 d5 16.♘xe7+ ♕xe7 17.♕d2 ♕h4 18.♘e2 ♖fe8 19.b3 ♖e7 20.♘g3 ♕f6 21.f3 ♗e8 22.♘e2 h6 23.♗f2 ♕g6 24.♘c1 d4 25.♘d3 ♕f6 26.♗g3 ♖d7 27.♖e5 ♕d8 28.♖de1 ♖d5 29.♖xd5 ♕xd5 30.♖e5 ♕d7 31.♕e1 ♖c8 32.b4 ♕d8 33.♖a5 ♕d7 34.h3

f6 35.♖xa7 ♕d5 36.♖a5 ♕d7
37.♖a7 ♕d5 38.♖a5 ♕d7
39.♕e4 ♗f7 40.♕f5 ♖e8
41.♔h2 ♕b7 42.a3 ♖d8 43.h4
h5 44.♘f2 ♕d7 45.♖a6 ♕e8
46.♕a5 ♗g6 47.♘d3 ♔h7
48.♕b6 ♖c8 49.a4 ♗f5 50.a5
c5 51.bxc5 ♗xd3 52.cxd3
♘xc5 53.♖a7 ♕g6 54.♖c7
♖xc7 55.♗xc7 ♘xd3 56.♕xd4
♘e5 57.♗xe5 1-0

Nezhmetidinov - Kotkov [C67]
RSFSR Ch. Krasnodar, 1957

1.e4 e5 2.♘f3 ♘c6 3.♗b5 ♘f6
4.0-0 ♘xe4 5.♖e1 ♘d6
6.♘xe5 ♗e7 7.♗d3 0-0 8.♘c3
♘xe5 9.♖xe5 ♗f6 10.♖e3 g6
11.♕f3 ♗g7 12.b3 ♘e8
13.♗a3 d6 14.♖ae1

With an edge.

14...♘f6 15.h3 ♘d7 16.♘d5
f5

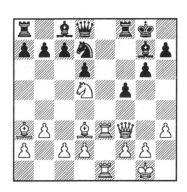

Nezmetdinov gives 16...♘e5
17.♖xe5! ♗xe5 (if 17...dxe5 18.♗e7!)
18.♖xe5! dxe5 19.♗e7 ♗g4 20.hxg4
♕b8 21.♗xf8 winning.

17.♘xc7!!

This brilliant piece sacrifice is typical
of Nezhmetdinov - who was an "old
style master."

17...♕xc7 18.♕d5+

No commentator has mentioned the
combination 18.♖e7 ♗f6 19.♗c4+
♔h8 20.♕f4! ♕d8 (forced) 21.♗b2!!
♘e5 (if 21...♗xb2 22.♕h6 wins)
22.♖1xe5! dxe5 23.♕xe5!! ♕b6
(forced) 24.♖f7 winning. The text
alternative is sufficient for victory also.

18...♔h8 19.♖e8!

Not 19.♗xd6 ♘f6!

19...♘f6 20.♖xf8+ ♗xf8
21.♗b2 ♗g7

Better is 21...♕g7 but after 22.♕d4
♘e4 23.f3 white is winning -
Nezhmetdinov.

22.♗c4 ♗d7 23.♗xf6

An inaccuracy. More efficient was
23.♕f7 ♖f8 24.♖e8!!

23...♗xf6 24.♕f7 ♕d8??

Catastrophe, but after 24...♗g5
25.g3 white is winning anyway.

25.♖e8+ 1-0

Keres - Unzicker [C67]
Hamburg (m/4), 1956

1.e4 e5 2.♘f3 ♘c6 3.♗b5 ♘f6
4.0-0 ♘xe4 5.d4 ♗e7 6.♕e2
♘d6 7.♗xc6 bxc6 8.dxe5 ♘b7
9.♘c3 0-0 10.♘d4

A strong alternative to the 10.♖e1 of my game with Lein.

10...♗c5

On 10...♘c5!? 11.♖d1 ♕e8 12.♘f5 white has a slight advantage but after 12...f6 13.♗h6 as given by Keres, the position is unclear because of 13...♘e6 14.♕g4 ♖f7.

11.♖d1 ♗xd4

After 11...♖e8?! there is 12.♕h5! g6 13.♕f3 ♗xd4 14.♖xd4 ♖xe5 15.♗f4 which gives white a strong initiative in compensation for the pawn.

12.♖xd4 d5 13.exd6 cxd6 14.b4!

White has a clear advantage.

14...♖e8

An older game continued 14...♕f6 15.♗e3 ♗f5 16.♖ad1 a6 17.g4! with an excellent position for white, Schlecter-Reti, Vienna 1914.

15.♗e3 ♗e6 16.♕f3 ♕d7?

The best chance was 16...d5!?

17.♘e4 ♗f5?

Better was 17...♗d5 18.c4! ♗xe4 19.♖xe4 with advantage - Keres.

18.♘g3! ♗xc2 19.♖c1 ♗a4 20.♘h5?!

More accurate was 20.♘f5! ♖e6 21.♖h4! -Keres.

20...f5! 21.♖f4 ♖e7

If 21...♖f8 22.♗d4! white has a crushing game.

22.♖xf5 ♖f7

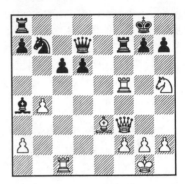

Now Keres finishes strongly.

23.♘xg7!! ♖xg7

Or 23...♖af8 24.♘e6!

24.♗h6 ♕e7

If 24...♖e8 25.h4 threatening 25.♗xg7 - Keres.

25.♗xg7 ♕xg7 26.h4 h6 27.♖c4! 1-0

Tarrasch - Alekhine [C60]
Karlovy Vary/Karlsbad, 1923

1.e4 e5 2.♘f3 ♘c6 3.♗b5 g6 4.d4 ♘xd4?! 5.♘xd4 exd4 6.♕xd4 ♕f6 7.♕d3

Alekhine gives 7.e5 ♕b6 8.♕xb6 (8.♕d3!?- ECO) ...axb6 9.♘c3 ♗g7 10.♗f4 with advantage.

7...♗g7= 8.♘c3 c6 9.♗c4 ♘e7 10.♗e3

Better is 10.0-0 - Alekhine.

10...b5! 11.♗b3 a5 12.a4

If 12.a3 ♗a6 is very strong - Alekhine.

12...b4 13.♘d1 0-0 14.0-0 d5!-+ 15.exd5 ♗a6 16.♗c4 ♗xc4 17.♕xc4 cxd5 18.♕d3 d4 19.♗d2 ♖ac8 20.♖e1 ♖c7 21.b3 ♖fc8 22.♖c1 ♕f5!

White's pawn at c2 is a serious liability.

23.♖e4 ♘d5 24.♘b2 ♘c3 25.♗xc3 ♖xc3 26.♕e2 ♗h6 27.g4 ♕f6 28.♖e8+ ♖xe8 29.♕xe8+ ♔g7 30.♖f1 ♖xc2-+ 31.♘d3 ♕f3! 32.♘e5 ♕d5 33.♘d7

Threatening 34.♕f8+ mate.

33...♕d6 34.♖d1 ♗e3! 35.♖f1 ♗g5

Intending 36...♗e7.

36.♕e5+ ♕xe5 37.♘xe5 ♗f4 38.♘c4 d3 39.♖d1 ♖c3! 40.♘xa5 ♔f6! 41.h4 ♔e5 42.♔g2 ♔d4 43.♔f3 ♗c7

44.♘c4 ♖xb3 45.♘e3 ♖c3 46.♖b1 ♗a5! 47.♘d1 ♖a3 48.♘e3 ♖xa4 49.g5 ♖a3 50.♖g1 b3 51.♖g4+ ♔c5 52.♖c4+ ♔b5 53.♖c8 ♖a1!

Avoiding the final trap 53...b2? 54.♖b8+ ♗b6 55.♖xb6+ holding.

54.♖b8+ ♗b6!

For now if 55.♘d5 d2! wins.

0-1

Boleslavsky - Nezhmetdinov [C76] *USSR Team Ch. Vilnius, 1958*

1.e4 e5 2.♘f3 ♘c6 3.♗b5 a6 4.♗a4 d6 5.c3 ♗d7 6.d4 g6 7.0-0 ♗g7 8.♗e3 ♘f6!

The best place for the knight. If 8...♘ge7 9.dxe5! dxe5 10.♗c5 gives white some edge - Boleslavsky.

9.♘bd2 0-0 10.dxe5 dxe5 11.♗c5?!

A better plan is 11.♖e1!? ♖e8 12.♗g5 with the idea of ♘f1-e3.

11...♖e8 12.♖e1 b6 13.♗a3 ♕c8 14.♘f1 b5 15.♗c2 a5!

Theatening ...b4.

16.♗c5 ♘d8 17.a4 ♕b7 18.axb5 ♗xb5 19.♗a3 ♘e6! 20.♘xe5 ♖ad8 21.♕c1?

Better 21.♕f3!? and then 21...♘g5 22.♕f4 h6! with a comfortable game - Nezhmetdinov.

21...♘h5! 22.♘f3 ♘hf4 23.♘g3 h5 24.h4 ♗h6-+

**25.♔h2 ♔g7 26.♕b1 ♕b6
27.♔g1**

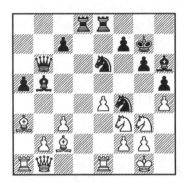

Instead if 27.♖e3 ♘xg2! 28.♔xg2
♗xe3 29.fxe3 ♕xe3 wins -
Nezhmetdinov.

**27...♘xg2! 28.♔xg2 ♘f4+
29.♔h1**

Loses instantly, but 29.♔g1 ♘h3+
30.♔g2 ♕xf2+ 31.♔xh3 ♗d7+
32.♘f5+ ♗xf5+ 33.exf5 ♕xf3+
34.♔h2 ♖d2+ is decisive also.

29...♕xf2 0-1

Kamsky - Ivanchuk [C61]
Tiburg (Interpolis), 1990

**1.e4 e5 2.♘f3 ♘c6 3.♗b5 ♘d4
4.♘xd4 exd4 5.0-0 ♗c5 6.d3
c6 7.♗a4 ♘e7 8.f4 f5 9.♗b3
d5 10.exd5 ♘xd5 11.♖e1+
♔f8 12.♕h5 g6 13.♕h6+ ♔g8
14.♘d2 ♗f8 15.♕h3 ♗g7
16.♘f3 h6 17.♘e5 ♕f6
18.♗xd5+ cxd5 19.b3 ♔h7
20.♗b2 ♕b6 21.♕f3 ♖e8
22.♕f2 ♗xe5 23.♖xe5 ♖xe5
24.♗xd4 ♖e2 25.♗xb6 ♖xf2
26.♗xf2 ♔g7 27.a4 ♗e6 28.a5**

a6 29.♗d4+ ♔f7 30.♔f2 ♖c8
31.♖a2 g5 32.♗e5 ♔g6
33.♔e3 ♔h5 34.♔d2 ♖g8
35.g3 ♔g4 36.♔e3 ♔h3 37.c3
d4+ 38.♔xd4 ♖d8+ 39.♔e3
♗xb3 40.♖b2 ♗d5 41.c4 ♗g2
42.♖b6 ♗f1 43.♖xh6+ ♔g2
44.d4 g4 45.c5 ♗c4 46.♖f6 1-0

Novik - Mejster [C61]
USSR Ch., 1991

**1.e4 e5 2.♘f3 ♘c6 3.♗b5 ♘d4
4.♘xd4 exd4 5.0-0 ♗c5 6.d3
c6 7.♗a4 d6 8.f4 f5 9.♘d2 ♘f6
10.♗b3 ♘g4 11.exf5 ♗xf5
12.♖e1+ ♔d7 13.♘f3 ♕f6
14.h3 h5 15.♘g5 ♘e3 16.♕f3
♖ae8 17.♘e4 ♗xe4 18.dxe4 g5
19.♗xe3 dxe3 20.f5 g4
21.♗e6+ ♔c7 22.♕g3 ♕xb2
23.♔h1 ♕xc2 24.e5 d5
25.♖ec1 ♕b2 26.♖ab1 ♕d4
27.♗f7 ♕xe5 28.♕xe5+ ♖xe5
29.♖xc5 ♖xf5 30.♗g6 ♖f2
31.♖e1 g3 32.♖c3 d4 33.♖c4
♖d2 34.a4 h4 35.♗e4 ♖e8
36.♗f3 e2 0-1**

Sax - Kortchnoi [C78]
Wijk Aan Zee (m/4), 1991

**1.e4 e5 2.♘f3 ♘c6 3.♗b5 a6
4.♗a4 ♘f6 5.0-0 b5 6.♗b3
♗b7 7.d3 ♗d6 8.c3 0-0 9.♖e1
♘a5 10.♗c2 ♖e8 11.b4 ♘c6
12.a4 ♗f8 13.axb5 axb5
14.♖xa8 ♕xa8 15.♗b3 ♘d8
16.♘a3 ♗c6 17.♗b2 d6
18.♘c2 g6 19.♘e3 ♗g7
20.♕a1 ♘e6 21.♕xa8 ♖xa8
22.g3 ♔f8 23.♘d5 ♘d7
24.♖a1 ½-½**

Short - Karpov [C86]
Linares (m/8), 1992

1.e4 e5 2.♘f3 ♘c6 3.♗b5 a6
4.♗a4 ♘f6 5.0-0 ♗e7 6.♕e2
b5 7.♗b3 0-0 8.c3 d6 9.d4
♗g4 10.♖d1 exd4 11.cxd4 d5
12.e5 ♘e4 13.a4 bxa4
14.♗xa4 ♘b4 15.h3 ♗h5
16.♘c3 ♗g6 17.♗e3 ♖b8
18.♘a2 c5 19.dxc5 ♘xc5
20.♘xb4 ♖xb4 21.♗c6 ♕b8
22.♗xd5 ♖xb2 23.♕c4 ♖c2
24.♕g4 ♕c7 25.♘d4 ♖c3
26.♘c6 ♖e8 27.♗d4 ♖c2
28.♘b4 ♖d8 29.♘xc2 ♗xc2
30.e6 ♗f8 31.exf7+ ♔h8
32.♖e1 ♗g6 33.♖e8 ♖xe8
34.fxe8=♕ ♗xe8 35.♗xc5
♗xc5 36.♕e6 1-0

Short - Timman [C86]
Amsterdam, 1992

1.e4 e5 2.♘f3 ♘c6 3.♗b5 a6
4.♗a4 ♘f6 5.0-0 ♗e7 6.♕e2
b5 7.♗b3 0-0 8.c3 d5 9.d3
♗b7 10.♘bd2 ♖e8 11.a3 ♗f8
12.♗a2 ♘b8 13.♖e1 ♘bd7
14.♘f1 c5 15.exd5 ♗xd5
16.♗xd5 ♘xd5 17.♗d2 g6
18.♖ad1 ♗g7 19.h4 ♘f8 20.h5
♕d7 21.hxg6 hxg6 22.♕e4
♖ac8 23.♕h4 f6 24.♘g3 ♘e6
25.♘e4 ♔f7 26.♕g4 ♖e7 27.c4
♘b6 28.♗a5 ♖c6 29.♗xb6
♖xb6 30.♘h4 ♘f8 31.♕f3
♖c6 32.♘c3 ♖d6 33.♘d5 ♖e8
34.♕g3 ♖xd5 35.cxd5 ♕xd5
36.b4 cxb4 37.axb4 ♗h6
38.♕f3 ♖d8 39.♕e4 ♕d6
40.g3 ♗g7 41.♖a1 ♕xd3
42.♕xd3 ♖xd3 43.♖xa6 ♖b3
44.♖c1 ♖xb4 45.♖c7+ ♔g8

46.♖a8 ♖g4 47.♔h2 f5 48.♖b7
♖a4 49.♖ab8 ♖a6 50.♖xb5
♔f7 51.♖8b7+ ♔f6 52.♘f3 e4
53.♘e5 ♘e6 54.♖d5 ♔g5
55.♘f7+ ♔h5 56.♔g2 ♗d4
57.♖b4 ♗f6 58.♖xe4 ♘g5
59.♖h4 mate 1-0

Geller-Salov [C76]
Moscow, 1987

1.e4 e5 2.♘f3 ♘c6 3.♗b5 g6
4.c3 a6 5.♗a4 d6 6.d4 ♗d7
7.0-0 ♗g7 8.dxe5 ♘xe5
9.♘xe5 dxe5 10.f4 ♘e7?!
11.f5 gxf5

Geller suggested 11...♗xa4
12.♕xa4+ ♘c6.

12.exf5 ♘d5 13.♕xd5! ♗xa4
14.♕xb7 ♗b5 15.f6! ♗xf6
16.c4! ♖b8 17.♕f3 ♕d4+
18.♗c3 ♕xc4 19.♘a3 ♕e6
20.♘xb5 ♖xb5 21.♕xf6 ♕xf6
22.♖xf6 ♖xb2 23.♖xa6 0-0
24.♖f1 ♖d8 25.♗h6 ♖b6
26.♖xb6 cxb6 27.♖f6 1-0

Part IV
Scandinavian Sabotage:
Encounters with the Center Counter

1.e4 d5 2.exd5 ♛xd5

The classical line. More popular at present is 2...♞f6, followed by 3.c4 c6 4.d4 (4.dxc6 ♞xc6 gives black excellent compensation for the pawn) cxd5 5.♞c3, transposing to the Panov Attack in the Caro-Kann. Another interesting gambit is 3...e6!? 4.dxe6 ♝xe6 but 4.d4 is better.

3.♞c3 ♛a5

3...♛d8 is also played, but is less active.

4.♞f3 ♞f6 5.d4

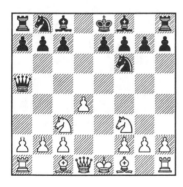

More cautious players prefer 5.♝c4 and then d3 and ♝d2, which hardly promises white opportunities for an advantage in the opening, but even such an active GM like David Yjanovsky had criticized the d4 move in this system because of the possible counterattack against this pawn. This comment was made over seventy years ago, but

nevertheless has some foresight as we shall see......

Here black has two very active possibilities: 5...♝g4 and 5...♞c6 (the rarer Mieses line 5...♝f5!? also is seen on occasion). In my practice, I have examined both such continuations with white, leading to double-edged and instructive games.

5...♝g4 6.h3 ♝h5!?

Theory also gives 6...♝xf3 7.♛xf3 c6, although the bishop pair will give white a long-term initiative. The text is more interesting and practically more promising for black.

7.g4 ♝g6 8.♞e5

Shamkovich - Zakharov [B01]
Moscow Ch., 1962

Threatening 9.♞c4, which black prevents with his next.

8...c6

The counterattack 8...♘e4 was met with 9.♗g2 ♘xc3 10.♕d2 c6 11.bxc3 e6 12.♖b1! with a strong position in Belyavsky-Bohm, Le Havre 1977. An interesting idea is 8...e6!? giving white the chance to play 9.♘c4 forcing the ugly move 9...♕a6. Nevertheless the Moscow Master Korolev employed this line with success e.g., 10.♗f4? ♕c6 11.♘d6+ ♗xd6 12.♗b5 ♗xf4 13.♕f3 ♗d6 14.♗xc6+ ♘xc6 with three very active minor pieces against the queen and a clear advantage as in Kremenetzky-Korolev, Moscow 1972. The idea itself was not a new one e.g., 8...♘bd7? 9.♘c4 ♕a6 10.♗f4 with advantage, Alekhine-Schroder, New York 1924. I liked this idea and decided to employ it with black in a serious tournament sometime. A good opportunity presented itself against the famous American opening expert Zuckerman, and a game was produced that was interesting and important for theory. We will examine the encounter Zuckerman-Shamkovich with 8...e6 in the next game. Let us return to Shamkovich-Zakharov ....

9.h4

A typical advance, exploiting the bishop's poor position on g6. White threatens h5 and ♗d2.

9...♗e4

A new move but dubious. Older attempts also favor white, e.g., 9...♘bd7 10.♘c4 ♕c7 11.h5 ♗e4 12.♘xe4 ♘xe4 13.♕f3 threatening 14.♗f4 winning - Em. Lasker.

10.♘c4 ♕c7 11.♘xe4 ♘xe4 12.♕f3 ♘f6 13.♗f4

By attacking the black queen, white wins a third consecutive tempo.

13...♕d7 14.g5

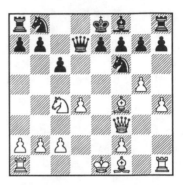

Emphasizing that more troubles are in store for the black queen.

14...♕d5

Necessary. On 14...♘d5 comes 15.♗xb8! ♖xb8 16.♘e5 ♕e6 17.♗h3 winning, and if 14...♘g8 15.♗xb8 ♖xb8 16.♘e5 ♕d5 17.♕xd5 cxd5 18.♗b5+ wins.

15.♕b3! b5

If 15...♕xh1 16.♕xb7, and black loses his entire queenside.

16.♘e5 e6

If 16...♕xh1, white continues 17.♕xf7+ ♔d8 18.gxf6 ♕e4+ 19.♗e3 with a very strong attack, as illustrated by such spectacular variations as 19...exf6 20.0-0-0! ♗e7 (if 20...fxe5 21.dxe5+ ♔c8 22.♗h3+ wins) 21.♗h3! ♖f8 22.♕e6 f5 23.d5 c5 24.d6 crushing or 19...gxf6 20.0-0-0 fxe5 21.♗h3! ♔c7 22.♕e6 a5 23.♕c8+ ♔b6 24.♕d8+! ♔a7 25.♕c7+ ♔a6 26.♗c8 mate. Trading queens with 16...♛xb3 17.axb3 would leave black's queenside fatally weakened.

17.gxf6! ♛xh1 18.♘f3!

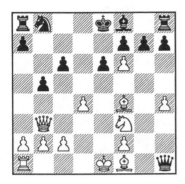

The trap has closed with a bang.

18...gxf6 19.0-0-0 ♗e7

The more stubborn 19...♖g8 could not resue black anyway, since 20.d5! (the methodical break) exd5 21.♗xb5! ♛xd1+ (or 21...♛h3 22.♗xc6 ♘xc6 23.♛xd5 wins) 22.♔xd1 cxb5 23.♛xd5 ♘d7 24.♛xa8+ ♔e7 25.♘d4 ♘e5 26.♛c8 is a mating attack.

20.♗h2

Threatening 21.♗h3, seizing the queen.

20...♗f8 21.♛d3 ♗h6+ 22.♔b1 ♘a6 23.c3 ♖d8 24.♗h3

Completing the hunting operation.

24...♘c5 25.♛e2 ♛xd1+ 26.♛xd1 ♘a4 27.♘d2 c5 28.♘e4 cxd4 29.♘d6+ ♔e7 30.♛h5 1-0

Zuckerman - Shamkovich [B01]
Cleveland, 1975

8...e6!?

We have already introduced this idea of Korolev, (see above).

9.♘c4

There are a number of alternatives and modern theory has not yet decided which is the best e.g., 9.♗g2 c6 10.h4 ♘bd7 11.♘c4 with an edge for white in Karpov-Larsen, Mar Del Plata 1982, where Karpov offered 10...♗b4!? as an improvement, or 9.h4 ♗b4 10.♖h3! with a clear advantage to white in Karpov-Rogers, Bath 1983, when the sharp break 10...c5!? deserves attention instead of the 10...c6 as played by Rogers, (see Supplemental Games). To my way of thinking, taking the bull by the horns with 9.♘c4 is the consistent choice.

9...♛a6 10.h4!

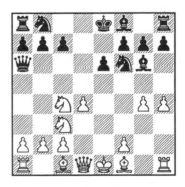

The solid 10.a3 was successful in Marjanovic-Rogers (Nis, 1983) after 10...♛c6 11.♖g1 ♘bd7? 12.♘e5! ♛b6 13.♘c4 ♛c6 14.♛e2! 0-0-0 15.♗g5 ♔b8 16.0-0-0 with a plus for white, but

11...♘e4! is an improvement, giving black a playable game.

10...♕c6

The alternative 10...♗b4 could transpose to the game after 11.♖h3 ♕c6. Instead, the cool 11...♘bd7 failed to 12.h5 ♗e4 13.g5 ♘d5 14.♘d2! ♘xc3 15.bxc3 ♕c6 16.cxb4 ♗xc2 17.b5! 1-0 in the game Shamkovich-Lowerence, Syracuse 1986. After 10...♗b4 the advance 11.h5 is also possible e.g., 11...♗e4? 12.♘d2! wins or 11...♗xc3+ 12.bxc3 ♗e4 13.f3 ♗c6 14.♘e5 ♕a5 15.♗d2 with a clear edge for white. We have to add that the desperate advance 10...h5 is dubious since 11.♘e5 ♕a5 12.♘xg6 fxg6 13.g5 ♘d5 14.♗d2 gives white a clear plus.

11.♖h3!

The old recommendation 11.f3 is questionable since 11...♗b4 (not 11...♘xg4? 12.♘e5! ♘xe5 13.♗b5 winning the queen) 12.h5 ♗e4! with counterplay for black (weakness of the white kingside and chances on the h1-a8 diagonal).

11...♗b4 12.h5 ♗e4

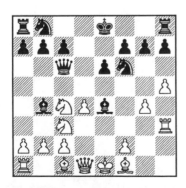

Now the game continued ...

13.♗d2? ♗xc3 14.♖xc3 ♕d7?

Better was 14...h6! 15.♗f4 ♕d7 16.♘e5 ♕e7 with an unclear position.

15.f3 ♗c6

If 15...♗d5 16.h6!

16.h6! gxh6 17.♗xh6 ♘d5 18.♖a3 ♕e7

Intending ...♕h4+

19.g5 ♗b5

19...♘d7? 20.♘a5! is very good for white.

20.♕d2 ♘c6 21.♘b6

Another possibility is 21.♘e3!? ♘xe3 22.♗xb5 ♘f5 23.0-0-0 ♕d6, unclear.

21...♘xb6 22.♗xb5 ♕d6 23.0-0-0 ♖g8! 24.♕e2 a6 25.♗xc6+

25.♗d3 ♘xd4 26.♕e3 0-0-0 is unclear.

25...♕xc6 26.♖c3 ♕d6 27.♕e4 ♘d5

Not 27...0-0-0 28.g6! with the threat of ♗f4.

28.♖b3 0-0-0 29.c4

If 29.♕xh7? black has the counter 29...♕f4+ 30.♔b1 ♖g6!

29...♕c6 30.♕xh7

Instead 30.♕c2 ♘e7 31.♕xh7 ♕xc4+ 32.♔b1 ♖xd4 33.♖c1 ♕d5 would be equal.

**30...♛xc4+ 31.♔b1 f5
32.gxf6 ♞xf6 33.♕f7 ♛e2??**

Correct was 33...♞d5! 34.♕xe6+
♔b8 35.♖c1 ♛a4 with good chances to
hold.

34.♖c1 ♞d5 35.♗f4! 1-0

But let us return to the previous
diagram. By playing 13.♞d2!! (instead
of 13.♗d2?) white could win the
hanging bishop at e4. The point is that
black cannot meet all three threats of
14.♗b5, 14.a3 and 14.g5 satisfactorily,
e.g., 13...a6 14.a3 ♗xc3 15.♖xc3 ♛d5
(if 15...♛d7 16.g5 wins) 16.f3!
winning a piece. If 13...0-0 then 14.a3
♗e7 15.g5 wins. Even the heroic
13...♗g2 hoping for an unclear queen
sacrifice with 14.♗b5 ♗xh3 15.♗xc6+
♞xc6, fails to 14.d5!.

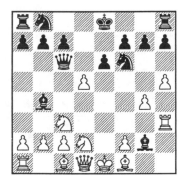

(analysis)

Thus, Korelov's idea with 8...e6
stands the test of serious analytical
scrutiny with great difficulty, especially
after 9.♞c4. Perhaps the continuations
briefly discussed after 9...♛c6 10. h4
♗b4 11.♖h3 h5!? 12.♞e5 ♛a5
13.♞xg6 fxg6 will offer a reasonable
defense.

After 1.e4 d5 2.exd5 ♛xd5 3.♞c3
♛a5 4.♞f3 ♞f6 5.d4, I mentioned
another interesting possibility with
5...♞c6, which forms the basis of my
next game with Leverett. This is a very
interesting battle because of two aspects
- a theoretical one because of my
original "indirect argument" with
Robert Fischer's viewpoint and because
of the dramatic course of the ensuing
middlegame.

Shamkovich - Leverett [B01]
USA, 1977

5...♞c6?! 6.♗b5!

Frankly speaking, over the board, I
had no self-doubts about this logical
developing move, which threatens 7.d5.
Many years after this game, I came
across Fischer's notes concerning his
game against Seidman (USA Ch.
1958-59), (see the notes to
Fischer-Robatsch, game #41 in the
classic "My Sixty Memorable Games"

"6.d5!? (possibly an improvement
over the usual 6.♗b5) ...♞b4 7.♗b5+
c6 (more crucial is 7...♗d7 8.♗xd7+
♞xd7 9.a3 ♞f6 10.axb4 ♛xa1 11.0-0
♛a6 12.♖e1 with a terrific attack)
8.dxc6 bxc6 9.♗a4 ♗a6? 10.a3 and
white is winning, Fischer-Seidman,
USA Ch. 1958-9."

Bobby's incisive insights are of
interest to us, because the same position
(after 11.0-0) arises in the present game
via a transposition of moves.
Practically, black cannot avoid this
situation as such variations as 6.d5 ♞b4
7.♗b5+ c6 8.dxc6 bxc6 9.♗a4 ♗d7
(Fischer's improvement) 10.♗b3! and
6...♗d7 7.d5 ♞e5!? 8.♞xe5 ♗xb5
9.♛f3! ♗a6 10.♗f4, followed by 0-0-0
are favorable to white. I have to add that

the alternative 6.♗c4 is not so promising since 6...♗g4 7.♗e3 e5! gives black good counterplay as in Bellon-Biriescu, Bucharest 1978.

6...♗d7

6...e6 7.♘e5 ♗b4 8.♕d3! is good for white.

7.d5 ♘b4!?

For the continuation 7...♘e5!? see the notes above.

8.♗xd7+ ♘xd7

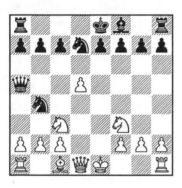

9.a3!

By the exchange sacrifice, white will gain a superiority in development and a strong attack. Is this risky attacking method really the best one available? I had recommended another way with 9.0-0 ♘f6 10.♕e2 sacrificing the pawn on d5 in the spirit of Alekhine. After 10...♘bxd5 11.♘xd5 ♘xd5 (if 11...♕xd5 12.♖d1) 12.♕e5! with plenty of compensation for the pawn, but 10...♖d8 11.♗g5 with an unclear game is a big improvement for black. So white's attack after the exchange sacrifice is more attractive. It is certainly not by accident that Fischer

only mentioned one manner of conducting the attack!

9...♘f6

Attacking the d4-pawn, the main target of black's counterplay.

10.axb4!? ♕xa1 11.0-0

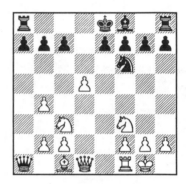

The critical position appears. Black's queen is almost trapped, and his kingside is still frozen. Attempts to release it immediately are not effective, e.g., 11...e6 12.dxe6 fxe6 (12...♗xb4 13.exf7+ ♔xf7 14.♘g5+ ♔g8 15.♘d5! with advantage to white) 13.♘g5 ♕a6 14.♖e1 favors white. Also good for white is 11...c6 12.dxc6 bxc6 13.♕e2 intending ♘f3-d4-b3 snaring the queen. Finally 11...g6 12.♘b5 ♖c8 13.♕d3 ♕a6 14.♖e1 ♗g7 15.d6! 0-0 (at last) 16.dxe7 ♖fe8 17.c4! doesn't offer black much hope for survival.

11...♖d8

By attacking the pawn at d5, black is relinquishing the possibility of evacuating the king to the queenside. The other reasonable alternative was 11...♕a6 to first safeguard the queen. In this case we remember that Fischer suggested 12.♖e1! while I had recommended 12.b5. Who is right?? Most probably Fischer as the following variations (after 12.♖e1) show: 12...♖d8 13.♗g5! c6 (13...e6 14.♗xf6 gxf6 15.♘d4 ♕c4 16.♕h5! ♕xd4 17.dxe6 wins) 14.♗xf6 gxf6 15.♕d4 ♗g7 16.♕g4! 0-0 17.♘h4 with a tremendous attack, or 12...c6 13.dxc6 ♕xc6 14.♘e5 ♕c8 (14...♕b6 15.♘c4! wins) 15.♕e2 a6 16.♘a4! ♕c7 17.♗f4 and black cannot save the game. As to my original idea 12.b5 ♕d6 13.♕d4, which looks to be as strong as well, 13...e6! 14.♗f4 ♕b4 gives black a defensible position.

12.♘d4!

From now on, the c7-pawn becomes a major target of white's attack. The threat is 13.♘db5. If now 12...♘xd5? 13.♘db5 wins.

12...♕a6

12...e6 13.♕e2 ♕a6 14.♘db5 favors white. If 12...a6 13.♘b3 wins. The best try was 12...c6 13.dxc6 bxc6 but after 14.♕e2! (threatening 15.♘b3) ♖xd4 15.♗e3 ♕xf1+ 16.♔xf1 ♖xb4 17.♕a6 white should win.

13.♘db5 ♖d7 14.♗f4 ♔d8

14...♘xd5 is answered with 15.♕xd5! ♖xd5 16.♘xc7+ ♔d8 17.♘xa6 ♖f5 18.♗e3 bxa6 19.♖a1 ♖f6 (if 19...e6 20.g4! would be very strong) 20.♗xa7 e5 21.♘d5 with a winning endgame.

15.♕e2?

Alas, sometimes it is possible to destroy a magnificent position by making quite "natural" moves. Fortunately, black fails to make the most of the fleeting chance offered to him. After 15.♕e2? we can see that 15...c6 16.♕e5 wins for white. But with the simple 15...e6! black has the opportunity to release his kingside. I had intended 16.♕e5, but 16...♗d6! favors black, (but not 16...♘xd5 17.♘xd5 ♕xb5 18.♗g5+! f6 19.♗xf6+ gxf6 20.♕xf6+ ♔e8 21.♕xe6+ ♗e7 22.♘xe7 ♖xe7 23.♕c8+ and white wins). Also if 16.♖e1 ♗xb4! (not 16:..exd5? 17.♘xd5! ♖xd5 18.♗xc7+ ♔c8 19.c4 and if 19...♖d7? 20.♕e8+! wins) 17.♕c4 ♗d6! is O.K. So where did white lose the correct attacking path?? Let us return to the previous diagram, and continue with the correct 15.♕d4!! followed by 15...e6 (if 15...c6? 16.♕e5 wins) 16.♗xc7+! ♖xc7 17.dxe6+ ♔c8 18.♖d1 ♗e7 19.♘xc7 ♔xc7 20.♕e5+ ♔c8 21.♘b5 ♕b6 22.exf7 and wins. Also failing is 15...♘xd5 16.♘xd5 ♕xb5 17.♕xa7! ♖xd5 18.♕b8+ ♔d7 19.♕xc7+ ♔e8 20.c4 ♖d7 21.♕b8+ ♖d8 22.cxb5 ♖xb8 23.♗xb8 and white should win this ending in view of the threat of ♖c1-c7. If 15...♕b6 16.♕d3! with an analogous attacking method viz., 16...e6 (16...c6 17.♗c7+ ♖xc7 18.dxc6+ ♔c8 19.♖d1 ♖xc6 20.♘a4! wins) 17.♗xc7+ ♖xc7 18.dxe6+ winning. Of course, it is not so easy to find such a problem-like winning plan over the board - and as such an examination in practical play would be beneficial. Nevertheless, black's position after 14...♔d8 is not without counterchances despite the dormant kingside.

15...♘xd5?

Missing his chance for 15...e6. Now black is really in trouble.

16.♘xd5 ♖xd5 17.♗xc7+ ♔c8

Here is one more "problem" variation. If 17...♔e8 18.c4 ♖d7 19.♘d6+!! ♖xd6 20.b5! ♖e6 21. ♕d1 wins.

18.c4 ♖d7

Now comes an unexpected and decisive combination.

19.♖d1! ♕e6

Trying to exchange the queens. The options are limited e.g., 19...♖xc7 20.♕d3 winning, or 19...♖xd1+ 20.♕xd1 b6 21.♕d8+ ♔b7 22.♕b8+ ♔c6 23.♘d4+ ♔d7 24.♕d8 mate.

20.♖xd7 ♕xd7

20...♔xd7 fails to 21.♕d3+ ♔c6 22.♘d4+ and of course if 20...♕xe2 21.♖d8 is mate. Let me present the final spectacular position. With the extra exchange and a reduced number of attacking pieces, my opponent may have been very optimistic at this moment.

21.♘xa7+!

Crushing, and destroying any last misconception of black's chances to hold the position.

21...♔xc7 22.♕e5+

Finally the undeveloped kingside plays a role. Black must sacrifice his queen to stave off immediate defeat. The point is that 22...♔b6 23.♕a5 is mate. The game is over.

22...♕d6 23.♘b5+ ♔d7 24.♘xd6 exd6 25.♕d5 ♗e7 26.♕xb7+ ♔e6 27.b5 ♗f6 28.b4 ♗c3 29.♕d5+ ♔e7 30.c5 ♖d8 31.c6 1-0

SUPPLEMENTAL GAMES

Karpov - Larsen [B01]
Mar del Plata, 1982

1.e4 d5 2.exd5 ♕xd5 3.♘c3
♕a5 4.♘f3 ♘f6 5.d4 ♗g4 6.h3
♗h5 7.g4 ♗g6 8.♘e5 e6
9.♗g2 c6 10.h4 ♘bd7 11.♘c4
♕a6 12.♗f1 b5 13.h5 ♗xc2
14.♕xc2 bxc4 15.g5 ♘d5
16.♕e4 ♖b8 17.♖h3 ♗e7
18.♗e2 ♖b6 19.♔f1 ♘f8
20.♘d1 ♕a4 21.♗d2 ♗b4
22.♗f4 ♘d7 23.♗h2 ♗e7
24.♖c1 ♕xa2 25.♗e5 c3
26.bxc3 ♘xe5 27.♕xe5 0-0
28.h6 f6 29.♕xe6+ ♔h8
30.hxg7+ ♔xg7 31.♗d3 ♖h8
32.c4 1-0

Karpov - Rogers [B01]
Bath, 1983

1.e4 d5 2.exd5 ♕xd5 3.♘c3
♕a5 4.d4 ♘f6 5.♘f3 ♗g4 6.h3
♗h5 7.g4 ♗g6 8.♘e5 e6 9.h4
♗b4 10.♖h3 c6 11.♗d2 ♕b6
12.h5 ♗e4 13.♖e3 ♗xc3
14.♗xc3 ♗d5 15.g5 ♘e4
16.♕g4 ♘d6 17.0-0-0 ♘d7
18.♗e1 ♘xe5 19.dxe5 ♘f5
20.♖h3 0-0-0 21.c4 ♕c5 22.b4
♗f3 23.♖xd8+ ♖xd8 24.♕xf3
♕xe5 25.♗c3 ♕d6 26.♗d3
♘d4 27.♕xf7 ♘f5 28.♗xf5
♕f4+ 29.♖e3 1-0

Part V
Overwhelming the Pirc:
Combatting the Modern Defenses

The Modern Defense/Pirc Defense complex has been featured in a number of my theoretically important and most memorable games. Many different spectacular plots have been seen in the ensuing middlegames but the common strategical point has been the thematic break e4-e5. We will examine a number of games in which I deployed a favorite system of development to combat this method of defense by black - namely a system involving ♘f3, ♗c4 and ♕e2. Although by no means the most theoretically critical lines of the Pirc/Modern - current fashion indicates that the Austrian Attack to be most critical - the attacking potential in white's position cannot be underestimated.

Shamkovich - Shapi [B06]
Moscow-Budapest (match), Moscow 1972

**1.e4 d6 2.d4 g6 3.♘f3 ♗g7
4.♗c4 ♘f6 5.♕e2 c6**

The most solid answer with the positional threat of 6...d5. In case of 5...♘c6 or 5...♗g4, black must reckon with the immediate break 6.e5.

6.♗b3 0-0 7.0-0 ♕c7

With the obvious idea 8...e5.

**8.e5 ♘d5 9.h3 dxe5 10.dxe5
♗e6 11.♖e1 ♘d7 12.♗g5**

This active lunge is unnecessary. Simply 12.c3 ♖ae8 13.♘bd2 was a good alternative as 13...f6? is met by 14.♘d4! winning.

12...♖ae8 13.♘bd2

13...♘c5?

After this move, white achieves a clear superiority in view of his strong control over the center and good chances for a kingside attack. More combative seems 13...f6!? because white's planned 14.♘d4 is not so clear after 14...♗xh3! 15.gxh3 fxg5 16.♘e6 ♕xe5 with sufficient compensation for the exchange. The correct course of action for white seems to be 14.♗h4 fxe5 15.♗g3 with an edge, but 14...♔h8! is playable for black.

**14.♘d4 ♗c8 15.♘2f3 ♘xb3
16.axb3 a6 17.♕e4**

Transferring the queen to the kingside, but it was better first to play 17.c3 (with the idea of 18.b4) c5 18.♘c2 with some advantage.

17...♖d8 18.♕h4 c5 19.♘e2 ♖fe8?

Here black misses his only chance to carry out a successful break with 19...f6! utilizing a temporary discord amongst white's forces (specifically the knight on e2). After 20.♗h6 g5! 21.♕h5 ♗f5 22.♗xg7 ♔xg7 23.c3 ♗d3 24.♕g4, a double-edged position is reached in which white is slightly better.

20.♘g3!

The concentration of white's pieces around black's king becomes menacing. Nevertheless my opponent decided in this moment to "clarify" the position. Psychologically this phenomenon is natural, having rejected the natural ...f6 for too long, black is governed by a "now or never" attitude. On the other hand, white's immediate and serious threat of 21.♗h6 followed by ♘g5 needs to be addressed.

20...f6 21.♗h6 g5?

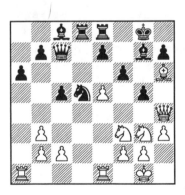

A decisive blunder. 21...♖f8 was absolutely necessary. Now comes a lightning bolt!

22.♘xg5! ♗xh6!

Black's only hope. If 22...fxg5 then 23.♕xg5 e6 24.♘h5 ends the discussion.

23.exf6!

Black was banking on 23.♕xh6 fxg5 24.♘h5 e6 with chances to survive, but this "in-between" move finishes black quickly.

23...exf6 24.♖xe8+ ♖xe8 25.♕xh6 ♕g7

Now the point of white's combination is clear, if 25...fxg5 26.♕xg5+ ♔h8 27.♕xd5 leaves white two pawns ahead with a dominating position. The rest is clear.

26.♕xg7+ ♔xg7 27.♘5e4 ♖e5 28.♘xc5 ♘b4 29.♘ce4 ♗e6 30.c4 ♘c6 31.f4 ♖a5 32.♖d1 1-0

Shamkovich - Zlotnikov [B06]
New York Open 1982

1.e4 g6 2.d4 ♗g7 3.♘f3 d6 4.♗c4 ♘f6 5.♕e2 c6 6.♗b3 0-0 7.0-0 ♗g4 8.♘bd2 a5 9.a4 ♘a6

9...e5!? is playable.

10.c3 ♘c7 11.h3 ♗c8?!

This retro-development is almost always a bad business (in open and half-open systems), but 11...♗xf3 12.♘xf3 or 11...♗e6 12.♗c2 is not that appealing for black either.

12.e5 ♘fd5 13.♘e4

White is better.

13...♘e6

Black threatens counterplay with 14...♘ef4. He would be O.K after 14.exd6 exd6 15.♗xd5 cxd5.

14.♘eg5! ♘ef4

Black plays it anyway! However, safer is 14...♘xg5 15.♗xg5 f6 although 16.♗d2! maintains better chances for white.

15.♗xf4 ♘xf4 16.♕e4 ♘d5

Now 17.e6 f5 18.♕h4 ♘f6 19.♖fe1 ♕b6 is unclear - how should white continue?

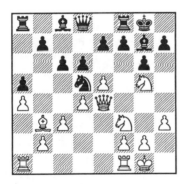

17.♘xh7!

A classical "destroying sacrifice" against black's castled position. I could not forsee all of the complications but believed this to be the correct path. Moreover, having authored the book, "The Modern Chess Sacrifice" I felt honor-bound to be brave in this situation.

17...♔xh7 18.♘g5+ ♔g8 19.♕h4 ♖e8 20.♗c2!

This long-range bishop, like a powerful laser, will play a decisive role in white's attack.

20...dxe5

Post-mortem analysis confirmed that after 20...f6 21.♕h7+ ♔f8 22.f4! or 20...♘f6 21.f4! white had a strong attack. If 20...e6 21.♕h7+ ♔f8 22.♘xf7! ♔xf7 23.♗xg6+ ♔f8 24.♖ae1! (threatening ♖e3) ...♘f4 25.♗xe8 ♕xe8 26.♖e4 wins for white.

21.♗xg6!

More fuel on the fire! A necessary sacrificial continuance of the attack. In case of the simple 21.dxe5 e6, black has chances to survive.

21...fxg6 22.♕h7+ ♔f8 23.♕xg6 ♔g8 24.♕h7+ ♔f8 25.♕g6 ♔g8

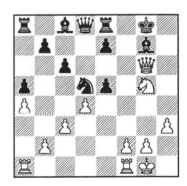

The critical position of white's attack has appeared. Having sacrificed two pieces, white can take a draw with perpetual checks or continue the struggle.

26.dxe5! e6 27.♕f7+ ♔h8 28.♕g6

A repetition to reach the time-control at move 30.

28...♔g8 29.♕f7+ ♔h8 30.♕g6 ♔g8 31.♖ad1!

With powerful threats, including 32.c4 and the rook-lifts ♖d4-h4 or ♖d3-f3.

31...♖e7?

This leads to the collapse of black's position. Black could have prolonged the struggle with 31...♕e7 32.♖d4 (not 32.♖d3? ♘f4! 33.♕h7+ ♔f8 34.♖f3 ♕xg5 and black wins) ...♖d8 and now white has a new chance to go astray with 33.♖h4 ♔f8 34.c4? ♕e8! and black wins. Instead 34.♖h3! is winning.

32.♖d3! ♖d7 33.♖f3 ♕xg5

Desperation. The rest passes without comment.

34.♕xg5 b5 35.♖d1 ♖f7 36.♕d8+ ♖f8 37.♖xf8+ ♗xf8 38.♖d3 ♘e7 39.♕e8 ♗b7 40.♖g3+ ♔h7 41.♕h5+ 1-0

Shamkovich - Botterill [B06]
Hastings 1977-78

1.d4 g6 2.e4 d6 3.♘f3 ♗g7 4.♗c4 ♘f6 5.♕e2 c6 6.♗b3

Sidestepping 6...d5.

6...0-0 7.0-0 ♗g4 8.♘bd2 e5!

This energetic move forever prevents the methodical break e4-e5, but creates a weakness at d6 that attracts white's knight. My opponent was well prepared

for this particular system as he is the author of a number of opening books on the Modern/Pirc.

9.dxe5 dxe5 10.♘c4 ♕e7 11.h3

11.♗d2!? ♘bd7 12.h3 ♗xf3 13.♕xf3 is possible as 13...♘c5? is rebuffed by 14.♗b4!

11...♗xf3 12.♕xf3 b5

Throwing back white's knight from the attractive square d6, but weakening the queenside pawns. The solid 12...♘bd7 is best met by 13.♗d2! when again 13...♘c5? is in error, i.e., 14.♗b4 ♘fd7 15.♖ad1 winning.

13.♘e3

13.♘a5 ♕b4! 14.♘b7 ♕e7 allows a draw by repetition. Not today!

13...♘bd7 14.a4 ♘c5!?

This leads to complications and a double-edged game. If instead 14...a6, maintaining control over the d5-square, then 15.♗d2 would still be very strong after 15...♘c5 16.♗b4 a5 17.♗xc5 ♕xc5 18.axb5 cxb5 19.c3 a4 20.♗d5 with an edge for white.

15.axb5 ♘xb3 16.cxb3 cxb5 17.♖a6!

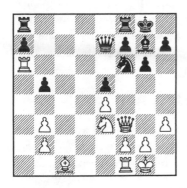

Preventing black from seizing the initiative with 17...♕b4.

17...♖fd8 18.♖d1 ♖d4?!

"Allowing Shamkovich to open a Pandora's Box of complications," - Robert Byrne. My opponent obviously overestimated his position. Correct was 18...♖xd1+ 19.♘xd1 and if 19...♘e8 (Robert Byrne's suggestion) then 20.♘c3 ♘c7 21.♖c6 or 20...♕b7 21.♖a1 a6 22.♗e3 ♘c7 23.♖d1 yields white slightly better chances. Better then is 19...♖d8 when both 20.♘c3 b4 and 20.♗g5 ♖d6 give black a playable game.

19.♖xd4 exd4 20.e5!

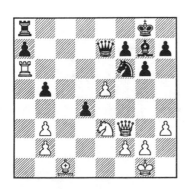

This break, which black safely

prevented in the opening, takes place instead in the middlegame. Black's rook and knight are under attack. The reply is forced.

20...♖c8 21.exf6 ♖xc1+ 22.♘f1

Not 22.♔h2? ♕c7+ 23.g3 dxe3 24.fxg7 exf2 25.♕xf2 ♕b7 and black wins.

22...♕e1

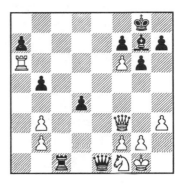

23.♖xa7!!

In view of the threat 23...♕xf1+, my opponent likely considered two answers, 23.♕d3 and 23.fxg7, but in both lines black is on top or white is looking to draw, e.g., 23.♕d3 ♗f8 24.♖xa7 ♖d1 25.♕xb5 ♖d2! (not 25...d3?? since 26.♖a8! ♕xf1+ 27.♔h2 ♕e2 28.♖xf8+! ♔xf8 29.♕c5+ mates) 26.♕d5 ♕xf2+ 27.♔h2 ♕f4+ with a draw. Even worse is 23.fxg7 ♕xf1+ 24.♔h2 ♕h1+ 25.♔g3 ♖c5! (threatening 26...♖g5+, R. Byrne) followed by 26.h4 ♖f5 27.♕e2 ♔xg7 28.♖xa7 ♕c1! and black has an edge.

The text move is much stronger. White is threatening both 24.♖a8+ ♗f8

25.♖xf8+ and 24.♕f4, but black can attack and counterattack as well. From this moment the chessboard becomes a minefield. Let me quote Robert Byrne's comments from his column. "Shamkovich's plan was the beautiful knight sacrifice 23.♖xa7!! so that on 23...♕xf1+ 24.♔h2 ♕e1 (24...♖e1 and 24...♖e1 fail to 25.fxg7 - Shamkovich) 25.♖a8+ ♗f8 26.♕f4!! black could not cope with the threat of 27.♕d6."

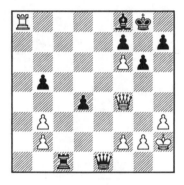

(analysis)

Now, for example, 26...♕b4 (if 26...♖a1 27.♖d8! wins) 27.♕h6! ♕d6+ 28.f4 threatening 29.♕g7 mate, is final. (Shamkovich).

"Moreover, the alternative defense 23.♖xa7!! ♕xf1+ 24.♔h2 ♕g1+ 25.♔g3 ♕e1 loses to 26.♖e7!! ♕b4 27.♕d5!" - Robert Byrne.

Note that in this line 26.♖a8+? is a mistake after 26...♗f8 27.♕f4 ♖c2! and white can only draw by perpetual check after 28.♖xf8+ ♔xf8 29.♕d6+ ♔e8 30.♕b8+.

This excellent analysis by Byrne made my own complicated combination more precise and artistic. The study-like moves 26.♕f4!! and 26.♕d5!! produce

an especially strong impression. We have to emphasize also the tremendous role in white's attack of the f6-pawn, which did hasten to take the black bishop.

23...♗f8

The most natural and cautious reply which seems to admit the erroneous nature of black's counterattack.

24.♕d5 ♕e6

The alternative 24...♕e8 allows 25.♖a8! (not 25.♕xd4? ♗c5!) ...♖c8 26.♖xc8 ♕xc8 27.♕xd4 and white wins.

25.♕xd4 ♕e2?

Here, Byrne suggested 25...♖c6 but after 26.♖b7! ♕xf6 (not 26...b4 27.♖b8! ♕xf6 28.♕xb4 wins) 27.♕xf6 ♖xf6 28.♖xb5 white should win the ending - R. Byrne.

26.♖a8! ♖xf1+

If 26...♕xf1+ 27.♔h2 ♕g1+ 28.♔g3 ♕d1 29.♕b4 wins - R. Byrne.

27.♔h2 ♖xf2 28.♖xf8+ ♔xf8

Has black survived??

29.♕c5+! 1-0

Let me present in conclusion a couple of games with the Uitelky system - an unusual variation of the Modern Defense.

Shamkovich-Ivkov [B06]
Amsterdam 1968

1.♘f3 g6 2.e4 ♗g7 3.d4 d6 4.♘c3 a6!?

An unusual, even "irregular," move. Normal is 4...c6 or 4...♗g4, but the text is extremely flexible, retaining black's options for ...b6, ...b5, ...c6, ...c5 and ...♘c6.

5.a4

Preventing ...b5, but 5...♗g4 is a strong answer. Modern theory recommends 5.♗c4.

5...b6?!

The Yugoslav grandmaster probably intended to play the well-known Uitelky System, in which black is content to develop his pieces and pawns within the first three ranks. Today's analogous system against the English Opening, the Hedgehog, demonstrates how hard these constructions are to crack.

6.♗g5!

The standard opening texts don't even consider this move, although it creates profound difficulties for black's kingside development. White is favored by both 6...♘f6 7.e5! ♘fd7 8.♗c4 dxe5 9.dxe5 ♘xe5 10.♕xd8+ ♔xd8 11.0-0-0+! ♔e8 12.♘d5 and 6...h6 7.♗h4 g5 8.♗g3.

6...♗b7 7.♗c4 h6 8.♗h4 ♘d7 9.0-0 c6?

Black continues his super-passive approach. Inadequate is the natural 9...♘gf6 10.♕e2 e5 (otherwise white plays 11.e5) 11.dxe5 ♘xe5 12.♘xe5 dxe5 13.♖ad1 winning; but white has only a slight edge after 9...c5! 10.♗d5 ♗xd5 11.♘xd5 ♘gf6 or 10.♖e1 cxd4 11.♘xd4 ♘gf6.

10.♕e2 ♕c7 11.♗b3

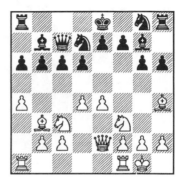

Black finds himself in a unique positional Zugzwang due to the strong posting of white's bishops. In fact, black has no active possibilities, since white has a distinct advantage after, for example, 11...c5 12.♘d5; 11...e5 12.♕c4; and 11...♘gf6 12.e5.

11...e6 12.♖ad1 ♘e7 13.♖fe1

White is fully developed with an excellent position. Black, on the other hand, has failed to castle, and his king falls just short of sanctuary.

13...♔f8

An attempt to build an artificial castle.

14.♗g3

Why not help him along?

14...♔g8 15.h4!

Serving notice to black that his king is no safer on the kingside than in the center.

15...♔h7 16.h5 ♖hg8?

Offering more resistance is 16...♘f8.

17.hxg6+ ♘xg6 18.♖d3

The rook is headed for the kingside to deliver a critical blow.

18...♖ae8?

Better is 18...♖af8 19.♘d2! b5 (otherwise, 20.♘c4) 20.f4! f5.

19.♗h2

Also strong is 19.♘d2.

19...b5?

This is tantamount to capitulation, but black's position is already hopeless: e.g., 19...♖h8 (preventing 20.♘g5+) 20.♘d2!

20.♘g5+! hxg5 21.♕h5+ ♗h6 22.♖h3 ♘h4 23.♕xf7+ ♔h8

White wins elegantly after 23...♗g7 24.♗f4! ♖gf8 25.♕h5+ ♔g8 26.♗xg5.

24.♗xe6 ♗c8

The sacrifice 24...♖xe6 provides no relief: 25.♕xe6 ♖g6 26.♕f7 ♖g7 27.♕h5 ♔h7 28.e5!.

25.♖xh4! gxh4 26.♗f5 ♘f6 27.♕xc7 1-0

Shamkovich - Riddell [B06]
World Open, Philadelphia 1992

1.e4 g6 2.d4 ♗g7 3.♘f3 d6 4.♗c4 c6 5.♗b3 ♘a6 6.0-0 ♘c7 7.♕e2 e6!?

The normal move is 7...e5, but followers of the Uitelky order usually don't contemplate moving pawns beyond their third rank without a special reason.

8.♗f4 ♘e7 9.♘bd2 0-0 10.♖ad1 b5?

Inconsistent. More in the spirit of the system is 10...b6 11.♘c4 ♗a6.

11.c4 a6 12.c5! ♘e8

Alternatives like 12...d5 13.♗d6 and especially 12...dxc5 13.dxc5, menacing 14.♘c4, are desperate for black.

13.cxd6 ♘xd6 14.♖c1

Taking control of the weakened c5- and c6-squares.

14...a5 15.♘e5 ♗b7 16.♖fd1 a4

Black wrongly believes that white's

light-squared bishop will be out of active play at the b1-h7 diagonal.

17.♗c2 f5

The only possible way to create counterplay, threatening 18...fxe4.

18.♗g5! ♘f7

Now if 18...fxe4 19.♘xe4 ♘df5 20.♘c5 ♘xd4 21.♕e4 ♕d5 22.♖xd4 ♕xe5 23.♕xe5 ♗xe5 24.♖d7 ♗xb2 25.♖b1 and all black's light pieces are hanging.

19.♘xf7 ♖xf7 20.♘f3 h6 21.♗d2!

Utilizes the weakness of the b4-square, where white's bishop will take up a very strong and comfortable position.

21...♔h7

Protecting the two weak pawns at g6 and h6. The dangerous opposition of black king and white's bishop at c2 does not seem to trouble black yet.

22.♗b4 ♘g8?

Black's position is desperate in any case, e.g., 22...fxe4 23.♗xe4 ♘d5 24.♘e5 ♗xe5 25.dxe5 with a superiority or 22...f4 23.♘e5 ♗xe5 24.dxe5 ♕e8 25.♕g4! ♘c8 26.♗b1! intending a3 and ♗a2, but the text loses quickly.

23.♘e5 ♖c7

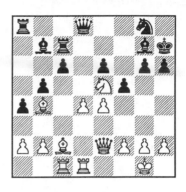

24.♘xg6!

Retribution for ignoring the power of the bishop on c2.

24...♔xg6 25.exf5+ exf5 26.♕e6+!

26.♕g4+? would be a serious inaccuracy because of 26...♕g5 27.♗xf5+ ♔f6 and black is winning.

26...♗f6

If 26...♘f6 or 26...♕f6 27.♗xf5+ mating.

27.♕xf5+ ♔f7 28.♕g6+ ♔e6

The king is dragged out to meet its doom in the center of the board.

29.♖e1+ ♔d5 30.♗b3+

Black resigned in view of 30...axb3 31.♕e4 mate.

1-0

Of course, white's final combination is not too complicated, but it is a methodical one. However there are in the world more complicated and effective combinations based on this topic, e.g., I recommend you to see the missed brilliancy in the Euwe-Smyslov game (see below)

Euwe - Smyslov
World Championship Match Tournament 1948

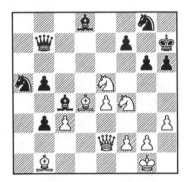

Ex-World Champion Max Euwe had achieved the following position against Vasily Smyslov...

33.♘exg6!!

Euwe had found intuitively the correct prelude to the winning combination. The elegant threat is 34.♘f8 mate. Black must accept the bold sacrifice.

33...fxg6

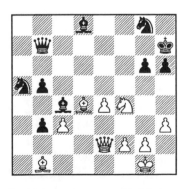

34.♕g4!

Euwe continued 34.♘xg6? - a blunder - as black's king slips away out of fire - very likely Euwe overlooked that after 34...♗xg6 35.♕g4+ ♚f7 36.♕g7+ ♚e8 all black's pieces are protected. He tried 35.e5+ ♚f7 36.♕h5+ but his attack fell short after 36...♚f8 37.f4 ♗b6, Euwe-Smyslov, WCh. M-T 1948.

Sometimes you can sacrifice a first piece intuitively, but a second sac and especially a third one (as in this case) demands precise calculation.

34...♗f7 35.e5 ♗g5

After 35...♘e7 36.e6 ♗e8 37.h4! white wins.

36.e6 ♗e8 37.♘xg6!

The second sacrifice.

37...♗xg6

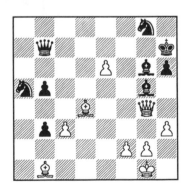

38.♕f5!! ♕g7

The only defense as 38...♗xf5 39.♗xf5 is mate.

39.♕f7!!

The third sacrifice. The self-sacrifice of white's queen is amazing.

39...♕xf7

If 39...♘f6 40.♗xg6+ ♔h8 41.e7 is winning, or 39...♗f6 40.♗xg6+ ♔h8 41.e7 ♕xf7 42.♗xf7 ♘xe7 43.♗xf6+ ♔h7 44.♗xe7 b2 45.♗a2 wins.

40.exf7 ♗xb1 41.f8♘ mate!

Two knights sacrificed to give birth to a third which exacts immediate revenge!

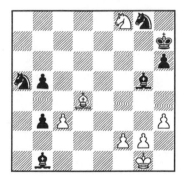

Part VI
Storming The French Fortress

The French Defense after 1.e4 e6 2.d4 d5 is not as popular as the Sicilian with 1...c5 or with those defensive systems which arise from 1...e5 because white obtains a clear space advantage early in the game before black can arrange counterplay. Nevertheless the French Defense has always attracted the attention of strong players in view of its clear strategical motifs and the chances for counterplay offered to black in the middlegame.

The French is an original opening which demands great interpretation and excellent preparation from black if he is to obtain good results. I remember many French masterpieces by the great specialists of this opening, such as Botvinnik, Bronstein, Petrosian, Kortchnoi and Uhlmann. Later on we can add such inventive masters such as Vaganian, Gulko, M. Gurevich, Short and Bareev among others. Each of them has contributed greatly to the theory of the French and introduced many new interesting ideas into its everyday practice.

I invariably used to play 1.e4 and often was faced with the French, playing both 3.♘c3 and 3.♘d2. Here we will look at some games where I played 3.♘c3.

RUBINSTEIN SYSTEM

1.e4 e6 2.d4 d5 3.♘c3 dxe4 4.♘xe4

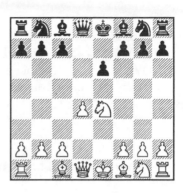

The early exchange 3...dxe4 is premature according to many theorists. For instance: "The text move relaxes the central tension too soon and gives white a good command of the center." S. Gligoric and W. Uhlmann in "The French Defense" - 1975. But the practice of the great "French knight" Tigran Petrosian has shown that black's counterchances are not so bad in skilful hands (for example see his games against Tal (Curacao 1962), Spassky (USSR 1976 and 1977) and Portisch (Palma de Mallorca 1967). I also think of some of the great games by Akiba Rubinstein for whom this system is named.

Shamkovich-Lepioshkin [C10]
Moscow, 1962

4...♘d7

4...♘f6 is really premature since 5.♘xf6+ ♕xf6 (5...gxf6 6.♘f3 is very good for white as black has weakened his kingside and white has two very strong bishops) 6.♘f3 h6 (Necessary as

6...♗d7 allows 7.♗g5 ♕g6 8.♗d3 ♕h5 (if 8...f5 then 9.h4! intending 10.♘e5 or 10.h5 as in Tarrasch-Lasker, Match 1907) 9.h3 winning. A curious trap can occur after 6...b6 7.♗d3 ♗b7? 8.♗g5 ♗xf3 9.♕d2!! winning the queen.) 7.♗d3 (One more trap emerges after 7.h4 ♘c6 8.♗g5? hxg5 9.hxg5 ♕xf3! 10.♕xf3 ♖xh1 when black has full material compensation for the queen and active pieces, e.g., 11.0-0-0 ♘xd4!) ...♗d6 8.0-0 and white is much better.

5.♘f3 ♘gf6 6.♘xf6+ ♘xf6 7.♗g5 ♗e7 8.♗d3

Probably more accurate is 8.♗c4 right away.

8...c5 9.♕e2 0-0 10.0-0-0!?

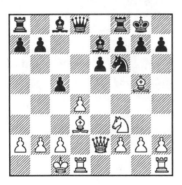

This active move seems to me to be more promising for white than Paul Keres' recommendation of 10.dxc5 ♕a5+ 11.c3 ♕xc5 12.0-0-0 ♖d8 13.♘e5 in ECO, because of 13...h6! 14.♗h4 b6 15.♗xf6 ♗xf6 16.♕e4 ♗b7! 17.♕h7+ ♔f8 and white's attack is hampered. Yet, 14.♗xf6 ♗xf6 15.f4 is an improvement, albeit still unclear after 15...♔f8!? The text allows white

to create even more unpleasant pressure on the d-file.

10...cxd4

Black's primary problem is the development of his bishop on c8. 10...♗d7 is met by the unpleasant 11.dxc5! (threatening 12.♗xf6 followed by 13.♗xh7+. 10...♕a5 looks more sensible intending to meet 11.♗c4 with 11...b5! 12.♗xb5 ♕xa2 with complications, but 11.♔b1 ♗d7 12.♘e5! would be very strong as 12...♖fd8? fails to 13.♗xf6 ♗xf6 14.♗xh7+! ♔xh7 15.♕h5+ ♔g8 16.♕xf7++- winning. Black's best would be 12...♗c6, minimizing white's edge.

11.♗c4

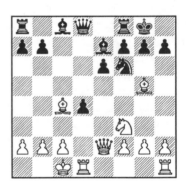

The critical moment. Very likely 11.♔b1! was best, preventing 11...b6 and preparing 12.♘d4. Note that the immediate 11.♘xd4 is wrong as 11...♕xd4! 12.♗xh7+ ♘xh7 13.♖xd4 ♗xg5+ 14.f4 ♗f6 15.♖d3 b6 16.♖h3 g6 gives black three strong minor pieces for the queen.

11...b5?!

This witty attempt to develop the bishop on c8 and seize the initiative should prove ineffective. Black should have played more simply with 11...♕c7 12.♖xd4 b6! completing development.

12.♗xb5 ♕a5 13.♗c4 ♗b7

The attempt to save the d4-pawn with 13...♖d8 backfires after 14.♗f4! intending 15.♗e5.

14.h4 ♖fd8 15.♘xd4 ♗d5

Has black tried to exchange the strong bishop at c4? No, he provoked the next move. We will see later on the reason for this decision. Other attempts are also favorable for white, e.g., 15...h6 16.♗f4 or the even more aggressive 16.♘xe6!? and now 15...♗xg2 16.♘xe6! fxe6 (16...♗xh1 17.♘xd8+- wins) 17.♕xe6+ ♔h8 18.♕xe7 ♖e8 19.♕xf6!+- winning.

16.♔b1 ♗xg2?!

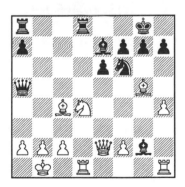

The point of this brave pawn capture at this moment is that the aforementioned attack with 17.♘xe6 no longer works because of 17...fxe6! 18.♕xe6+ ♔h8 19.♕xe7 ♗xh1! White

cannot play 20.♗xf6 or 20.♕xf6 in view of the loose rook at d1 and if 20.♖xh1 ♖e8 21.♕xf6 ♖e1+ and black wins. A fine tactical trap, if my opponent really took it into consideration, but the text had other grounds. 16...♗xc4 17.♕xc4 is definitely bad for black because of the threat of the "family fork" with 18.♘c6. Objectively speaking 16...♖ac8 17.♗b3 ♕b6 (not 17...♗xg2 18.♘xe6 again) was best.

17.♖hg1 ♗d5 18.♕e5!

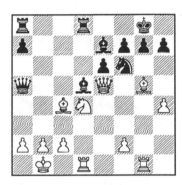

By pinning the bishop at d5, white creates direct threats against the black king (19.♗xf6) and after 18...♗d6 19.♕xf6! gxf6 20.♗d2+ ♔f8 21.♗xa5 white wins. If 18...♔f8 19.♘c6 would be very strong, but what about 18...♘d7?

18...♘d7! 19.♕g3!

Avoiding the exchange combination 19.♕xg7+ ♔xg7 20.♗d2+ which here is favorable to black after 20...♔f8 21.♗xa5 ♗xc4 22.♗xd8 ♗xd8 23.♘c6 ♗d5! White's threats are now very strong and unavoidable. How to parry the simultaneous threats of 20.♗xe7 and 20.♗d2? Here 19...♗f8 fails to 20.♗xd8 ♖xd8 21.♘b3 and 19...♗xg5 loses quickly to 20.♕xg5 g6 21.♘c6+- (or 21.♘f5+-). My opponent used his last chance for counterplay.

19...♗xc4 20.♗xe7 ♕xa2+

We see now why black 5 moves ago forced the prophylactic 15.♔b1 - he can capture the a2-pawn with check.

21.♔c1 g6

In case of 21...♕a1+ 22.♔d2 ♕a5+ white can play 23.c3 g6 24.♗xd8 winning.

22.♗xd8 ♖xd8

23.♕c7!

The winning move, as queen takes control over all critical squares. However, in analyzing this game again I found the secondary forced solution 23.♘c6 which would lead to more complications after 23...♕a1+ 24.♔d2 ♕xb2 25.♘xd8 ♘f6! 26.♕e3! (If 26.♕f4 ♕b4+! is equal as is 26.f3 ♕d4+) ♘d5! 27.♖b1! ♕f6 28.♖b8 (Threat 29.♘xe6+) ...♔g7 29.♖b7 ♘xe3 30.♖xf7+ ♕xf7 31.♘xf7 ♔xf7

32.fxe3+- and white should win the ending thanks to the passed pawn at c2. I have to emphasize that two different solutions in a critical position are not typical for fighting practical games. It means that here white's advantage is really great.

23...♖b8 24.♘b3! ♗xb3

The alternative 24...♖xb3 would not help black since 25.cxb3 ♗xb3 26.♖xd7 ♕a1+ 27.♔d2 ♕xg1 (or 27...♕xb2+ 28.♔e3 winning) 28.♖xf7 ♕d1+ 29.♔c3 and white wins.

25.♖xd7 ♖a8 26.♖d8+ ♖xd8 27.♕xd8+ ♔g7 28.♕d4+ ♔g8 29.♖g3!

White has repulsed all black's threats and with the advantage of the exchange, he can now consolidate his winning advantage.

29...♕a1+ 30.♔d2 ♕a5+ 31.♖c3 ♗d5 32.♕f6 ♗c6 33.♔e3 ♕b5 34.♖b3 ♕c5+ 35.♕d4 ♕f8 36.♕e5 1-0

Shamkovich - Osmanagovic [C11]
Sarajevo, 1965

1.e4 e6 2.d4 d5 3.♘c3 ♘f6 4.♗g5 dxe4

More popular at the present time is the classical line 4...♗e7 5.e5 ♘fd7.

5.♘xe4 ♗e7

The alternative 5...♘bd7 is more flexible, see as an example, Fischer-Petrosian, Stockholm izt 1962.

6.♗xf6 gxf6

This is more ambitious than 6...♗xf6, although the deformation of black's kingside pawns can create some difficulties for him.

7.♗c4!?

The normal continuation is 7.♘f3 b6 8.♗c4. With the text, I was trying to confuse my opponent with threats such as 7...b6 8.d5?! and 8.♕f3?! but 8...♗b7 in the first line and 8...♕xd4 in the second one should destroy white's illusions. After 7...b6, white could transpose to the game with 8.♘f3 ♗b7 9.♕e2 c6.

7...c6?!

Too cautious.

8.♘f3

A good alternative is 8.c3 intending 9.♕h5. Keres-Minev, Varna Ol. 1962, continued 8...f5 9.♘g3 ♕d6 10.♘f3 ♘d7 11.♕e2 ♕f4 12.0-0 0-0 13.♖fe1 and white has the upper hand, e.g., 13...♗d6 14.♗xe6!

8...b6 9.♕e2 ♗b7 10.0-0-0 ♕c7

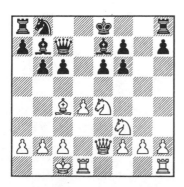

This is one of the critical positions of the Rubinstein Defense. The "book line" is 11.♔b1 ♘d7 12.♖he1 0-0-0 13.♗a6 ♗xa6 14.♕xa6+ ♕b7 with a small plus to white as in Klovan-Petrosian, USSR Ch. 1975. However, white's advantage in this line is not too considerable (Petrosian, in fact, won his game). Can white utilize his better development in a more radical way?

11.♘fd2!?

Freeing a path to the h5-square for the white queen: an attractive post for her in similar pawn structures found in the Sicilian and French Defenses. This action prevents queenside castling by black as black is unable to counterattack white's center. The power of this plan is demonstrated in a variation such as 11...♘d7 12.♕h5 ♘f8 13.g3 ♘g6 14.f4 0-0-0 15.f5! and white is winning. The text leads to dynamic and interesting play.

11...f5

Too risky is 11...♘d7 12.♕h5 f5 13.♗xe6! fxe4 14.♕xf7+ ♔d8 15.♘xe4 ♖f8 16.♕xh7 ♕f4+ 17.♔b1 ♘f6 18.♘xf6 ♕xf6 19.d5! with a very strong attack.

12.♘g3 ♕d6?

An inaccuracy in a new and complicated position. Black should have tried 12...♘d7 13.♖he1 (Idea ♘xf5) ...♕d6 (13...♘f6 fails to 14.♗xe6! fxe6 15.♕xe6 ♖f8 16.♘xf5+-) avoiding an unpleasant attack by ♕h5. However, it is not really fatal for black, as we shall see.

13.♕h5!

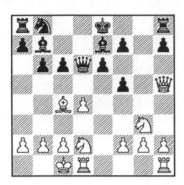

Forcing black to castle kingside, where his king will find life uncomfortable. One point is 13...♘d7 14.♗xe6! ♛xe6 15.♖he1 ♛g6 (15...♛xa2 16.♘xf5+-) 16.♛e2! with a clear plus. So white's threats at e6 and f5 are in the air and black must be on alert. Nevertheless, 13.♖he1 ♘d7 14.♘f3, holding black's center, seems to be more sound.

13...0-0 14.♛h6

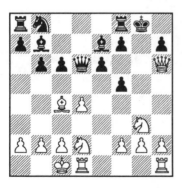

Threatening 16.♘h5. But what about 14...♛xd4 protecting the critical f6- and g7-squares? If 15.♘h5 ♛g4! would be a strong reply to safeguard black's king. White's best attacking method would be 15.♗xe6! (again!) ...fxe6

16.♛xe6+ ♖f7 17.♘de4! (better than 17.♘xf5 ♛f6) with a decisive attack.

14...♚h8

If 14...♘d7 15.♘h5 ♗f6 16.g4! with a strong attack.

15.♘f3

The knight returns to "his" position so as to participate in the attack. The alternative 15.♘h5 ♖g8 16.♘f6 is not dangerous for black because of 16...♗xf6 (16...♖g7?? fails to 17.♛xg7+ or 17.♘e8) 17.♛xf6+ ♖g7 18.♘f3 ♘d7 19.♛h4 ♖eg8 and black holds. Instead, if 19...♖g4?! then 20.♘e5! would be strong.

15...♘d7 16.h4! ♖g8 17.♘g5

17...♗xg5+?

The opening of the h-file is fatal for black. More stubborn is 17...♖g7! when 18.♘h5?? would be a criminal blunder since 18...♗xg5+ 19.hxg5 ♖g6 traps white's queen. Again and again, you must make certain to be absolutely accurate in "winning" positions, where plenty of hidden traps await those who are careless. After 17...♖g7, white should play 18.♔b1!, followed by 18...♘f6 19.♕xh5 ♖f8 21.♕h6 with some pressure.

18.hxg5 ♖g7 19.♔b1

19.♘xf5 gives nothing after 19...♕f4+ 20.♘e3 ♕xg5. Now 20.♘xf5 is a real threat.

19...♕e7 20.f4!

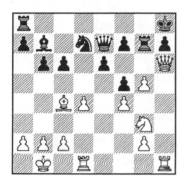

After this consolidating move, white completely dominates. The alternative 20.♘h5 is wrong since 20...♖g6! forces a draw after 21.♕xh7+ ♔xh7 22.♘f6+ ♔g7 23.♖h7+ ♔f8 24.♖h8+ ♔g7. Note, however that 20...♖xg5? fails to 21.♘f6!+-.

20...♘f8 21.♕h3 ♖d8 22.♘h5 ♖g6 23.♕c3!

A sudden shift in the attack. Major things are about to happen on the long diagonal. The primary threat is 24.d5+.

23...♔g8 24.g4!

Opening lines for a decisive attack, for if 24...fxg4 25.♗d3 c5 26.dxc5 ♗xh1 27.♖xh1 bxc5 28.♗xg6 fxg6 29.♘f6+ ♔f7 30.♘xg4 and white wins. The straightforward and immediate 24.d5? is a mistake after 24...exd5! 25.♘f6+ ♖xf6 26.gxf6 ♕d6 and black holds.

24...c5 25.gxf5 cxd4 26.♕e1!

More accurate than 26.♕h3 exf5 and black can put up some resistance.

26...♗xh1 27.fxg6 ♗f3

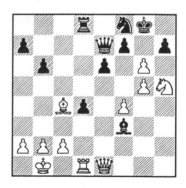

Here comes the final combination based on the long diagonal theme.

28.♘f6+ ♔g7

If 28...♔h8 29.g7+ ♔xg7 30.♕e5+-.

29.♕e5! ♘xg6

29...♗xd1 fails to 30.♘d5++- and 29...♔xg6 to 30.♗d3++-.

30.♘h5+ 1-0

MacCUTCHEON VARIATION

1.e4 e6 2.d4 d5 3.♘c3 ♘f6 4.♗g5 ♗b4!?

This active method of counterplay has been well known for a long time, but its theory still contains some "white spots" and unclear assessments. It is not very popular at present although the black bishop's development at b4 fully corresponds to contemporary opening practice. The major line is 5.e5 h6 6.♗d2 ♗xc3 7.bxc3 ♘e4 where black (according to ECO C12) has sufficient counterchances, mainly because he can exchange off the strong bishop at d2. A question is: can White prevent his bishop from being exchanged to keep it for an eventual kingside attack? The rather strange move of D. Yanovsky, 6.♗e3!?, attracted my attention many years ago, dsepite its poor theoretical reputation. I have tried it 5 or 6 times against strong opposition with good results. Let us examine further......

5.e5 h6 6.♗e3 ♘e4 7.♕g4

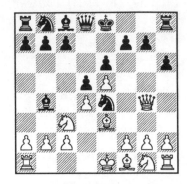

The key position of Yanovsky's variation. Black may choose between 7...g6 and 7...♔f8 (I have met both in my career).

I present two of my most dynamic games in this variation.

Shamkovich-Chistiakov [C12]
Moscow TCh. 1961.

7...g6 8.a3

An improvement over the classical line 8.♗d3 ♘xc3 9.♗d2 (or 9.a3 ♘a2+ 10.♗d2 ♗xd2+ 11.♔xd2 c5 12.♖xa2 ♘c6 with advantage to black) ...♘xa2 10.c3 ♘xc3 11.bxc3 ♗e7 and black was better in Yanovsky-Marshall, Ostende 1907.

8...♗xc3+ 9.bxc3 c5

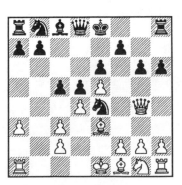

Accepting the gambit with 9...♘xc3 10.♗d3 ♘c6 can be dangerous after 11.h4 ♘e7 (11...♕e7 12.h5 g5 13.f4! was good for white in Klovan - Makarichev, USSR 1978.) 12.f3! with advantage in Kurajica-Dvorecki, Wijk aan Zee I 1976.

10.♗d3 ♕a5 11.♘e2 cxd4 12.♗xd4

White's pieces are well developed and ready to attack the weakened black kingside.

12...♘c5?!

Provoking the following piece sacrifice. More reliable was 12...♗d7 or 12...♘c6.

13.0-0 ♘c6 14.♗xg6! ♖g8

Of course, black cannot take the bishop immediately - 14...fxg6? 15.♕xg6+ ♔f8 when either 16.♗e3 or 16.f4 gives white a strong attack.

15.♗xf7+! ♔xf7 16.♕h5+ ♔e7 17.♕xh6

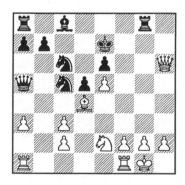

White already has three pawns for the piece with a raging attack, but the success of white's intuitive sacrifice depends on whether black has chances to evacuate his king to the queenside and consolidate his forces. My opponent almost succeeded.

17...♔d8 18.♘f4 ♘e7

Intending to protect the kingside. 18...♖e8 looks more sensible, but it fails to 19.♕f6+ ♔c7 (19...♖e7 20.♘g6+-) 20.♘xd5+!+-.

19.♖fd1!

Threatening to attack the d5-pawn with 20.c4. Such forcing threats are the best tactical resource in positions where the opponent has not finished his development. 19.♗xc5 ♕xc5 20.♘xe6+ ♗xe6 21.♕xe6 is weaker.

19...♗d7 20.c4

Consistent. 20.♗xc5 ♕xc5 21.♕xe6 ♖f8 22.♕h6 ♔c7 looks attractive but is unclear.

20...♖c8

Not 20...dxc4? 21.♗xc5 ♕xc5 22.♘xe6++-.

21.♕h4?

A serious error. Correct was 21.cxd5 exd5 (or 21...♘xd5 22.♘xd5 exd5 23.♕f6+ ♔c7 24.♕d6+ ♔d8 25.e6 wins) 22.c4! with a decisive attack.

21...♘e4 22.cxd5 ♘g5!

I overlooked this nice resource. The threat of 22...♘f3+ gives black a chance to organize a counterattack.

23.♔h1

Not 23.♘xe6+ ♗xe6 24.dxe6 ♘f3+
25.♔h1 ♘xh4 26.♗b6+ ♔e8 27.♗xa5
♖xg2-+.

23...♘f5 24.♕h5 ♔c7

Intending to safeguard the king, and
at the same time, to connect the rooks.
Other tries are likely to favor white, e.g.,
24...exd5 25.♘xd5 ♘xd4 (if 25...♖xc2
26.e6! or 25...♖c4 26.♘f6) 26.♖xd4
♕c5 27.♖ad1 with the initiative.

**25.♕e2 ♔b8 26.c4 ♕a6
27.♖ac1**

Black has consolidated his forces and
is now on top. He has the option of
pursuing a number of promising
continuations, e.g., 27...exd5 28.♘xd5
♘xd4 29.♖xd4 ♘e6; 27...♘xd4;
27...♗a4 28.♖d2 ♗b3; 27...♕a4 with
sufficient counterplay in all lines.

27...♕xa3?!

My opponent - a glorious chess
veteran who always sought active play
- had planned to transfer his queen to the
kingside for a counterattack, but he
underestimated the threats on the other
side of the board. This was a super-bold
idea although 27...♘xd4 28.♖xd4
♕xa3 seems a better way of capturing
the a-pawn.

28.♗b2!

Avoiding the trap 28.♖a1? ♘xd4!
29.♖xa3 ♘xe2-+.

**28...♕e7 29.♖a1 ♕h7 30.h3
♕h4?!**

Attacking the white knight, a key
element in white's king fortress.
However, black could play more
interestingly - utilizing the long-ranging
queen at h7, e.g., 30...♘e4!? (Idea
31...♘eg3+) 31.♖a3 ♖g3! but 32.♖e1!
still wins for white, or 30...exd5
31.cxd5 ♖c2!? 32.♕xc2! ♘g3+ 33.fxg3
♕xc2 34.♗d4 a6 35.e6! and white is
still on top. As we shall see, black's
counterattack is by no means naive in
concept.

31.♗c1 ♖cf8 32.c5

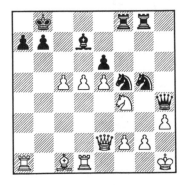

With the horrible threat of 33.c6. If
now 32...exd5 33.e6! My opponent
now tried a desperate counterattack.

32...♘xh3!? 33.♘xh3 exd5 34.e6 ♗c6 35.♗f4+!

A horrible blunder would be 35.♕e5+ ♔c8 36.♖xa7? because of 36...♕xh3+!! 37.gxh3 d4+ 38.♔h2 ♖g2+ and black wins.

35...♔c8 36.♖xa7 ♔d8

Now 36...♕xh3+ doesn't work because of 37.gxh3 d4+ 38.f3 ♘g3+ 39.♔h2 ♘xe2 40.♖a8#.

37.♗d6 1-0

Black resigned as mate can only be avoided by great material loss.

Even more exciting was this next game where my opponent (one of Moscow's best masters) played 7...♔f8, where white's fierce kingside attack was met by black's ferocious queenside counterattack.

Shamkovich - Prokhorovich [C12]
Moscow Ch., 1961

1.e4 e6 2.d4 d5 3.♘c3 ♘f6 4.♗g5 ♗b4 5.e5 h6 6.♗e3 ♘e4 7.♕g4 ♔f8

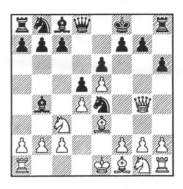

This alternative to 7...g6 seems to be more reliable for black, despite the unavailabity of castling.

8.a3!?

The same idea as the previous game. With the pawn sacrifice white can achieve a significant initiative. After 8.♘ge2 c5 9.0-0-0 ♘xc3 10.♘xc3 ♘c6 11.♘b1 c4 black got the superior position in the old game Spielmann-Vidmar, Vienna 1907. Forget about the c3-pawn - the Chess Terrorist understands the advantages in development and the quick preparation of an attack.

8...♗xc3+ 9.bxc3 ♘xc3 10.♗d3 b6!?

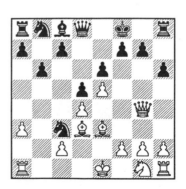

An interesting concept aimed at

exchanging off one of white's strong bishops with ...♗a6. Hort has played 10...c5 against me but did not equalize after 11.dxc5 ♕a5? 12.♗d2 ♕a4 13.♕b4! ♕xb4 14.axb4+− (Shamkovich-Hort, Marianske Lasne 1965). However the up-to-date recommendation of 11...♘c6 12.♘f3 f5! is an improvement. More promising for white is likely 12.♕f4 f5 13.h4.

11.h4 ♗a6 12.♖h3

Threatening 13.♖g3 g6 14.♗xg6 winning.

12...h5

12...♗xd3 is met strongly by 13.cxd3 ♘d7 14.h5 (Idea 15.♖g3). However, after the text, the g5-square becomes weak and serves as a nice outpost for the white pieces.

13.♕f4 ♕e7 14.♖f3

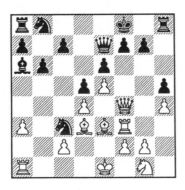

White now threatens 15.♗xg6 (and also ♘h3-g5). Therefore black's reply is practically forced.

14...♔g8 15.♘h3 ♗xd3 16.cxd3 ♘a6

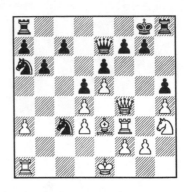

16...♘d7 fails to 17.♖c1.

17.♕g3!

Liberating the g5-square for the bishop.

17...c5!

Beginning a sharp counterattack.

18.♗g5 ♕e8

If 18...♕f8 19.♘f4 intending both 20.♘xe6 and 20.♘g6.

19.♗f6 ♕f8 20.♕g5 ♘b5

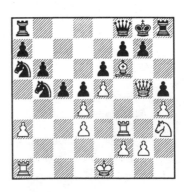

A tense and uncompromising position has been reached. If only black can repulse white's basic threats, he can look forward to success.

21.♖g3 ♖h7 22.♘f4 ♘xd4

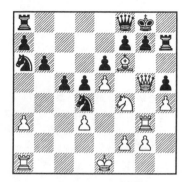

The black knight re-enters the fray. Now white's attack is difficult.

23.♗e7!

Not 23.♘xh5 g6! 24.♗e7 (24.♘f4 ♕h6-+) ...♖xh5-+.

23...f6!

My opponent once again finds the best defense. 23...♕e8 loses to 24.♘xh5 (Threat 25.♘f6+) ...♔h8 25.♘xg7 and wins.

24.exf6

The alternative 24.♗xf6 is weaker because of 24...♘f5!

24...♕f7 25.♘g6!

With the new threat of 26.♘e5.

25...♘c6

25...gxf6 26.♗xf6 is crushing.

26.♔f1!

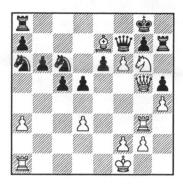

26...♘c7

Black also brings his forces to the fight. A blunder would be 26...♘xe7 27.♘xe7+ ♔f8 28.♘g6+ ♔e8 29.♖f3! and white wins.

27.♖e1 ♘b5 28.fxg7 ♘bd4

Black's knights are very active and are willing to fall in battle to secure the release of their monarch.

29.♗f6 ♘f5

Necessary because of the threat of 30.♘f8. Now black threatens both 30...♘xg3+ and 30...♖h6.

30.♖f3

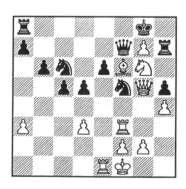

Parrying both threats. The battle reaches its peak.

30...♖h6!?

Forcing further complications which are eventually advantageous to white. But black did not have anything better, e.g., 30...♘xg7 31.♗xg7 ♕xg7 32.♖xe6 ♘d4 33.♖e7+- or 30...♖e8 31.♘f8!+-.

31.♖xf5! ♕xg6

The alternative 31...♖xg6 fails to 32.♕xh5 ♖xg7 33.♗xg7 ♕xh5 (33...♕xf5 34.♕h8+ ♔f7 35.♕xa8+-) 34.♖xh5 ♔xg7 35.♖xe6+-.

32.♖xe6 ♘d4

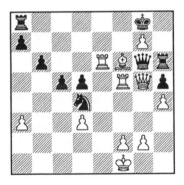

Now the position is transferred prosaically to a won ending for white.

33.♕xg6 ♖xg6 34.♖xh5 ♘xe6

If 34...♖xf6 35.♖xf6 ♔xg7 36.♖d6+-.

35.♖h8+ ♔f7 36.♖xa8 ♘xg7 37.♗xg7 ♔xg7 38.♖xa7+ 1-0

TARRASCH SYSTEM [C07]

Shamkovich-Seirawan
US Championship, 1980

This exciting game, played with the Tarrasch variation, ♘d2 (which according to theory is "quiet" and "peaceful") was a wonderfully sharp battle.

1.e4 e6 2.d4 d5 3.♘d2 c5 4.♘gf3 cxd4 5.exd5 ♕xd5 6.♗c4 ♕d6 7.0-0 ♘f6 8.♘b3 ♘c6 9.♘bxd4 ♘xd4 10.♘xd4 a6 11.♖e1!?

This sharp move, intending ♘f5 or action against e6, was introduced by that virtuoso of sharp openings, Paul Keres, against Pal Benko in Curacao, 1962, when white landed a big advantage after 11...♗e7 (the book recommendation) 12.c3 e5? 13.♘f3 ♕xd1 14.♖xd1 e4 (14...♗g4 15.♖e1 wins) 15.♘e5. Black's 12th move was, of course, a positional error, activating the bishop at c4. ECO suggests 12...0-0 13.♕e2 (threatening 14.♘f5) ...♕c7 14.♗g5 ♘d5 (14...♘g4? 15.♕xg4 ♗xg5 16.♗xe6!, Peters-Berry, USA 1976) 15.♗xe7 ♘xe7 16.♖ad1, giving white only a slight advantage. I am not so sure this is true. How is black to finish developing his pieces? Crushing is 16...♗d7 17.♘xe6!, and yielding little more in either line is 16...b5 17.♗d3 ♗b7 18.♘xe6! fxe6 19.♕xe6+ ♖f7 20.♗xh7+, followed by: 20...♔xh7 21.♕xf7 ♕c6 22.f3; or 20...♔f8 21.♖d7 ♕c6 22.♕xf7+!! Instead of 14...♘d5, Jack Peters recommends 14...♗d7, although white is clearly better anyway after 15.♗d3 ♖fe8 16.♕f3 ♖ad8 17.♕h3!

Curiously, the logical and strong 11.♖e1 has been ignored for many years in favor of the theoretical lines 11.b3 (also very strong), 11.c3, and 11.♗b3. This game is still one of the newest examinations of 11.♖e1.

My young opponent chooses the most energetic and thematic response.

11...♕c7 12.♗d3

A common alternative is 12.♗b3. Huebner-Nogueiras, Barcelona 1989 then continued 12...♗d6 13.♘f5! ♗xh2+ 14.♔h1 ♔f8 15.g3 exf5 16.♗f4 ♕c6+ 17.♔xh2 ♗e6 and black holds, but recently some master improved white's idea by 15.♕d4! and seized the initiative, e.g. 15...exf5 16.♕xf6! or 15...h5 16.♘xg7! ♔xg7 17.♗g5 with an attack.

12...♗d6 13.♘f5!?

This was an innovation, but a very natural one. Opening theory and commentators suggest 13.h3 (see Adams-Gulko, Groningen PCA 1993 in the Supplementary Games). Instead, white sacrifices the pawns for an attack.

13...♗xh2+ 14.♔h1

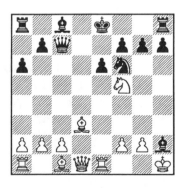

14...h5?!

Not 14...0-0 15.♘xg7! ♔xg7 16.♕d2! with a strong attack. More circumspect is the cooler 14...♔f8!, as 15.♘xg7? ♔xg7 16.♕d2 h6! is to black's advantage and if 15.g3!? exf5 16.♗f4 ♕c6+ 17.♔xh2 ♗e6 gives black a slight edge, but not 17...b5? 18.♗xb5!! and white wins.

15.g3 ♔f8 16.♗f4 ♕b6 17.♗d6+

Black's position is already critical.

17...♔e8

Black loses the queen after 17...♔g8 18.♘e7+.

18.♘xg7+

Simpler is 18.♔xh2 ♕xf2+ 19.♔h3.

18...♔d7 19.♗e5 ♘g4

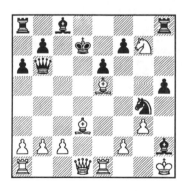

White has a choice of winning ways, e.g., 20.♗f5+ ...♔e7 21.♗xg4! hxg4 22.♘f5+, followed by 23.♗xh8. Even more convincing is 20.♗b5+ ♔e7 21.♘f5+ ♔f8 (21...exf5 22.♗d4+)

22.♗d4! ♕xb5 (or 22...♕c7 23.♕d2!)
23.♗g7+ ♔e8 24.♘d6+, etc.

20.♗f1+?

Time pressure.

♔e7 21.♗d4 ♕a5 22.♗g2 ♖d8
23.♕f3!

White is still better.

23...f6!

Seirawan never loses self-control in
difficult positions.

24.c3?

And now 24.♘f5+! ♔f7 25.♘h6+
would be crushing.

24...e5!

And the game ended in a draw after
a crazy mutual time-scramble, spoiling
my shot at a nice miniature.

25.♘xh5!? ♖h8 26.b4 ♕c7
27.♗h3 ♕c6! 28.♕xc6 bxc6
29.♗c5+ ♔f7 30.f3 ♗xg3!
31.♘xg3 ♖xh3+ 32.♔g2 ♖h2+
33.♔g1 ♖h3 34.♔g2 ♖h2+
35.♔g1 ½-½

This exciting game with new analysis
clears up some of the questions
concerning the attack with ♖e1 and
♘f5. The latest conclusion is: the
sacrifice of the h2-pawn is questionable
in both main lines; 12.♗d3 since
14...Kf8! and 12.♗b3 since 14...0-0!
Therefore most players prefer 13.h3.

SUPPLEMENTAL GAMES

Wolff - Gulko [C07]
USA Ch., 1993

1.e4 e6 2.d4 d5 3.♘d2 c5
4.exd5 ♕xd5 5.♘gf3 cxd4
6.♗c4 ♕d6 7.0-0 ♘f6 8.♘b3
♘c6 9.♘bxd4 ♘xd4 10.♘xd4
a6 11.♗b3 ♕c7 12.♖e1 ♗d6
13.♘f5 ♗xh2+ 14.♔h1 0-0!
15.♘xg7 ♖d8! 16.♕f3 ♔xg7
17.g3 b5 18.♔xh2 ♗b7
19.♕f4 ♕c6 20.♖g1 ♖d1!
21.♗e3! ♖xa1 22.♕h6+ ♔g8
23.♕g5+ ♔f8 24.♕c5+ ♔e8
25.♕xc6+ ♗xc6 26.♗xa1
♘g4+ 27.♔h3 ♘xe3 28.fxe3
♖d8 29.a4 b4 30.♗c4 a5
31.♗b5 ♖c8 32.♗d3 ♔e7
33.g4?! ♖g8 34.♔h4 h6
35.♖f1 ♖g5 36.b3 ♖e5 37.♖e1
f6 38.♔g3 h5 39.gxh5 ♖xh5
40.e4 ♔d6 41.♔f4 ♔c5 42.e5
f5 43.♗c4 ♖h4+ 44.♔g5
♖xc4! 45.bxc4 ♔xc4 46.♖d1
♗xa4 47.♖d6 ♗xc2 48.♖xe6
♗a4! 49.♖a6 ♔b5 50.♖a8 b3
51.e6 ♔b4 52.♖b8+ ♔a3
53.♔xf5 b2 0-1

Adams - Gulko [C07]
Groningen PCA, 1993

1.e4 e6 2.d4 d5 3.♘d2 c5
4.♘gf3 cxd4 5.exd5 ♕xd5
6.♗c4 ♕d6 7.0-0 ♘f6 8.♘b3
♘c6 9.♘bxd4 ♘xd4 10.♘xd4
a6 11.c3 ♕c7 12.♗b3 ♗d6
13.h3 0-0 14.♖e1 b5 15.♗g5
♗b7 16.♗c2 ♘d5 17.♕h5 g6
18.♕h4 ♗h2+ 19.♔h1 ♗f4
20.♗e4 ♖ab8 21.♖ad1 ♗xg5
22.♕xg5 ♘b6 23.♗xb7 ♕xb7

24.♘f3 ♘d5 25.♕h6 ♖fd8
26.♖d4 ♕e7 27.♖h4 ♘f6
28.♘e5 ♖d6 29.♘g4 ♖bd8
30.♘xf6+ ♕xf6 31.♕xh7+
♔f8 32.♕h6+ ♔g8 33.♖f4
♕g7 34.♕g5 ♖d2 35.♕e7 ♕f8
36.♖xe6 fxe6 37.♕xe6+ ♔g7
38.♕e5+ ♔g8 39.♖xf8+ ♖xf8
40.♕g5 ♖fxf2 41.♕xg6+ ♔h8
42.♕h6+ ♔g8 43.♕xa6 ♖xb2
44.a3 ♔h7 45.♕c6 ♖fc2 46.h4
♖c1+ 47.♔h2 ♖bc2 48.♕xb5
♖xc3 49.a4 ♖c4 50.♕h5+♔g7
51.♕g5+ ♔h7 52.a5 ♖c7
53.a6 ♖1c6 54.♕e3 ♖c4
55.♕d3+ ♔g7 56.♕g3+ 1-0

Part VII
Total War!

Our final excursion examines some spectacular fighting games with immense tactical complications and ferocious attacks and counterattacks in the middlegame - I often think of such encounters as TOTAL WAR! This type of chess struggle is uncompromising to the bitter end where the resolution to a crisis is often resolved by a spectacular or unexpected resource. I present to the readers four examples of all out no-holds barred TOTAL WAR!

Shamkovich - Hort [B14]
Leningrad, USSR, 1967

1.e4 c6 2.d4 d5 3.exd5 cxd5 4.c4

The Panov Attack, which is still popular today.

4...♘f6 5.♘c3 e6 6.♘f3 ♘c6

More common is 6...♗e7 7.cxd5 ♘xd5 8.♗d3 a'la Queen's Gambit Accepted or Tarrasch Defense.

7.c5 ♗e7 8.♗b5 ♗d7!?

Something new. After 8...0-0 9.♗g5 the game could transpose to the famous Botvinnik-Kmoch game (Leningrad, 1934) where 9...♘e4 did not equalize.

9.0-0 0-0 10.♖e1 a6

More cautious is 10...♘e4 aspiring to simplifications, but my opponent had more aggressive ideas in mind. An interesting alternative was 10...b6 but it seems 11.♘e5! would be a strong reply.

11.♗d3 b6 12.cxb6 ♕xb6 13.♘e5 ♖fc8!?

This looks normal - to consolidate further with 14...♗e8, but in fact Hort erred here. Curiously this is just the kind of mistake that can initiate a "Total War." 13...♗e8 was correct, but not 13...♘xd4? 14.♗e3+- or 13...♘xe5 14.dxe5+-.

14.♘xd5! exd5

Perhaps Hort was concerned about 14...♘xd5 15.♗xh7+ ♔xh7 16.♕h5+ ♔g8 17.♕xf7+ ♔h7 but now what?? Perpetual check?? If 18.♗h6 then 18...♗f6 19.♘xd7 ♕xd4 is unclear. Best seems 15.♘xd7 ♕xd4 16.♘e5! with advantage to white.

15.♘xc6 ♖xc6 16.♖xe7

So white has won a pawn, maintaining the bishop pair. However, the weakness of the d4-pawn and the unstable position of the rook at e7 give black good chances for counterplay.

16...♗e6

Trapping the white rook - threatening 17...♔f8. Now white seeks to rescue his rook.

17.♕a4

Intending to meet 17...♔f8 with 18.♕a3. A terrible blunder would be 17.b3 ♕b4!

17...♔h8

My opponent is bent on snaring the rook on e7 - the threat is 18...♞g8! More sensible is likely 17...♖ac8 18.♗f4 ♕xb2 19.♖f1=.

18.♕b3

This move seemed to me to be the only one, but 18.♗d2 deserves attention as well. After 18...♞g8 19.♗a5 ♕xb2 20.♕xc6 ♕xa1+ 21.♗f1 ♖c8 22.♖c7 the position is about equal.

18...♕xd4

Now black's queen becomes very active.

19.♗e3 ♕h4 20.♖a7 ♖ac8

20...♖xa7 21.♕b8+ ♖c8 22.♕xa7 is very good for white.

21.h3

21.g3?! is dubious as the light squares become too weak, e.g., 21...♕h5! with the idea 22...♞g4.

21...♞e4!?

Now black threatens to crush white right away with 22...♗xh3 23.gxh3 ♖g6+ or 22...d4. Also dangerous was

21...d4 followed by 22.♕a4 ♖c4!! 23.♗xc4 dxe3 24.♗b3 ♕xf2 with a tremendous attack. Better is 22.♕b4 ♖c4 23.♗xc4 dxe3 24.fxe3 ♗xc4 25.♖c1 with a small edge for white.

22.♕a4! ♗xh3!?

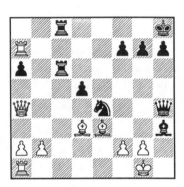

A fascinating tactical struggle evolves from this point on with chances for both sides. The threat is 23...♗xg2. White cannot capture the bishop with 23.gxh3 since 23...♖g6+ 24.♔h2 ♖g3! 25.♗f1 ♖xe3 wins for black. If 23.♗f1 ♖g6! would be very strong, while 23.♖xf7 fails to 23...♗xg2! 24.♔xg2 ♕g4+ winning either the queen after 25.♔f1 ♞g3+ or the rook after 25.♔h2 ♕h5+.

23.♖xa6!!

A significant move, which prevents the ...♖g6 threat, protects white's queen and at the same time threatens 24.♖xc6. Additionally the text prevents another threat of 23...♖c1+ 24.♖xc1 ♖xc1+ 25.♗f1 (25.♗xc1?? ♕xf2+-+) and white wins using the motif of the back-rank weakness. Desperate sacrifices such as 25...♖xf1+ won't work as after 26.♔xf1 ♗xg2+ 27.♔xg2

♕g4+ 28.♔f1 ♕h3+ 29.♔e2 ♕g4+ 30.♔d3 the white king slips away from pursuit. Nor will the bold attempt 23...♗xg2 work. After 24.♔xg2 ♕g4+ 25.♔f1 ♖xa6 26.♕xa6 ♘g3+!? 27.♔e1 ♕b4+ 28.♗d2 ♖e8+ 29.♔d1 white wins, although this puzzling line could deserve further examination.

So white has achieved a great advantage?? No! It is not clear yet at all, because black's pieces are very active and the real skirmish around white's king is about to begin.

23...♕g4 24.♗f1 ♖xa6 25.♕xa6 d4?!

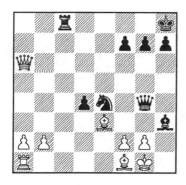

The post-mortem analysis suggested that black's position is dangerously close to losing. During the game we were both entranced by this advance of the d-pawn. We both thought that 26.♗xd4 favored black after 26...♘d2 or 26...♘g5 with the terrible threat of 27...♘f3+ 27.♔h1 ♗xg2+ mating. Actually the first attempt should be met by 27.♕d3! ♘xf1 28.♕xh3 winning, and the second one with 27.♕e2! ♕xd4 28.gxh3 with a small edge for white. Obviously black needs to make "luft" so correct was 25...h6! followed by

26.♕d3 ♖c6 or 26.f3 ♕g3 27.♕d3 (27.♗d4 ♔g8 28.fxe4? ♖c2 wins for black) ♘g5 with a double-edged game. Note that 26.♗xh6 ♘xf2! 27.♔xf2? ♖c2+- wins for black. Back to the game, where I opted for the complicated 26.f3!?

26.f3!? ♕g3 27.♖d1

White again uses the weakness of the back rank, for if 27...dxe3 28.♕xc8+! mating. Yet the simple 27.♗xd4 is also possible as 27...♖c2 fails to 28.♕a8+ ♖c8 29.♕xe4.

27...♘c5 28.♕b6 ♘e6!

Black now threatens ...♗xg2 and ...♘f4.

29.♗xd4!

Here we go. Frankly I could not calculate everything here, I just trusted my instinct and the counterattacking resources that I felt were lurking in the position.

29...♗xg2?!

This almost loses. More practical chances were provided by 29...♘f4! intending 30.♖d2 (If 30.♗f2 ♕g5) ...♗xg2! 31.♖xg2 ♘xg2 32.♗f2! (Not 32.♗xg2? ♖c1#) ♕xf3 33.♗xg2 ♕d1+ 34.♔h2 ♕h5+ 35.♗h3 ♕e5+ with a draw. However, the fine 30.♗e5! is winning, e.g., 30...♘e2+ 31.♔h1 ♗xg2+ 32.♗xg2 ♕h4+ 33.♗h2 ♘g3+ 34.♔g1 ♘e2+ 35.♔f1+- and black cannot capture the bishop at h2.

30.♗f2!

Bad is 30.♗xg2 ♘f4. Also not good is 30.♗e5 ♕xe5 (30...♕xf3? 31.♖c1!+-) 31.♗xg2 g5. I would like to emphasize that the difference between winning and losing in Total War! games is hardly perceptible.

30...♕xf3 31.♖d3!

More accurate than 31.♖c1 ♖d8 32.♗xg2 ♖d1+ 33.♖xd1 ♕xd1 with drawing chances.

31...♕f5!

The heroic bishop at g2 is still invulnerable.

32.♖c3! ♖d8?

Hort is the first to go down to the pressure. 32...♗c6! left him chances to escape, e.g., 33.♖xc6 ♕g4+ 34.♗g2 ♕d1+ 35.♔h2 ♕h5+ 36.♗h3 ♕e5+ etc. A fitting and fair outcome to our dramatic struggle.

33.♗xg2

The game is over, as 33...♖d1+ is met by 34.♗f1 ♕g4+ 35.♖g3.

33...h5

Too late - this desperate counterattack is insufficient.

34.♗f1 ♖d2 35.♕e3 ♖d4 36.♗d3 ♕g4+ 37.♔h2 ♖d8 38.♕e4!

Removing the queens and black's fading hopes because of the mate threat.

38...♘g5 39.♕xg4 hxg4 40.♔g2 g6 41.♗h4 1-0

I have crossed swords over the board

with the great David Bronstein about a dozen times in different events since 1942 when we were 18-19 years old. Almost all of our battles have been uncompromising. Our unofficial match stands at +4 =4 -4 unless I fail to recall some other games. Will we meet again?? I remember with pleasure some details of our chess duels. Tbilisi 1942 (our first game - which I won.), games from strong USSR Championships, the Moscow Championship of 1964 where we tied for first place (I succeeded in our individual encounter), the ensuing playoff match where David triumphed +2 -1 =3 and Amsterdam 1967 (he beat me) amongst others. I am proud to be an admirer of this uniquely talented chess artist. I present to the reader one of my most memorable games against this legend.

Bronstein - Shamkovich [A13]
USSR Ch. Leningrad, 1960

1.c4 e6 2.♘f3 d5 3.e3 ♘f6 4.b3 c5 5.cxd5 exd5 6.d4?! ♘c6 7.♗e2 cxd4 8.♘xd4 ♗b4+ 9.♗d2 ♗d6!

Now white must spend a couple of tempi to improve the position of the bishop on d2.

10.♘xc6 bxc6 11.♘c3 0-0 12.0-0 ♗f5 13.g3 ♕d7 14.♖e1 h5

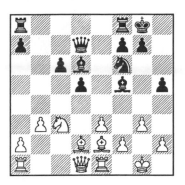

The h-pawn is used as a battering ram in a classical attack against the king's fortress.

15.♗c1 h4 16.♗b2 hxg3 17.hxg3

White has managed to strengthen the position of his dark-squared bishop, but white's king position has become weakened. Nevertheless, the demolition of white's kingside will be no easy task.

17...♘g4!

Now 18...♗xg3 is a real threat.

18.♗f3

White organizes the strong counterthreat e3-e4. 18.e4 at once is premature because of 18...♗xg3 19.fxg3 ♕d6 20.♕d3 ♕c5+-+.

18...♖ae8 19.♖c1 ♕e6 20.e4! ♗c5!

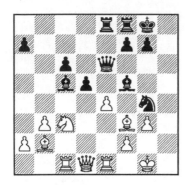

The beginning of a real "Total War" which flares up with great intensity even to the end of the game.

21.♗xg4 ♗xg4 22.♕d2

The alternative 22.♕d3 is weaker because of 22...f5 23.exd5 ♕xe1+ 24.♖xe1 ♖xe1+ 25.♔g2 f4! and black has much the better game.

22...♗f3 23.♕f4

If 23.♕g5 f6 24.♕h4 ♔f7! threatening 25...♖h8.

23...f5! 24.e5

White cannot play 24.♕xf3 because 24...fxe4 gives black a crushing attack.

24...♗e4

Who is better? Black's ideas include both ...♕g6-h5 and ...♗e7 followed by ...g5 with a strong attack. But white has serious pressure along the c-file. True, 25.♘xd5? doesn't work because of 25...♕xd5 26.♖ed1 ♕f7 27.♖xc5 ♕h5! winning.

25.♘e2! ♗e7 26.f3

The best move again. 26.♘d4 is a

blunder since 26...♕g6 gives two threats (27...♗g5 and 27...♕h5).

26...♕g6!

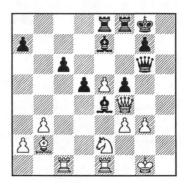

Black's bishop is still invulnerable; 27.fxe4 fxe4 28.♕d2 ♖f3 29.♔g2 ♖ef8 30.♖f1 ♗h4 with a tremendous attack. But my famous rival discovers a new resource for counterplay.

27.♔g2 ♗g5 28.♖xc6! ♕h5

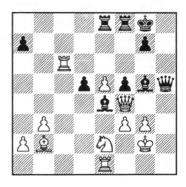

I intended to trap white's queen in any case, but the cost is too much for black. Correct was 28...♕xc6 29.♕xg5 ♕c2! 30.♗d4 ♖e6 31.♕e3 (31.fxe4? ♕xe4+ 32.♔f2 ♖h6-+) and black has some advantage.

29.fxe4!! ♗xf4 30.♘xf4 ♕f7 31.exd5

The table is suddenly turned as white gets a tremendous attack as his two minor pieces and strong central pawns dominate black's queen. But white must still be careful.

31...♕b7

32.♗a3?

After the game, we discovered the shot 32.♖g6!! which comes close to punishing me for the super-optimistic 28...♕h5. But in sharp time pressure, it is never too easy. After 32...♖d8, there is 33.♖d1 ♖c8 34.♖d2 ♕b4 35.♖e2 ♖c3! 36.e6 ♖fc8 37.♘h5 (37.e7! ♔f7 38.♖xg7+ ♔xg7 39.e8♕ ♖xe8 40.♖xe8 ♔f7 41.♗xc3 ♕xc3 42.♖e2 is equal) ...♔h7 38.♖xg7+ ♔h6 is unclear; or 33.e6 ♖xd5 34.♖xg7+ ♕xg7 35.♗xg7 ♖d2+ 36.♔f3 ♔xg7 37.a4 with a roughly level game.

32...♖c8 33.♖ec1

33.♗xf8 ♖xc6 34.dxc6 ♕xc6+ 35.♔f2 ♔xf8 36.e6 g5 with a clear edge for black.

33...♖fe8 34.e6 ♖xc6 35.♖xc6

35.dxc6 ♕a6 36.c7 g5 is good for black.

35...g5!

36.e7!?

Despair, as knight moves lose, e.g., 36.♘h5 ♖xe6!-+.

36...gxf4 37.gxf4 ♕b5

The fight is over, as black's queen is free at last.

38.♖f6 ♕xd5+ 39.♔h3 ♕f3+ 40.♔h2 ♕xf4+ 41.♔h3 ♕g4+ 42.♔h2 ♕h4+ 43.♔g2 ♕xf6 0-1

In the previous two games, the role of attacker passed from hand to hand, almost move by move. The following two games demonstrate a clearer situation in which the role of the attacker was clearly defined in the opening stage of the game.

Zaitsev,A - Shamkovich [B48]
RSFSR Ch., Rostov-on-Don, 1961

My opponent - a strong attacking

player and talented young Grandmaster from Vladivostok - sadly died at only 36 years of age.

1.e4 c5 2.♘f3 e6 3.d4 cxd4 4.♘xd4 a6

The Classical Paulsen system.

5.♘c3 ♛c7 6.♗d3 ♘c6 7.♗e3 ♘f6 8.0-0

More common at present is 8.♘b3, avoiding the trade of knights.

8...♘xd4   9.♗xd4   ♗c5 10.♗xc5 ♛xc5

The exchange of dark-squared bishops gives the game a specific character - it both facilitates white's kingside attack and black's queenside counterattack. It is hardly surprising that the game soon takes on a very double-edged nature.

11.♛e2 d6 12.a4

A questionable prophylactic, weakening the b4-square. Apparently 12.♔h1 is better, followed by 12...b5 13.f4 (13.a3 ♗b7 14.f4 is a little better for white.) b4=.

12...♗d7 13.♔h1 e5

This methodical advance is reasonable, in view of white's eventual threat of e4-e5. e.g., 13...0-0 14.f4 ♗c6 15.e5 dxe5 16.fxe5 ♘d5 17.♘e4 ♛d4 18.♛h5! h6 19.♘g5 with a dangerous initiative. However, 16...♘d7 17.♖ae1 ♖ae8 is playable for black and more likely a safer course for black than the text.

14.f4!

The beginning of a direct attack on the black king. Black must be very careful, e.g., 14...exf4 15.♖xf4 ♛e5 16.♖af1 0-0 17.♖xf6! gxf6 18.♘d5 f5 19.g4! f4 20.g5! ♔h8 21.♘f6+- threatening both 22.♘xd7 and 22.♛h5. If 16...♗e6 17.♖f5! ♗xf5 18.♖xf5 ♛e7 19.e5 with a tremendous attack. An alternative here is 18...♛d4 when 19.♘d5! ♘xd5 20.exd5+ ♔d8 (better is 20...♔f8 21.♛e6 f6 22.♛xd6 which is somewhat better for white) 21.♖xf7 ♖e8 22.♛f3 ♖e1+ 23.♗f1 which is winning for white due to the vulnerability of the black king.

14...♖c8 15.♖ae1 0-0 16.f5!?

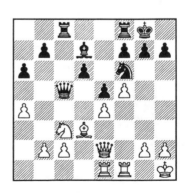

Is this correct? With the text move,

white opens a way to the black king's fortress for his heavy artillery, but makes black's counterplay with ...d5 and ...♕b4 easier. More reliable was 16.♕d2. Black's next move demonstrates my opponent's great courage.

16...♗c6 17.♖f3

17.g4 is met by the unpleasant 17...d5! with the long-range bishop at c6 making its presence felt.

17...♕b4!

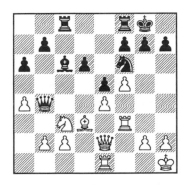

Only active play can maintain the promise of black's game. The alternative plan with 17...d5 is no longer effective as white obtains a crushing attack after 18.exd5 ♘xd5 19.♘e4 ♕e7 20.f6.

18.♕d2 h6 19.♖h3

If 19.♖g3 ♔h7! holds.

19...d5!

Attention! Serious military operations are commencing. The more solid 19...♖fd8 allowed 20.♖xh6!? gxh6 21.♕xh6 ♕xb2 22.♘d1 ♕a1 23.♕xf6 ♕c1 24.♗c4 and black's king is not too safe.

20.exd5 ♘xd5!?

More solid and adequate was 20...♗xd5 maintaining the strong defender knight at f6 and control of the key e4-square. If 21.♖xe5 ♕xb2! and white should not take the bishop at d5; 22.♘xd5? ♕xe5-+; 22.♖xd5? ♘xd5 23.♘xd5 ♕a1+-+. The best continuation is 22.♗f1 ♗c6 (22...♖fd8? 23.♖d3+-) 23.♖d3 ♖fe8 24.♖xe8+ ♖xe8 25.♖d8 leading to a rather tame position. No way! Both of us were resolved to a sharp struggle.

21.♖e4!

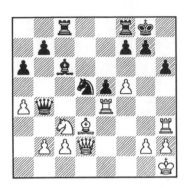

Transferring to the kingside with tempo.

**21...♕xb2 22.♘d1 ♕a1
23.♖g4**

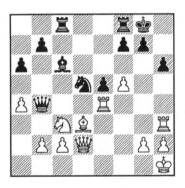

White's idea to attack the black king with heavy pieces is appearing to come to pass - he threatens mate in three with 24.♖xg7+. If 23...♘f4 24.f6!+-

23...e4!

Connecting the black queen to the kingside. The pin on the knight is black's main source of counterplay.

24.♗xe4

Closing the diagonal with 24.c3 fails to 24...e3!

24...♖fe8 25.c3?

Closing the diagonal and renewing the threat of 26.♖xg7+. But this is a decisive mistake! White's back rank is weak and black's pieces are very active. An exchange combination like 25.♗xd5 ♗xd5 26.♖xg7+!? (not 26.c3 ♕c1! winning) ♕xg7 27.♖g3 ♖xc2! 28.♖xg7+ ♔xg7 29.f6+ ♔g8! 30.♕b4 ♖xg2 (or 30...♖e4) exploits the weakness of the first rank. However, white has something better than 25.c3 or 25.♗xd5 - that is 25.♖hg3! when the direct threat is 26.♖xg7+, e.g., 25...♖cd8 26.♖xg7+ ♕xg7 27.♗d3! ♗xa4 28.♔g1 is a roughly level position. If 25...♘f6? luring white's rook into black's position, then white wins elegantly with 26.♖xg7+ ♔f8 27.♕d6+ ♖e7 28.h3 ♗xe4 29.♕xf6!! ♕xf6 30.♖g8#. However, after 25.♖hg3!, black could play 25...♖xe4! 26.♖xe4 ♘f6! 27.♖d4 ♘e4 28.♖d8+ ♔h7 29.♕d4 ♕xd4 30.♖xd4 ♘xg3+ 31.hxg3 ♖e8 and he stands well. Instead 25.c3? leads to further complications.

25...♘f4!

This "problem move" is now an effective one. Black simultaneously breaks the communication of white's queen with the black kingside and attacks the rook at h3 and the bishop at e4. Black also threatens the terrible 26...Rcd8. This threat is actual after 26.Rxf4 Bxe4 and 26.Bxc6 Rcd8 (26...Qc1! is a nice alternative). White needs a new resource!

26.f6!

This powerful thrust threatens 27.Rxg7+ Kf8 28.Qd6+ and mate. On the natural 26...Rcd8 my rival had prepared the brilliant 27.Bh7+!! Kf8 28.fxg7+ Ke7 29.Re3+ Ne6 (29...Kf6 30.Rxf4+ Kxg7 31.Rxf7+! is crushing) 30.Rd4 with a decisive advantage. Now it's black's shot.

26...g5!

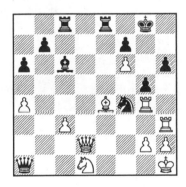

The only and sufficient defense, frustrating white's bold attack.

27.Bh7+

A last attempt.

27...Kxh7

27...Kh8? loses to 28.Rxh6 Rcd8 29.Bc2+! Kg8 30.Rxg5+ Ng6 31.Rgxg6+ fxg6 32.Bb3+ mating.

28.Rxg5

Threatening mate in two.

28...Rg8!

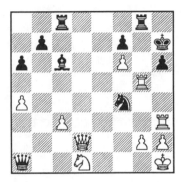

Parrying all threats.

29.Qc2+ Rg6

The smoke clears. The last moves are easy to understand.

30.Rxg6 fxg6 31.Re3 Rd8 32.Re1 Nxg2 33.Re7+ Kh8 0-1

The following game is one of the most spectacular and dramatic ones. Playing black with the Grunfeld Defense, I employed a rare system in the Modern Exchange variation with ...Bg4 and tried to break up the pawn chain with ...c5 and ...b5 on the queenside and ...g5 and ...e6 on the kingside. In the game, white faced two unpleasant surprises - the temporary piece sacrifice with 19...Nxe5 and the stunning rook sacrifice 20...Rxd5.

White's king was lured to the center of the board. But a rook is a rook - how to mate white's king?? Read on....

Fedorowicz - Shamkovich [D85]
New York, 1980

1.d4 ♘f6 2.♘f3 g6 3.c4 ♗g7 4.♘c3 d5 5.cxd5 ♘xd5 6.e4 ♘xc3 7.bxc3 c5 8.♗e3

The popular alternative is 8.♖b1, preventing the development of the ♗c8, but 8...0-0 9.♗e2 ♕a5 is fine for black.

8...♗g4!?

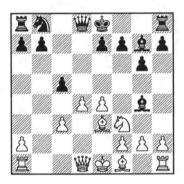

8...0-0 9.♕d2 ♗g4 10.♖c1 ♗xf3 11.gxf3 ♘c6 12.h4!

9.♖c1 ♕a5 10.♕d2 ♗xf3

This is better than 10...0-0 11.♘g5! with an active game for white, as in Portisch-Kortchnoi, Bad Kissingen (m/2) 1983. Black played 8...♗g4 to exchange his bishop and intensify the pressure on white's center.

11.gxf3 ♘d7 12.d5 b5

This plan originated in this game. The methodical 13.c4 is met by 13...b4

with the threat of 14...♗c3. White finds another way to build an imposing pawn center.

13.f4 ♖d8

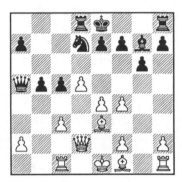

An important move aimed at breaking up white's center. If 13...0-0? 14.h4!

14.c4 b4 15.e5

Limiting the activity of the ♗g7 (for a while...).

15...g5! 16.♗h3

In order to meet 16...gxf4 with 17.♗xd7+! ♖xd7 18.♗xf4.

16...e6

Proceeding to break up the white center.

17.♖g1

If 17.dxe6 ♘xe5.

17...gxf4 18.♖xg7 ♘xe5!

The first surprise. Black's knight enters the fray and threatens the fork 19...♘f3+. My opponent likely

calculated 18...fxe3 19.♕xe3 only,
e.g., 19...b3+ 20.♔f1 b2 21.♖e1 ♕b4
22.dxe6! b1♕ 23.♖xb1 ♕xb1+ 24.♔g2
♕b7+ 25.♔g3 - unclear.

19.♔e2?

A decisive blunder. Correct was
19.♔f1 but black is already better, e.g.,
19...♕a3! 20.♗xf4 ♕xh3+ 21.♔e2
♕f3+ 22.♔f1 ♕d3+!

19...fxe3 20.♕b2

If 20.fxe3 ♕a6!

20...♖xd5!!

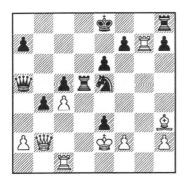

Another deadly surprise. White must
take the rampant rook as replies such as
21.♔xe3 ♖d4! or 21.fxe3 ♕a6 clearly
favor black.

21.cxd5 ♕a6+ 22.♔xe3 ♕d3+
23.♔f4

White's king sets off on a journey of
no return.

23...f6!

Setting a mating net - an important

part of black's attack. The direct threat
is 24...♕f3#.

No good is 23...♘g6+ 24.♖xg6 and
23...♕xh3 24.♕xe5 (24.♔xe5 ♕f5+
25.♔d6 ♕xd5+ 26.♔c7 ♕d7+ 27.♔b8
♔e7+-+) allows black only a draw after
24...♕xh2+.

24.♕b3 ♘g6+ 25.♖xg6 e5+
26.♔g4 h5+ 27.♔h4 ♕e4+!
0-1

The final point; 28.♔g3 h4 is mate,
and 28.♗g4 (or 28.♖g4) ...hxg4+
mating. Pay attention to the treacherous
role played by the ♖h8 - up to now it
was out of the battle.

Shamkovich - Sakharov [A17]
USSR Ch., Kiev, 1964

**1.c4 ♘f6 2.♘c3 e6 3.♘f3 ♗b4
4.g3 b6 5.♗g2 ♗b7 6.0-0 0-0
7.♕c2 a5 8.b3 d5 9.♗b2 ♘bd7
10.cxd5 exd5 11.♘b5 ♗a6
12.♘bd4 ♗c5 13.d3 ♗b7
14.♖ac1 ♖e8 15.♗h3 g6
16.♕c3!?**

Lucky. Correct was 16.e3.

**16...♗xd4! 17.♘xd4 c5
18.e3!!**

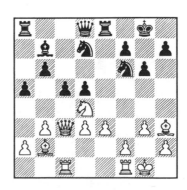

By sacrificing the piece, white aims to control the long diagonal. The trivial alternatives 18.♘b5 d4! 19.♘xd4 ♘d5! 20.♕c4 ♘e5 or 20.♕d2 cxd4 21.♗xd4 ♘c5 favor black.

18...cxd4?

Not all gifts are good. Black should have declined the sacrifice with 18...♘e5! 19.f4 ♘eg4 20.♗xg4 ♘xg4 21.♘c6 d4! 22.exd4 cxd4 (22...♗xc6 23.d5 is good for white) 23.♘xd4 f6! and black has more than sufficient compensation for the pawn.

19.♕xd4 ♖e6 20.f4!

No exchanges - even bishop for rook. The correct strategy for white entails intensifying the pressure along the long diagonal and on the kingside.

20...♖c8 21.♖xc8 ♕xc8 22.f5 gxf5 23.♗xf5 ♕e8 24.♕h4!

Avoiding the temptation 24.Bxe6? Qxe6 and black can hold.

24...♖e5 25.♕g5+ ♔h8 26.♗xd7 ♘xd7 27.♖f5! f6 28.♖xf6!

28...d4 29.♗xd4 ♕c8 30.♗xe5 ♘xe5 31.♕xe5 1-0

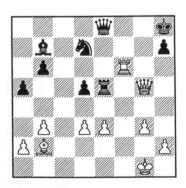

The final blow - if 28...♖xg5 29.♖f8 mate!

Index of Complete Games